MOMMY
DIAGNOSTICS™

Shonda Parker

Loyal Publishing
www.loyalpublishing.com

D1733275

Mommy Diagnostics

Loyal Publishing, Inc.
P.O. Box 1892, Sisters, OR 97759

Third Edition

Copyright © 1998 by Shonda Parker

All rights reserved. No part of this book may be reproduced or transmitted in any form or by any means, electronic or mechanical, including photocopying, recording, or by any information storage or retrieval system, without written permission from Loyal Publishing, Inc., except for the inclusion of quotations in a review. We hereby grant permission for the forms: Dietary Analysis Sheet, Health Analysis Survey, Complete Family Health History as well as the Mommy Diagnostics^{TM} Evaluation to be reproduced for personal use only; professional use is prohibited without written permission of Loyal Publishing, Inc.

WARNING-DISCLAIMER
Loyal Publishing, Inc. and the author have designed this book to provide information in regard to the subject matter covered. It is sold with the understanding that the publisher and the author are not liable for the misconception or misuse of information provided. The purpose of this book is to educate. The author and Loyal Publishing, Inc. shall have neither liability nor responsibility to any person or entity with respect to any loss, damage, or injury caused or alleged to be caused directly or indirectly by the information contained in this book. The information presented herein is in no way intended as a substitute for medical care and counseling.

Cover Art by Robert Duncan, Robert Duncan Studios
Cover Design by Bill Chiaravalle
Clip-art courtesy of ArtToday.com

ISBN: 1-929125-11-9

00   01   02   03   04   05   06   07   08   /   12   11   10   9   8   7   6   5   4   3

For they who began this book by causing me to learn the art of mothering—
May God be praised that you've survived your mother's learning curve,

Zachary, you were birthed from the battle place
to stand pure and clean as an example to us all,

Emily, we worked hard, you and I, for you to be born,
Your arrival in our family confirmed for me God's mercy,

Eryn, whose birth brought such peace to my life—
you inspired your mother to poetry,

Eliana, whose birth changed our family's course—God answered with you,

Zebediah, our man-child of God, your birth stands as a
living testimony to God's faithfulness.

Other books by Shonda Parker:

The Naturally Healthy Pregnancy,
The Essential Guide to Nutritional and Botanical Medicine for the Childbearing Years

The Naturally Healthy Family
Home Study Course

Pregnancy, The Naturally Healthy Way
booklet

TABLE OF CONTENTS

ACKNOWLEDGEMENTS

This work is my basket of thank-you's to:

Melinda Stokes, for all those hours you put up with me sitting in your home and office, pouring through your books, watching you with clients, and, graciously being given the opportunity to try out my newfound knowledge of medicinal herbs. You created an herbalist.

Kristy Bell, for all the "learning" you provided about whole grains and bread making. The section, entitled, "Bread: The Staff of Life," is a direct result of me sitting in Kristy's kitchen one morning watching her bake while she gave me a lesson in whole foods.

Charles Walker, Ph.D., for teaching me about looking at people as a "whole" and not just "parts is parts." Your kindness and encouragement is remembered.

Lynn Marie Myers, M.D., for respecting and trusting my care of my children. You set an example for other physicians to follow.

Sheila Page, D.O., for answering my questions regarding illnesses and helping in my research process with wonderful suggestions for medical textbooks.

Susie McAllister, for the wonderful work of editing you did on this book. I've gained a good friend, indeed, in you. Any problems left herein are a result of my stubbornness, not Susie's handiwork.

Vivian Mock, Tana Basinger, Carrie Hurd and Shelley Treadway, for all the times of listening to my newest idea for this book and still remaining my very good friends.

Additionally, I wish to thank Tana Basinger for her sacrificial work designing my book cover. You make the cover look so nice, you make me glad to be its author.

Shelvia Carroll, for loving my mother, Virginia Bond Carroll, and for making me your daughter. You're a good daddy.

My dearest Keith, your love supports me, enfolds me, emboldens me. You are my beloved, and you are my friend.

FOREWORD

If you want to make the best decisions about your child's health and medical care, it is vitally important that you learn what your options are. When my children were young I did not know there were any health care choices except what conventional doctors offered. I trusted one of these doctors to take care of my daughter. Instead, he prescribed months of psychiatric drugs for my daughter's bladder infections, then withdrew her from these addictive drugs "cold turkey." My daughter was left ill for three years as a result.

To protect my family from anything like that ever happening again, I went to medical school at the age of 39 to learn what doctors learn. I felt compelled to go to medical school in self-defense and in defense of my family.

What I discovered in medical school was that doctors are taught a lot about prescribing drugs but very little about nutrition and virtually nothing about herbs or any other natural means for healing or keeping the body healthy. Every child deserves the opportunity to grop up as healthy as possible and every parent deserves to know what options and choices are available to keep their children healthy. No one knows your child better than you, the parent and no one else is going to care as much as you do.

Once I became a physician and with my children healthy, my goal was to share information and resources which would help put the power of health in the hands of parents and patients. *Mommy Diagnostics* is certainly a book I recommend for parents. I wish I had found a book like this one with all of its information, resources and options, when I was a young mother searching for answers to my own health child's health problems. Even today, as a physician, I refer to it. It is well organized, easy-to-read and understand and is very comprehensive. I hope this book helps you on your road to better health.

Mary Ann Block, D.O.
Medical Director of the Block Center
Author
No More Ritalin
A Mother's Journey, a Physician's Approach

and

No More Antibiotics
Treating Ear and Respiratory Infections Without Antibiotics
(Previously title: *No More Amoxicillin*)

INTRODUCTION

As a revival of interest in natural health care occurs, we, as families, do well to educate ourselves in the art of family health care. Family health care is an art that mothers practice on a daily basis. We observe our children. We evaluate the need for intervention. We medicate as necessary. We seek other opinions when appropriate. Mothers, by nature of our calling, become family health practitioners.

This book is designed to provide a continuing education class for Mothers as family health practitioners. As we proceed to educate and equip you in this learning process, we will encourage you to look upon the home practice of family health care as a heritage to teach to your children so that they may then teach this to their children and so on through the generations.

Mom, you are an artist. God endows us with the unique ability to house and nurture His new creations in our wombs. Just as our health habits, spiritual and physical, provide the background colors onto our children's divinely-designed, body blueprints, our mothering attitude and actions paint the color in our children's lives that will one day be a complete portrait of God's creation. What an amazing job we have! What a blessed job we have! We, women, are called to an awesome career and ministry, that of stewarding our children. We steward their environment, the home. We steward their health, by nourishing them and caring for their illnesses. We steward their spirits, by teaching them the wonder of their design and their own purpose in God's creation.

May the Lord bless our learning together. May we present ourselves as willing vessels for His use in the creation of our masterpieces, our children.

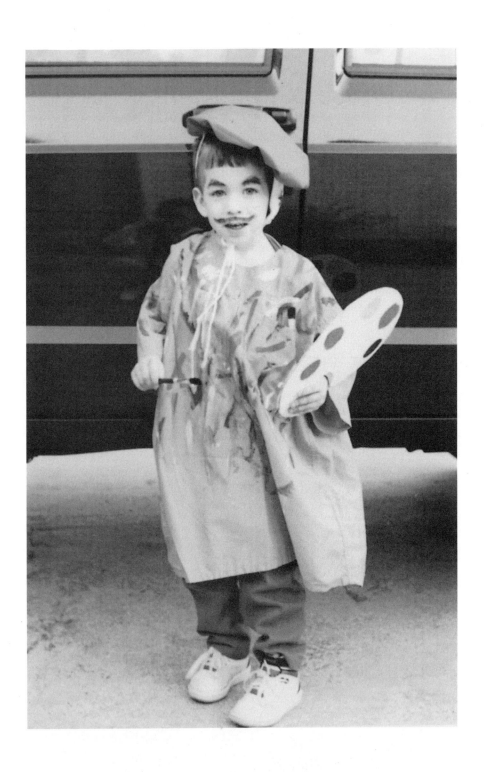

Part One

DRAWING THE BLUEPRINT

The Ladder Approach to Health™

The "ladder-approach" to health is based on the idea that health is maintained by following the health practices outlined in God's Holy Word, and that we repair our health through a step-by-step process. As we climb the "ladder of repair" upwardly from the least interventive means, our risk increases. If we fall off the first rung of a ladder, our risk of great injury is quite small; if we fall off the top rung of a ladder, our risk of injury is great. This increase in risk may become necessary in some health situations in order to repair areas of heavy damage, or in acute health crises.

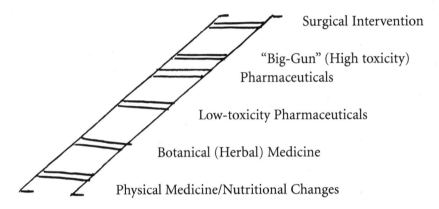

Surgical Intervention

"Big-Gun" (High toxicity) Pharmaceuticals

Low-toxicity Pharmaceuticals

Botanical (Herbal) Medicine

Physical Medicine/Nutritional Changes

The "ladder-approach" acknowledges the aspect of "re-building" in attaining health. After we have climbed the ladder to repair problem areas, we generally will need to utilize the therapies on the lower rungs as we descend the ladder restoring our health. Restoration to health often involves using a combination of therapies. The sooner we begin to intervene when an illness begins, the less intervention we probably will need to use.

Many times we can solve our health concerns with a simple change in diet or lifestyle (physical medicine). Using herbs for healing should be considered botanical medicine. Medicinal amounts of herbs are medicine. We do not have to be fearful of herbs as medicine. We do need to become knowledgeable about their medicinal actions and respect the chemical components of herbs.

Climbing the ladder above botanical medicine into pharmaceuticals is required for certain health crises. Again, we do not have to fear pharmaceuticals to the extent of never using them for medicine. We can read about the effect a particular pharmaceutical has on the body, seek professional counsel and make an informed decision weighing risk versus benefit. The key factor in home health care is knowing when to seek professional help. Obviously, obtaining pharmaceuticals and surgery is accomplished under the guidance of a licensed physician. Often, those who begin to practice nutritional and botanical medicine eschew any form of allopathic medicine to include all use of pharmaceuticals. I believe this to be unwise as we look at the big picture.

I believe our acknowledgement of the great benefit of allopathic medicine in crisis situations is an important aspect of relaxed and confident family health care. The comfort of knowing I have alternatives if my home care is not succeeding or if I have encountered an illness so acute that home measures would not have time to work allows me to practice with a greater confidence. Nutritional and botanical medicine are not alternative forms of medicine. They are the essential and foremost forms of medicine. Allopathic medicine is the alternative that we can be thankful is available when necessary.

DEVELOPING GOOD
DIAGNOSTIC SKILLS

Good Mommy Diagnostics™ is a skill to be finely-honed. The lasting benefit and financial savings gained over the years is substantial. Doctors recognize that children naturally respond better to mom. This positive response and trust is essential to successful diagnostics. Caring for our families during illness requires our availability. We must consider before beginning new projects the possibility of an illness in the family and determine if we will still be available to our family during the project. If we would be unable to tend to our families, that particular project may be unwise to undertake at that point in our lives.

Education is the foundation of good diagnostics. I have read everything I could get my hands on in the last ten years on anatomy, physiology, microbiology, biochemistry, pharmaceuticals, herbs and nutrition. After a time, I was finally able to combine these areas together during illnesses to reach several possibilities and begin to rule them out until I was left with the most likely. From that point I proceeded to my favorite herbals and textbooks to point to a therapeutic regime.

Good diagnostics basically follow five steps:

1. Identify the chief complaint,
2. Accumulate the facts,
3. Evaluate the facts likely to fit,
4. Prepare a hypothesis,
5. Choose the leading hypothesis.

Many times, the best thing to do is wait and observe the symptoms. For example, if a child is running a fever with no other symptoms, the best thing may be to wait three days to see if a rash occurs. If other symptoms develop during that time, they should be written down and compared to possible illnesses to see which one most likely fits. I have found that my Merck Manual and a Nelson's *Textbook of Pediatrics* have been invaluable in *Mommy Diagnostics.*™

I am the one with my children more. I am the one most likely to have the whole picture if I am paying attention. If the illness is something that I feel needs to be further evaluated by a physician, I am able to bring in a full and accurate description that will aid the physician, who has limited time, in his diagnosis.

At the beginning of an illness, the first priority is to decide if this is an illness that should be medically evaluated immediately. Then we must decide whom we should see? An M.D., a D.O., N.D., a chiropractor, herbalist, nutritionist? Some situations require immediate support, such as breathing difficulty. If a child is having difficulty breathing, respiratory support should be immediately sought. Choosing pharmaceuticals or botanicals for daily treatment can come after the child is breathing easier.

The home diagnostic tools that will pay for themselves many times over are: otothermometer, otoscope, stethoscope, blood pressure cuff and a watch with a second-hand. After purchasing these tools, learn to use them. Check out books from the library, or better yet buy some good ones, that show color pictures of how the eardrum looks when it is healthy as well as how it looks during illness. Listen to your children's heartbeats and lung sounds when they are not ill so that there will be a baseline comparison when they do become ill. Learn to use the otothermometer. The Thermascan requires a little art to using it accurately. It must be held in the ear longer than the directions say since the fiber optic has to have time to bounce off the surface of the eardrum for an accurate reading. A watch with a second-hand will allow you to time respirations or heartbeats (this can also give dad something fun [for him] to do when you are having contractions). The blood pressure cuff is not an essential; however, during the childbearing years, I find it to be a help for checking my blood pressure when I am pregnant.

After several texts, including the Merck, have been consulted and a tentative diagnosis has been reached, we must next decide what to use for treatment. The choices at home, in order of least intervention up, are dietary change, physical therapy, vitamins, and herbs. Constipation, many times, can be simply remedied by the addition of more water to the diet. In this instance, there is no need to use herbs. More water is needed. We need to accept that the simple choices are sometimes the best. If vitamins and/or herbs are to be used, herbals can be consulted to decide what therapeutic regimen to follow.

When deciding upon our regimen, we do well to consider the whole family in our deliberations. As much as I prefer to avoid pharmaceutical drugs and use natural alternatives, there are situations where acetaminophen may relieve the pain in child or adult to allow sleep, which helps the whole family to heal and restore. This rescue should be very infrequent due to acetaminophen's liver toxicity. If it is used, I would definitely take some milk thistle along with it since milk thistle protects the liver from the toxic effects of acetaminophen.

Seeking Wise Counsel

There are times when we encounter those illnesses at home that are beyond our ability to handle them alone. These illnesses require our close attention, diligent home care as well the seeking of professional counsel from qualified health care providers. As I firmly believe that we individuals and parents are responsible for our own health care, I believe it to be of utmost importance to seek out those health care professionals who are willing to join us in a health care partnership.

A health care partnership with a physician or herbalist or nutritionist or midwife involves our willingness to follow our health history, chronicle our illnesses and call the professional for their counsel when appropriate. Since physicians, particularly M.D.s and D.O.s, are those health care providers that many feel intimidated by or uncomfortable with sharing all of our home health care practices, I will address seeking their counsel in this section.

A good physician/client relationship, more than likely, will begin with a referral from a friend who likes the physician. From there, an interview should take place to see if the physician is of like-mind or at least open-minded to responsible preventive health practices. After the interview, an exam can be set up for the child's or parent's check-up or for a mild illness so that doctor and child or parent can get comfortable with one another. Some tips for the interview and good doctor/client relationships are provided below.

Tips:
- Dress nicely for the interview.
- Unless you specifically want to see little Susie's reaction to the doctor, it is probably best to leave her at home.
- Do not go in with an "attitude." We usually do not allow our children to take an "attitude" with others. Let us not do the same. A doctor is still a person, no greater and no less than we.
- If we want to be respected, we must respect. Respecting another human being does not mean we have to bow to their every command with fear and trembling. That worshipful fear belongs to the Lord. Respect does mean we allow others to render their opinion without denigrating them. We would not want the physician to do this to us, let us not repay evil with evil.
- Smile and relax. The doctor should not bite. If he does, leave.
- Be specific about what you are looking for: partnership in health care, someone whose counsel you will seek when unsure about method of treatment or diagnosis, simple diagnostic tools sometimes rather than full medical evaluations, respect in regard to parent's ability to know the child's normal behavior and body signs.

- If all is going well and the relationship is warm, respectful and trusting, be clear about the therapies you regularly employ at home. There is no need to delve into specifics. Simply state that many times, you have found altering the diet or adding botanical medicines when safe and appropriate has helped to avert or limit illnesses or symptoms. Add that you are researching this continually to make certain those botanicals you will use are safe and effective. Mention some of the mainstream herbs such as Echinacea for colds and flu or Ginger for stomach upset.
- If the immunization question comes up, a cautious approach is wise. Let the doctor know that you evaluate the need for each immunization based upon each child's individual needs as well as proper timing of immunizations in regard to the rest of the world's immunization schedules. Asking the doctor how he/she feels about this as you discuss it is probably wise. Before this topic comes up, I would try to get a feel for how much the doctor respects a parent's right to parent the child medically. Know the laws of your state in this regard.
- Interview the physician before the child gets sick. A crisis is no time to establish a relationship. We all act differently when confronted with our child's miseries.
- Take the child in at least once yearly to maintain the relationship. Choose a time of day when the office will not be crowded and doctor is still in a good mood (first thing in the morning is good).
- Take the child's health history in for the first visit, and then at each sick visit, take the illness chronicle with you. This chronicle will allow you to be specific and not leave anything out about the course of the illness that might be helpful for the physician to know.
- Learn the language of doctors. Read the Merck Manual and other medical texts so that you understand the terminology and are able to use it as needed. Act like a peer, and you may be treated (somewhat) as a peer.
- Be willing to pay for phone consultations. This is service of my physician that I find invaluable. We have sometimes eliminated the need for visits by talking over the phone.
- Learn how to properly describe the symptoms: "Red rash that began on the trunk, within hours became like blisters with clear fluid, burst and scabbed over. I think it is chicken pox. Don't you?" This is like going to the mechanic. Imitate the sounds made if needed. "The cough sounds like…, whoop, whoop. Can we come in for a sputum culture?"

WARNING SIGNS of a Potential Poor Relationship:

- Doctor does not want to take time to talk with you or does not even introduce himself to you.
- Pooh-pooh's nutritional and botanical medicine as quackery.

- Believes the state should govern the child medically.
- Does not listen to the child's description of symptoms or your description.
- Diagnoses the problem before listening to the whole picture.
- Does not discuss procedures with you before implementing said procedures.
- Refuses to have you as patient unless you comply with all well-child checks as his office demands.
- Talks down to you, not with you.
- Does not return phone calls or letters.
- Tries to cheat the insurance company.

M.D.s are not the only ones who can act like the doctor in the Warning Signs section above. Many other health care providers can be just as unkind or irresponsible. The key to seeking wise counsel is just that: recognize that it is counsel you are seeking, not a magic pill or potion. Evaluate the counsel as you would anything else in your life. Pray about the path God would have you walk during this particular illness and follow that path. Seek counsel from several sources and see where there is agreement and disagreement.

As we seek wise counsel, we must remember not to take the time to seek out this counsel only to throw it out just because it "violates" our natural philosophy. God has provided botanical medicines and nutrients from food for our health. He has also allowed medical knowledge to increase. We do not have to eschew modern medicine nor do we have to embrace it blindly; rather, we can combine the two to complement and balance out one another. Surgery can be lifesaving, and it can be wisdom to yield to His guidance rather than our own, sometimes prideful, philosophies.

Our society can greatly benefit from a more respectful relationship between healthcare providers and their clients/patients. Doctors should be grateful to find patients who choose to take responsibility for their family's healthcare rather than placing all the responsibility squarely upon their shoulders. A diagnostician's dream patient is one who is informed and willing to assume responsibility for choices in treatment. Families, likewise, should be grateful for those physicians who have educated themselves enough to provide alternatives to home family healthcare, rather than placing all the responsibility to know everything about illnesses, diagnostic testing and drugs squarely upon their shoulders. A parent's dream doctor is one who is informed and willing to give choices in treatment.

The Professional Herbalist

What exactly *is* a Professional Herbalist? I wish the answer were as easy as saying "One who has certification in such and such areas;" however, this is not the case. Currently in the United States, there is no "official" certifying body for herbalists. Translated, this means that we are basically self-taught and self-governed. The American Herbalist's Guild does provide a designation of "Herbalist, AHG," which means that the AHG has decided that that herbalist has fulfilled their education requirements. Many individual organizations and herbal education institutions provide this type of "certification." The AHG is desirous to be the certifying body that is nationally recognized and accepted.

While I do not see a problem with being self-taught (I am primarily self-taught), I think there are a few guidelines to follow when seeking a professional herbalist for herbal medicine recommendations. Since anyone could "hang out an herbalist's shingle" without actually being well-versed in the properties and actions of herbs, the consumer must shoulder the responsibility for making certain his/her herbalist is truly knowledgeable in the field of botanical medicine. I have set forth a few suggestions for the herbal consumer as he/she seeks professional herbal care:

- Where did the herbalist receive his/her training?
  - Herbal Correspondence Course - What texts were used? Training in anatomy and physiology? Biochemistry? Herbal pharmacognosy? Basic pharmacology? Actual medicine-making with the herbs?
  - Apprenticeship - Who with? Were the above areas studied in addition to field work with the plants?
  - Self-Taught - Same questions as with herbal correspondence course as well as clinical experience? Can the herbalist work with the actual plant? Years of study?

- Does the herbalist only work with one brand of herbal supplements?
  While preferring certain supplements is actually the norm in botanical medicine, is the herbalist willing to concede that one company does not hold the "corner" on the "best" of medicines? One company cannot fill every need. Some will have better products in one area than another and vice versa. A willingness to explore a variety of companies' products is essential to achieving the best for the client.

- Does the herbalist read only books from a folklore/historical use standpoint, or is she also knowledgeable in the scientific findings regarding herbal medicine?
  While we certainly would not want to ignore the historical data, we must, as herbalists, strive to integrate scientific evidence with the clinical data we compile.

- Is the herbalist willing to refer out to other specialists, including physicians, when necessary?
  There are times in acute situations when allopathic medicine or pharmaceuticals could and should be employed; the herbalist must be willing to concede that he/she do not have "all the answers."

- Are the fees for services reasonable and customary?
  $ .50 - $1.00 per minute for phone consultations is common with evaluations ranging from $25.00 - $50.00 according to time involved.

- Is the herbalist aware of the implications and cautions regarding herbal medicine during pregnancy and lactation?

- Does the herbalist take a complete health history?
  The whole picture of health must be taken into consideration to arrive at the appropriate measures to be taken.

- Does the herbalist employ diagnostic techniques that may be objectionable to you, personally?
  I find it ideal to find a health care professional, regardless if herbalist or doctor who is in agreement with one's beliefs and practices; however, this is not always easy. At least, seek someone who is not hostile to your own beliefs.

Finding a good herbalist is most often accomplished through the recommendation of a friend or other health professional. Consumers still must ask their own questions regarding the issues with which they are most concerned.

THE NATUROPATHIC DOCTOR

One seeking a Naturopathic Doctor for health care needs must be aware of the different factions in the natural health community that are currently "warring" over that title. The group of licensed Naturopaths, who have received advanced on-site training at an accredited Naturopathic college or university, desire that the title Naturopathic Doctor only be allowed for their group. The reason for making this distinction would be to ensure the consumer knows what kind of medical care to expect when they contact a naturopath for care: Licensed naturopaths, in the states in which they are licensed, are able to provide integrated medical care that incorporates both natural medicine and conventional medicine when warranted.

The other group is made up primarily of naturopaths who have received their doctor's degree through correspondence study. They believe that the licensed group is trying to usurp their ability to provide traditional naturopathic care to their clients. They oppose any licensure or regulation of the natural health professions, believing that licensure is sure to oust certain members of the natural healing community. An unlicensed naturopath, who has received learning through correspondence work, functions primarily as a professional herbalist, more than being able to provide primary physician care. The correspondence-degreed naturopath will not be able to prescribe herbs or pharmaceuticals or legally diagnose and treat illness.

I am a strong believer in supportive health care, including the use of herbal and nutritional medicine. I believe that the majority of self-limiting illnesses can adequately be cared for in the home. I believe that we benefit from the increased knowledge of those who have learned through self-teaching and correspondence work. I also believe that when a professional has a doctor's designation of initials after the name, that certain diagnostic and treatment expectations are communicated through that licensed initial designation.

I do not wish to see only licensed naturopaths being able to counsel families as to the medicinal use of herbs and foods. I do see a place for a separate category of naturopaths who receive the N.D. as a sign that they are able to provide both natural health care and conventional health care. Licensed naturopaths have had on-site "book learning" and actual clinical training, which I believe to be essential to render complete services as a physician.

Those naturopaths who have received correspondence degrees should still be able to provide naturopathic counseling, perhaps with a separate professional designation of initials after their name.

Part Two

Personalizing the Plan

THE HERITAGE OF A COMPLETE HEALTH HISTORY

I find as I grow older and begin to see familial patterns of illness in my family that I wish someone had chronicled my grandparents' health history, my parents' health history and my own health history. I am currently trying to backtrack and piece together at least a partial history based on hospital and physicians' records. This is not the ideal way to provide a health history for our children because some records are destroyed after a number of years in hospitals and physicians' offices as well as some are nearly impossible to release if the relative is deceased with no will having been filed.

My children and their children will need to know those illnesses which "run" in our family. Having a complete health history will enable them to practice aggressive prevention in those areas of their bodies where familial weaknesses or tendencies toward disease process lie. Knowing that several members of the family have experienced colon polyps or cancer would make one definitely avoid refined and processed foods such as white flours, white sugars and white rice and add to the diet plenty of fruits, vegetables and whole grains for their antioxidant properties and fiber.

Another benefit of maintaining a record of growth and illnesses is that it provides documentation that we are actively pursuing family health. Since we do not visit the doctor's office very often, having a health history allows our physician a better sense of what is normal for that particular child. This documentation can alert us to any problem areas that need to be addressed which we might miss if we did not have a written history in which to refer.

A family health history is not an area to neglect in a complete preventive health plan. This is family history, not just health history.

Name _____ **Birthdate** _____

Birth Information:

Weight _____ Length _____ Head Circumference _____ Chest Circum. _____

Gestational Age at Birth _____ Apgar, 1-minute _____ Apgar, 5-minute _____

Blood type _____ Newborn screening results _____

Health Information:

Breastfed? _____ If bottlefed, formula type _____ Reactions to formula _____

Age vegetables introduced _____ Food allergies observed _____

Age fruits introduced _____ Food allergies observed _____

Age grains introduced_____ Food allergies observed _____

Age dairy introduced _____ Food allergies observed _____

Age meats introduced_____ Food allergies observed _____

Environmental allergies observed _____

Medicines given regularly _____
Allergies to medicine observed _____

Vitamin/mineral supplements regularly given 1-4 yrs _____
5-12 yrs _____
13-18 yrs_____
19 yrs and up_____

Height and Weight:

6 weeks _____ long,	_____ lbs.,	_____ oz.	_____ cm head circumference	
2 months _____ long,	_____ lbs.,	_____ oz.	_____ cm head circumference	
4 months _____ long,	_____ lbs.,	_____ oz.	_____ cm head circumference	
6 months _____ long,	_____ lbs.,	_____ oz.	_____ cm head circumference	
1 yr _____ long,	_____ lbs.	10 yr_____ tall,	_____ lbs.	
2 yr _____ tall,	_____ lbs.	11 yr_____ tall,	_____ lbs.	
3 yr _____ tall,	_____ lbs.	12 yr_____ tall,	_____ lbs.	
4 yr _____ tall,	_____ lbs.	13 yr_____ tall,	_____ lbs.	
5 yr _____ tall,	_____ lbs.	14 yr_____ tall,	_____ lbs.	
6 yr _____ tall,	_____ lbs.	15 yr_____ tall,	_____ lbs.	
7 yr _____ tall,	_____ lbs.	16 yr_____ tall,	_____ lbs.	
8 yr _____ tall,	_____ lbs.	17 yr_____ tall,	_____ lbs.	
9 yr _____ tall,	_____ lbs.	18 yr_____ tall,	_____ lbs.	

Physical and Developmental Characteristics:

Hair color _____ Eye Color _____ Distinguishing Marks _____
Rolled over at _____ months   Sat up at _____ months   Walked at _____ months
Began talking _____ months

Vision and Audiometric Screening:

1 yr	_____ Right Eye	_____ Left Eye	_____ Right Ear	_____ Left Ear
3 yr	_____ Right Eye	_____ Left Eye	_____ Right Ear	_____ Left Ear
5 yr	_____ Right Eye	_____ Left Eye	_____ Right Ear	_____ Left Ear
7 yr	_____ Right Eye	_____ Left Eye	_____ Right Ear	_____ Left Ear
9 yr	_____ Right Eye	_____ Left Eye	_____ Right Ear	_____ Left Ear
11 yr	_____ Right Eye	_____ Left Eye	_____ Right Ear	_____ Left Ear
13 yr	_____ Right Eye	_____ Left Eye	_____ Right Ear	_____ Left Ear
15 yr	_____ Right Eye	_____ Left Eye	_____ Right Ear	_____ Left Ear
17 yr	_____ Right Eye	_____ Left Eye	_____ Right Ear	_____ Left Ear

Dental History:

First tooth at _____ months. Canine teeth at _____ months. First molars at _____ months.

First dental visit _____ yr. Comments _____
Dental problem areas identified at dental visits 3-18yrs _____
_____
_____
_____
_____
_____

Immunization Dates:

IPV and/or OPV Polio_____
DPT or DT with Acellular Pertussis (DTaP)_____
HIB _____
MMR _____
Hepatitis B _____
Rubella alone, evaluated for benefit by Rubella titre at age 12 _____
DT booster _____
Tetanus booster _____

Family Medical History:

Please write in the line the relation to you of the family member, if any, who has experienced the following conditions.

Allergies/Sensitivities _____

Arthritis _____

Anemia _____

Asthma _____

Blood Pressure, High _____

Blood Pressure, Low _____

Cancer _____

DES Exposure _____

Diabetes _____

Drug Allergies, Who and What _____

_____

Endometriosis _____

Emotional Problems _____

Epilepsy _____

Fibroids or Fibrocystic Breast Disease _____

Heart Disease _____

Hemorrhoids _____

Hepatitis _____

Hypoglycemia _____

Gastrointestinal Difficulties _____

Kidney Disease _____

Twins or other multiple birth _____

Pelvic Inflammatory Disease _____

Rh Problems _____

Rheumatoid Arthritis _____

Skin Problems _____

Stroke _____

Thyroid Problems _____

Tuberculosis or TB Medications _____

Varicosities _____

History of Illness:

Date of Illness _____ Diagnosis _____

Symptoms _____

_____

_____

Treatment Protocol _____

_____

_____

Treatment Professional Consultation Results _____

_____

_____

Laboratory Tests Performed/Results _____

_____

_____

If hospitalization necessary, Where, When, How long, Surgery or Treatment Performed

_____

_____

_____

Date of Illness _____ Diagnosis _____

Symptoms _____

_____

_____

Treatment Protocol _____

_____

_____

_____

Treatment Results _____

_____

_____

Professional Consultation Results _____

_____

_____

Laboratory Tests Performed/Results _____

_____

If hospitalization necessary, Where, When, How long, Surgery or Treatment Performed

_____

_____

Evaluating Family Nutritional Needs

The evaluation of family nutritional needs is not a matter of difficulty; rather, it is a matter of time. Evaluations take time to gather needed information, evaluate the available facts, do any necessary research, choose method of intervention. As I do nutritional evaluations for clients, I have them fill out a one-week food diary detailing everything they eat and drink for at least five days. I prefer to have a weekend in that five-day period since most of us tend to "blow it" on the weekends more than we would during the weekdays. I also have them completely fill out the Health Analysis Survey on page 36. The client is encouraged to elaborate on past medical conditions, medications and any health problem they may currently be experiencing. Completely filling out the previous Family Health History is vital to knowing what the "weak" areas are in our familial lines to aid in choosing preventive measures.

The key to being able to evaluate is to gain maximum information from the family member being evaluated. My husband often tells me I ask too many questions of our children when they are sick. While these repetitive questions can be irritating, I usually am able to elicit more information by repeating my questions in varying ways until my children finally understand the question and give me an answer. The danger here lies in pushing too hard and having them answer just to get you to leave them alone. I find that if I do not allow myself to become aggravated by their seeming reluctance to answer and recognize the communication problem, I can elicit honest answers.

Dietary Analysis

Analyzing the diet is quite simple. After the one-week food diary is complete, I merely go through the diet sheets highlighting all red flag areas (See Red Flags Chart on page 33). I then make recommendations for change based on the Whole Foods for Whole Health Healthy Substitutions Chart. My purpose is to offer the "ideal" diet as something to work towards, yet I am diligent to provide a realistic plan for getting to the ideal. Slow change is necessary so that the liver does not become overburdened by an abrupt change. A slow change to a healthful diet is also needed to prevent rebellion among the troops. Choose to eliminate one bad habit per week until healthy substitutions are the norm and not the exception. Some folks will be ready and willing to make all necessary changes right away. If the family is ready, go for it! If not, take it easy, exert some patience, and use lots of herbs and spices to add more taste, and health!, to the Whole Foods Diet. Tony Chacherie's spice combo is a staple at the Parker table!

DIETARY ANALYSIS SHEET

Day One:
Breakfast:

Mid-morning snack:

Lunch:

Afternoon snack:

Dinner:

Bedtime Snack:

Day Two:
Breakfast:

Mid-morning snack:

Lunch:

Afternoon snack:

Dinner:

Bedtime Snack:

Day Three:
Breakfast:

Mid-morning snack

Lunch:

Afternoon snack:

Dinner:

Bedtime snack:

Day Four:
Breakfast:

Mid-morning snack:

Lunch:

Afternoon snack:

Dinner:

Bedtime snack:

Day Five:
Breakfast:

Mid-morning snack:

Lunch:

Afternoon snack:

Dinner:

Bedtime snack:

Red Flags Related to Diet and Nutrition

1. Enriched flour in ingredients list: Flour must first be depleted in order for it to have to be enriched.
2. Amount of processing involved in food. The more processing, the more nutrients lost.
3. Preservatives: BHT, BHA, sodium nitrite and nitrate, propyl gallate, sulfur dioxide, and sodium bisulfate. Just why is it even bacteria won't touch the stuff?
4. Caffeine, alcohol, tobacco. All deplete the body of ESSENTIAL nutrients.
5. Artificial coloring: Esp., FD&C Red No. 1, Orange B, Red No. 3, Red No.40, Yellow No. 5, Blue No. 1 and Blue No. 2 and artificial flavorings: MSG(if you are allergic), quinine.
6. Chemicals of any kind, particularly artificial sweeteners: saccharine, aspartame.
7. Natural additives: sorbitol.

WHOLE FOODS FOR WHOLE HEALTH

The following is a list compiled to give an idea to the beginners of "whole food" eating what they can substitute for their usual processed ingredients.

Whole Food	Imitation/Processed Version
Freshly ground whole grain flour	Packaged white, wheat, rye, barley, oat flour
Purified water	Soda pop, Coke, Dr. Pepper, Kool-aid, etc.
Unsweetened fruit juices - fresh squeezed is best, frozen better, bottled okay	Juice "cocktails" or "drinks," powdered, artificial-flavored drinks
Herbal teas (no caffeine); green tea (caffeine)	Black tea, contains caffeine, coffee
Whole wheat pasta, spelt pasta, sesame pasta, etc.	White pasta of any shape
Brown rice, buckwheat, millet, barley, rye, oats, etc.	White rice, refined grains
Whole grains - whole, freshly cracked or rolled	Boxed cereals, processed grains
Whole grain toasted bread crumbs	Boxed croutons
Whole grain crackers	White flour crackers
Unrefined oils - cold-pressed or extra virgin olive oil	Hydrogenated fats and shortenings, refined oils
Butter	Margarines, spreads
Goat milk, Tofu milk, Certified raw milk	Homogenized, pasteurized milk
Certified raw milk cheese - "It's naturally white."	Dyed, added-to, homogenized, pastuerized cheeses
Plain yogurt with live cultures	Sweetened varieties or frozen varieties
Cultured dairy products	Uncultured, sweet dairy products
Unfiltered, unpasteurized apple cider vinegar	Distilled vinegar
Baking powder without aluminum or yeast	Baking powder containing aluminum
Low sodium baking powder (aluminum-free)	Baking soda
Carob powder	Cocoa, chocolate
Uncooked, unfiltered "Raw" honey - 1/2 c = 1 c sugar; Grade A Pure Maple syrup	White sugars (sucrose, dextrose, glucose, "raw" sugar, corn syrup)

Unsulphured molasses, fruit juices/purees, dried raw cane juice, fructose in small amounts	Brown sugar
Baked chips, popcorn, dried unsulphured fruits, raw nuts, granola	Fried chips, sulphured dried fruits, candy, snack items with added sugars, dyes, preservatives, other additives.
Organic fruits, vegetables and grains	Conventional fruits, vegetables and grains
Unhydrogenated peanut butter made with 100% peanuts without added sugar (or salt, if preferred), sesame butter (tahini), cashew butter, almond butter	Commercial peanut butter and other nut butters
Raw, lightly steamed, grilled vegetables	Boiled, fried vegetables
Raw fruits	Canned or frozen fruits with added sugars.
Clean (Leviticus 11) animals that can be completely bled - common ones we eat: chicken, turkey, deer, beef (in moderation)	Commercially raised animals fed grains/hay treated with chemicals and given chemicals to keep them "healthy"?
Beans, peas, lentils, whole grains, etc.	Eat less meat - Majority of protein should be from vegetable source for maximum health.

The Dietary Plan

After doing the dietary analysis, circling all poor nutrient-quality foods and listing the substitutions, a plan of attack may be made.

Foods to be Eliminated:

List all foods here that don't deserve a place in our pantry. Yo-Yos would qualify. As my good friend, Tana Basinger, once sagely said, "If you are going to indulge in a sweet, can't you do better than a Yo-Yo?"

Foods to be Limited:

List all foods under this heading that need to be reduced from their current priority place in the diet due to their health-reducing qualities. This is the place that those 6 cups of coffee daily should be listed or the 2 pounds of cheese on that homemade pizza!

Foods to Add to the Diet:

List the foods here that are missing from the diet according to daily requirements:
Whole grains, complex carbohydrates - 11 servings
Fruits and Vegetables - 5 servings
Meat - 1-2 servings
Oils, Fats - 1 small serving
If your idea of a fruit serving is fruit punch drink, much work is ahead of us!

HEALTH ANALYSIS SURVEY

Personal Information

Name _____ Date _____

Address _____ Phone _____

Age _____ Sex _____ Height _____ Weight _____

Health Habits

1. How much sleep do you get each night on the average? _____ hours.
   What time do you generally go to sleep? _____ o'clock.
   Do you sleep soundly? _____ Fitfully? _____ Insomnia often? _____

2. How often do you exercise? _____ hours per _____.
   What type of exercise do you do?

3. What is your daytime energy level like?

4. How often do your bowels eliminate? _____ per _____.

5. Do you observe a rest day each week?

6. Think of your personal hygiene habits. Are there areas needing work? Regular
   bathing _____ Hand-washing _____ Proper wiping after potty _____
   Tooth-brushing _____ Flossing _____ Hair care_____

7. Do you come into regular contact with others who are ill? _____
   Are you careful to observe precautions when in contagious situations? _____

8. In general, what is your daily emotional attitude? _____
   Have you had stressful life situations in the past year? _____ If yes, please
   explain how you've dealt with them? _____ With hope? _____ Despair?

8. Briefly describe your God-given character, the positive and negative?

9. What steps can you take to minimize the negative traits and maximize the positive
   ones?

Medical Information

1. Please list any surgeries or serious illness you have had in the past.

2. Generally speaking, how has your health been in the past?

3. What are your current health concerns?

4. Do you have a medical diagnosis of your condition? _____ If so, what is the diagnosis?

5. Are you under a medical doctor's care for your condition? _____ If so, what medications or therapies are you currently using?

Current Physical Symptoms

Do you have, or have you had, symptoms or problems related to the following body system and parts? If so, please describe.

a. Bones/Joints/Spine/Back
b. Brain/Nervous System
c. Eyes, Ears, Nose
d. Glandular System (Pituitary, Thyroid, Adrenals, Pancreas)
e. Hair/Skin/Nails
f. Hands/Feet/Legs/Arms
g. Heart/Circulation
h. Kidneys/Bladder
i. Liver/Gallbladder
j. Lungs/Sinuses
k. Lymphatic System/Lymph Glands
l. Muscles
m. Neck/Shoulders/Head
n. Reproductive Organs
o. Small and Large Intestines (Bowels)
p. Stomach
q. Other Symptoms Not Included Above

List any nutritional supplements currently being taken (vitamins, herbs, minerals, etc).

*All of the forms in this section may be reproduced for your personal use.

Evaluating Health Concerns and Nutritional Needs

After we have filled out the Health Analysis Survey and the Family Health History, we are ready to draw up a plan for nutritional supplementation.

Personal Information

If weight is above what is healthful for you, choosing a whole foods diet while limiting caloric intake to 1,500 - 2,000 daily would be wise. Limiting caloric intake should never be done during pregnancy or breastfeeding.

Health Habit

Sleep - If you are not getting at least 6 - 8 hours of sleep at night, this could create health problems for you. Most people need at least 8 hours of sleep. While some can manage on less, the majority of us need that sleep to feel rested and have our bodies functioning at optimal performance. Each hour of sleep gotten before 12:00 midnight counts as two hours of post-midnight sleep.

Exercise- A minimum of one hour of exercise two to three times weekly is necessary for circulatory health, insulin metabolism, weight-management, glandular health… Well, just about all of us benefit from regular exercise. Simple walking can do a body a world of good.

Energy Levels - If lagging energy levels are a continual problem, an underlying health condition may be present. After ascertaining that good foods are eaten, adequate water is consumed, sleep is restful and exercise is regular, other investigation may be required such as: thyroid panel (low-functioning thyroid can make one tired), hemoglobin values (anemia can cause tiredness), underlying infectious process checked out, and, of course, we must not forget the good ol' pregnancy test if we remember something was missed last month!

Bowel Elimination - Ideally, we would have a bowel movement (b.m.) every time we eat a meal per day (three meals would equal three b.m.s). However, most of us don't have that good of function in our intestinal tract. At least one bowel movement per day is necessary to allow our body to eliminate toxins produced from the foods being digested. If elimination is not occurring on a regular basis, resulting health problems can occur.

Rest Day - God instituted a day of rest as a gift to His people. We do well to observe this day as a day of renewal for the upcoming week. When neglected, stress levels may build resulting in increased nutritional needs.

Personal Hygiene

Washing our body is an important way of decreasing bacterial growth responsible for body odor and skin infections. Hand-washing is essential for reducing the risk of contracting disease in our surroundings. Females need to be aware of the utmost importance of wiping front to back to avoid bacterial contamination of the urethra, which could result in a bladder infection. Teeth need to be daily brushed and flossed to maintain gum health and freshen the breath. Our hair needs to be regularly washed and brushed to maintain a lovely sheen and help us avoid an oily face due to oily hair. All of these areas affect us personally, yet they also affect those around us. Since our health is positively affected by the number of supportive friends we have, regular personal hygiene is a health must!

Tending the Sick

If we are regularly tending the sick, we need to be especially careful in proper hand-washing technique. To effectively remove germs from hands, we need to wash for at least 10-15 seconds with soap under warm water. Standing back from cough spray is important as well. Germs spread when coughing can spray up to 20 feet; if mouth is covered, three feet is typical spray distance.

Emotional Attitude

"A merry heart doeth like good like a medicine, but a broken spirit drieth the bones" Proverbs 17:22. Our attitude does affect our entire life. If we are able to weather the storms of life with hope in the Lord, rather than despairing at man's evil, we will be giving ourselves good medicine; the Bible says so! Use this time as an opportunity to dwell on that, which has caused anxiety over the past year, and search God's Word for the promises of hope He gives His children. We do know that physically, when we are anxious, our body burns up its nutrients at a much higher rate than normal; therefore, we must be very diligent in supplementation during periods of burden.

Character Traits

Evaluate your positive character traits as well as the negative traits. Think of ways to minimize the negative traits. Ask the Lord for help and make a plan of ways to react better in whatever situations are your weak points.

Medical Information Analysis

According to your confirmed health conditions, look up in herb books those nutritional supplements that are known to benefit your particular condition. If any surgeries have been performed, look for herbs used to support the body systems that were affected by the surgery. Check in your herbal/pharmaceutical books to make certain that any nutritional supplements chosen will not cause adverse reactions when combined with any pharmaceuticals currently being taken. At the next doctor's visit, let the doctor know what nutritional supplement therapies you are going to be undertaking and for how long you will utilize said therapy.

Physical Symptoms Cross-Referenced with the Family Health History

Check your Family Health History to see if current symptoms are part of a recurring problem, or if the current symptoms are early signs of health problems experienced by extended family members. Look in *Food-Your Miracle Medicine* by Jean Carper for foods that help prevent/treat specific health problems. Also look up your different symptoms in medical texts, with a goal of narrowing down possible diagnoses. After narrowing down the categories, you can then look up those illnesses in your herbal texts to find the nutritional supplement recommendations specific to those illnesses.

The Plan

Body Systems Needing Support:

List those areas of the body needing specific nutritional and herbal medicine support.

Lifestyle Changes Necessary for Health:

List those changes in health habits and attitude that need to take place for healthy living.

Medicinal Foods Needed:

List the foods needed to prevent/treat health concerns.

Medicinal Supplements (Vitamins, Minerals, Herbs) Needed:

List the supplements needed to prevent/treat health concerns. If several health problems are present at the same time, prioritize the most concerning down to that of least concern. Do not try to treat everything at one time. Take things one health concern at a time.

Part Three

ASSEMBLING THE TOOL-CHEST

ASSEMBLING A HOME HEALTH CHEST

Creating a home health chest does not have to be an expensive endeavor. Many of the items essential to the home health chest are items commonly found in all homes. Some herbal preparations are necessary to purchase, yet these may be ordered inexpensively through certain suppliers (please see Resources for Food and Products).

Over the years of practicing home health care, I find that I try to keep a good supply of essentials on hand. When a member of my family is ill, we generally do not want to go to the health food store at that time to shop. I try to use what I do have on hand; however, I do not hesitate to go out and purchase preparations I consider essential to my healing program.

The list below may seem long to many of you. I assure you that the ability to begin a nutritional and botanical medicine regime upon the first hint of illness can make the difference between successfully treating at home and having to seek outside assistance from a professional health care provider. One of the nicest things about having these items on hand is that I am able to share that which I may not currently need with a neighbor or friend who is in immediate need of a particular product. If I list a source in parentheses for something, you can find the address and/or phone number in the Resource section.

At the very least, a home health chest should include those items needed to cover the following health issues: fever, colic, teething, colds, flu, "stomach bugs" and ear infections.

Essentials to the Home Health Chest
Tools for Making Herbal Preparations
Medium stainless steel or glass pot with cover (avoid aluminum)
Double boiler, glass or stainless steel
Crock pot
Wooden spoons (avoid aluminum utensils)
Cheesecloth (a very old, very thin clean t-shirt may be used in lieu of cheesecloth)
Ladle
Strainers, fine and course
Clean Ball jars, quart size
Blender or food processor
Coffee filters, unbleached
Coffee grinder
Amber jars

Foods and Herbs for Making Herbal Medicines:

- Garlic
- Onion
- Unsweetened carob powder
- Unsweetened applesauce
- Oatmeal
- Carrot
- Beets
- Parsley
- Barley
- Black tea
- Dry mustard
- Sea salt
- Baking soda
- Green clay
- Bentonite clay
- Olive oil (the greener, the better - Organic, Extra Virgin is the best
- Castor oil (available at any pharmacy store, the odorless is okay)
- Apple-cider vinegar
- Purified water (Fred's Essential Water and Air can answer questions and recommend purifiers. See page 271)
- Lavender essential oil - (available from co-ops, Frontier Herbs or Blessed Herbs)
- Cayenne pepper (also known as capsicum)
- Slippery elm powder - (Frontier Herbs, Blessed Herbs or through co-ops)
- Chamomile flowers or tea (Frontier Herbs, Blessed Herbs or through co-ops)

Home Health Instruments:

- Infant bulb syringe
- Earscope (Otoscope - I purchased one from Wal-Mart that is not top-quality but functional)
- Otothermometer (Thermascan - Fiber optic thermometer)
- Ultrasonic humidifier (clean with white, distilled vinegar)
- Clear, bubble umbrella
- Steam infuser (Self-Care Catalog has some excellent ones)

Essential Nutritional Supplements:

- Liquid calcium/magnesium (NF Formulas has a tasty peppermint-flavored liquid cal/mag - another option is a total herbal calcium (mineral) supplement such as the Blue Green Minerals by Tri-Light)

- Good prenatal for mom - NF Prenatal Forte from NF Formulas, Opti-natal from Eclectic Institute
- Good vitamin/mineral supplement for Dad - Spectra 2C without iron/copper from NF Formulas
- Chewable kids' vitamins with no calcium (calcium should come separately in liquid)
- Quality acidophilus and bifidus probiotic powder - Buy a refrigerated product for maximum "friendly" bacteria
- Omega-3 oils (from fish, Cod Liver oil, or flax seed oils)
- Buffered vitamin C powder (health food store or co-op)
- Bioflavonoids (good source for kids is from rosehips syrup)
- Zinc (Enzymatic Therapy and Twinlab has good zinc wafers, 23mg elemental zinc)

Single Herbs

I either purchase these herbs in combinations, if available, or purchase them in singles. I have put an asterisk (*) beside those herbs which I keep on hand as liquid singles to add to my combinations or to make up my own TincTract combinations.

- Echinacea (Echinacea angustifolia, purpurea - I keep tablets or capsules and a liquid TincTract combination with Echinacea in it)
- Peppermint and/or Spearmint (Mentha piperita and Mentha Spicata - I keep both a TincTract combination product with Peppermint in it as well as Ginger/Peppermint capsules from NF Formulas on hand)
- Milk Thistle (Silybum marianum), (liquid TincTract by Tri-Light's Liquid Light Products, tablet by Ethical Nutrients or capsule, Thisylin by Nature's Way and Simply Milk Thistle by Enzymatic Therapy)
- Yarrow (Achillea millefolium)
- Elder berries and/or flowers (Sambucuscanadensis, nigra)
- *Boneset (Eupatorium perfoliatum)
- Thyme (Thymus vulgaris - I keep both a liquid TincTract combination with thyme on hand as well as loose thyme herb for baths)
- Elecampane (Inula helenium)
- *Licorice (Glycerrhiza glabra)
- *Mullein (Verbascum thapsus)
- *Osha root (Ligusticum porteri)
- *Ginger root (Zingiber officinale)
- *Goldenseal (Hydrastis canadensis - I like to keep a small amount of goldenseal powder on hand from Spirit-Led Childbirth, a single TincTract of goldenseal and a combination TincTract with goldenseal in it)
- Myrrh gum (Commiphora myrrha)

- Black haw (Viburnum opulis)
- *Lobelia (Lobelia inflata)
- *Lomatium (Lomatium disectum)
- *Usnea (Usnea barbata)
- *Nettles (Urtica spp.- Because my family has allergies, I like to keep freeze-dried nettles capsules from Eclectic Institute on hand as well as a nettles TincTract for the children)
- *Ginkgo (Ginkgo biloba - I keep this TincTract single for my asthmatic child to be given daily as a preventive, also used to keep circulation flowing well in adults in our family)

Herbal Combination Products I Purchase:

- Intestinal Care (by Ethical Nutrients, a division of Metagenics - powder)
- ImmunoComp (by Enzymatic Therapy - capsuled herbs)
- Immuplex (by Standard Process Labs - capsuled glandulars)
- Phytobiotic (by Enzymatic Therapy - capsuled herbs)
- SinuCheck (by Enzymatic Therapy - capsuled herbs with standardized amount of Ephedrine. I only use this for major sinus pressure and blockage)
- AL-C (by Nature's Sunshine - I use this herbal combination for colds with sinus congestion. I personally find the standardized Ephedra products to be too strong for simple colds)
- FV (by Nature's Sunshine - I really like this for flu; however, I find the ImmunoComp with added Ginger to be effective also)
- Soothing Salve Drops (a Liquid Light product by Tri-Light Company - I have found no salve or other antiseptic drops to work as well at healing as Soothing Salve. We even use these on chapped lips or mouth sores and inflamed gum tissue)

INVESTING IN FAMILY HEALTH

After we have gone through all of the preceding information, many moms feel over-whelmed at the thought of extended study, health records, diet sheets and dollars walking out the door for supplements and such. The specter of a life consumed with diet and health is scary. When our dietary habits begin to take precedent over the other God-given duties of our days, then we must reevaluate our motivation. Establishing and maintaining good health through following Biblical principles is important, and I am certainly not minimizing their importance. I am encouraging a relaxed approach, which will over time build confidence in the Mommy Family Health Practitioner.

What I hope to avoid teaching is an investment of all our time in thinking about family health. Healthcare is a part of life, not our whole life. If we find that our thoughts and actions are consumed with family healthcare, an evaluation of our focus is neces-sary. Certainly, we will have times when family health is practically consuming to our days, say, during a family illness. At other times, we may relax and enjoy God's creation rather than focusing on a part of the fall of creation, illness.

An encouragement I would like to share is for those of us who feel very secure in our ways of family health to be cautious when dealing with others whom may not share our family health ways. Let us respect the God-given freedom of others to choose another way of healing. We may share what we have learned, if asked or given opportunity; however, zealous conversion to natural healthcare should never be our focus. God, in His infinite wisdom, will give us requested opportunities to share about stewarding our bodies with those whom He has prepared to receive the information. Let us trust Him in this.

Family Health Tools Investing

There are investments to make over the long haul. These investments are sometimes monetary, yet most of the investment will be in time. Mom will have to take time after the little ones are in bed for their naps to read her herbals and medical texts. She can then formulate a plan for purchasing her home health care tools.

I have outlined a plan below for establishing a Home Health Chest. This is how I would approach investing in the tools for health if I were beginning today. Some of us can purchase all of our needs at one time; others may need months or several years to save up for them all. The plan below provides for all the tools over a year's period of time. This plan may be adjusted according to your family's individual needs. My plan is chronological from January to December for ease of understanding. I've also put into each month what a family might need for that time of year. Of course, we hope you will continue through these months your herbal learning through the *Naturally Healthy Family*™ *Home Study Course.*

January

Physical Tools	Botanicals
Castor oil	ViraMune
Natural Alternatives to OTC & Prescription Drugs	Scout Out
Otoscope (Earscope)	LymphaRub

February

Physical Tools	Botanicals
Unsweetened carob powder	Buffered Vitamin C powder w/ Bioflavonoids
Herbal Prescriptions for Better Health	Lungs Plus
Otothermometer (Thermascan)	Omega-3 Oil (Cod Liver oil or Flax oil)

March

Physical Tools	Botanicals
Bentonite clay	Liquid Calcium/Magnesium or Blue Green Minerals.
Food - Your Miracle Medicine	*Acidophilus* & *Bifidus* powder
Lavender essential oil	Nettles (freeze-dried & TincTractTM)

April

Physical Tools	Botanicals
Soothing Salve Drops	Yummy Yarrow w/Elderberry
What the Bible Says About Healthy Living	Ginger
Ultrasonic Humidifier	Zinc lozenges w/23mg zinc gluconate

May

Physical Tools	Botanicals
Green Clay	The Pure Body Program - Adults
Treating Respiratory and Ear Infections video	Worm-Out TincTract™
Clear, bubble umbrella	Grapefruit Seed Extract

June

Physical Tools	Botanicals
Cheesecloth	NR Glow TincTract™
The Green Pharmacy by James Duke, Ph.D.	Usnea TincTract™
Dry Mustard	ImmunoComp (Enzymatic Therapy)

July

Physical Tools	Botanicals
Thyme (bulk herb - 1 pound)	Echinacea & Thyme w/Elderberry TincTract™
The Merck Manual	Goldenseal TincTract™
Chamomile flowers (bulk herb - 1 pound)	SinuChek (Enzymatic Therapy) or AL-C (NSP), Breathe-Aid (NW)

August

Physical Tools	Botanicals
Goldenseal powder	Lomatium TincTract™
Encyclopedia of Natural Medicine	Mullein TincTract™
Steam Infuser	Phytobiotic (Enzymatic Therapy)

September

Physical Tools	Botanicals
Water purifier	FV (NSP)
Kid Smart! By Cheryl Townsley	Lobelia TincTract™
Slippery Elm powder (bulk herb)	Licorice TincTract™

October

Physical Tools	Botanicals
Grain Mill	Black haw TincTract™
Encyclopedia of Nutritional Supplements	BactaMune
Ginger Powder	Bromelain 2400

November

Physical Tools	Botanicals
Take a break this month!	

December

Physical Tools	Botanicals
Bread machine, such as the Bosch	Restock any winter herb products
The Botanical Safety Handbook	Wild Cherry Coffaway

I saved the big expenses of a water purifier, grain mill and bread machine until the end of the year so that you could save most of the year to be able to purchase these. These purchasing suggestions may be adapted for your family's individual needs.

HARVESTING, DRYING AND STORING HERBS

Many of us will choose to purchase the bulk of our herbs from health food stores, co-operatives or mail-order businesses. Some of us will choose to grow some of our herbs in our own garden to make inexpensive herbal preparations for our family, and a few of us may be entire "do-it-yourself-ers." I find that there is nothing quite like anticipating spring so that I may get out in my gardens and dig in the dirt. A part of health for me is being able to dream up new garden designs, plant new herbs, flowers, shrubs and trees. Merely walking through a garden with the ability to reach down, ruffle some rosemary with my fingers, then inhale that wonderful scent is a delight for me.

When harvesting herbs, we will want to collect the healthiest plants in our garden. We certainly don't want to make herbal medicines with sick or "bug-gy" plants. Herbs should not be collected if heavy pesticides have been regularly used in our gardens. And, as my mother always says of her purple-hulled, pink-eyed peas, we must not let the herbs "go through a heat" after collecting. Bring the herbs home before wilting and decomposition can begin and keep them in a cool place. My mother uses a small fan to gently blow over her harvested vegetables to keep them cool in a non-air-conditioned room.

We must be careful not to over-pick our gardens lest we have nothing to harvest next year. If gathering seeds, spread some around to encourage new growth. I find that harvesting some herbs (such as rosehips, echinacea flowers, etc) encourages new production.

Parts of Plants Used to Make Medicines:

Flowers: Pick on a warm, dry day after the dew has evaporated. Flowers should be fully mature and looking at their liveliest - bees buzzing around them are a good sign of health. Spread on a screen to dry. For example: *Echinacea, calendula, chamomile.*

Leaves: After the dew has dried off the plant on a warm morning, leaves may be harvested just before flowering or when setting buds. Collect the whole stems and strip off the leaves after drying. Examples: *Mints, lemon balm, nettles.*

Seeds or fruit: Pick when fully grown, just as they ripen. Examples: *Hawthorne, rosehips.*

Bark: Harvest in early spring when the sap is rising or in the fall when the sap is about to fall - notice the last colored leaf. Dry whole or cut into 1-inch strips. Examples: *Crampbark, wild cherry, willow.*

Roots or rhizomes: For biennials, harvest the root in the autumn of the first year or spring of the second year before much foliage growth has occurred. *Burdock.* With periennials, gather in the autumn before the first deep frost after the tops have died back or in the very early spring before new foliage appears. Wash and chop into 1/2 inch pieces before drying. For example: *Comfrey, elecampane.*

Whole Herb: The term "whole herb" refers to all aerial (above the ground, in the air) parts of the plant: leaves, flowers and stems. Harvest after the dew has dried in the morning of a warm day. Flowers should just be starting to bloom with the plant heavy with buds. Dry on the stem in small bundles. Examples: *Catnip, hyssop.*

Drying

Plants are a large part water, just as we are! Moisture must be removed to avoid molding, bacterial-growth, enzymatic or chemical changes. Some herbs change during the drying process making them more medicinal than in their fresh state, such as gentian, wild cherry, valerian. Direct sunlight is to be avoided during drying to prevent undesirable physical and chemical depletion of the plants. Some roots, containing tannins or anthraquinone glycosides, may need sunlight during the drying process, but generally, we will choose a dark room or a room with indirect sunlight.

A well-ventilated room is essential during the drying process. A small fan may be used to facilitate proper air circulation and prevention of mold growth. DO NOT OVERDRY. Crumbly or very brittle leaves and flowers will not be as potent in their medicinal qualities.

Dried Herb Storage

As with any long-term storage, air is the enemy causing oxidation to occur. Fill containers to the top with the herb or place cotton in the jar so that air space is not allowed. O_2 packs may be used in large jars along with these other measures to further prevent oxidation. We, then, can transfer small amounts of our stored herbs to smaller containers allowing more frequent use of the small amounts without endangering the potency of our larger, stored amount.

Light is another foe to our stored herbs. Light causes photo-oxidation and accelerates chemical changes in the herbs. I prefer amber jars and bottles; opaque containers are best. Clear glass jars may be used if they are hidden in a closed cabinet, away from heat sources.

Speaking of heat, temperature affects the rate of chemical reaction in plant material. We must keep the heat away from our stored herbs to maintain their potency. Ideal storage temperature is 55 degrees F. to 65 degrees F.

Before storing, remove all extra debris, such as insects, fungus, bacteria, and other contaminants. Store in an air-tight, glass container, preferably the amber bottles available from herbal preparation suppliers. Before filling the jars with our herbs, we should heat the container slightly, then cool, and fill our jars immediately. This eliminates condensation. Mold can be a problem if any excess moisture is in the jar.

Most dried leaves and flowers may be kept up to a year and replenished with a new harvest. Roots, barks and seeds will store longer, 18 to 36 months.

HERBAL PREPARATIONS FOR THE FAMILY

There are many herbal preparations that are helpful for the family, especially when dealing with infants and small children. The following are some guidelines for preparing and using herbal preparations with family members.

Teas

Teas are water extracts. There are two types of medicinal herbal teas: **decoctions** and **infusions**. Infusions are made from the aerial parts of the plant, such as leaves and flowers, and, sometimes, soft berries and seeds. Decoctions are used for the hard or woody parts of the plant, such as the roots, seeds and barks.

Infusion Preparation:
- Steep 1 tsp. of herb(s) in 1 cup of water (pour the boiling water over the herb) at least 10 minutes, maximum 30 minutes (the longer steeped, the stronger the infusion).
- Use within 8 to 12 hours or store in the refrigerator up to 3 days.

Decoction Preparation:
- Place 1 tsp. of the herb(s)in 1 cup cold water; bring water to a boil.
- Turn heat down and slow-simmer the herbs 5 to 20 minutes.
- Remove from heat and strain.
- Use within 8 to 12 hours or store in the refrigerator up to 3 days.

When using teas medicinally for an infant or child, a teaspoonful dose once every hour is necessary to keep the medicine level up until improvement is seen. Herbal teas may be sweetened with raw sugar, rice syrup, glycerine. Honey should NEVER be used for a child under 1 year of age due to the inability of the child's digestive system to inactivate the botulism spores naturally found in honey.

Baths

Baths treat the whole body. This is accomplished through the skin absorbing the chemical constituents thus passing these constituents into the bloodstream. Water, in and of itself, is medicinal: hot water can reduce pain and tension; lukewarm water is comforting and healing; cold water is tightening and astringent. Our olfactory receptors in the nose cause the aromas from any herbs to potentially be aesthetically appealing. The olfactory receptors are part of the limbic system, which is responsible for the "happy" feeling we experience.

When using a bath as a way of administering medicine, we must stay in the tub at least 20 minutes, preferably 30 minutes. The body is hydrating in the first 10 minutes, then the next 10 to 20 minutes allow the medication to penetrate. Use one quart of an infusion or decoction depending on the herb. Always strain the herbs out of a decoction before adding to water.

During an illness with fever, a hot bath is dehydrating. Since a hot bath can make us so much more comfortable when experiencing body aches, we can oil the child with castor oil to seal the skin before putting him/her in the bath. A hot bath with Epsom salts added can relax achy muscles as long as the child is oiled prior to placing in the bath.

Tepid water baths may be done during a febrile illness; however, the child should be oiled after the bath to seal in the water that has been absorbed.

Body Rubs

Body rubs can decrease muscle spasm to help with coughs, lower back pain and colic. Body rubs penetrate muscle tissue to bring about relaxation and stimulate healing. Aromatic herbs should be used for body rubs because of their high volatile oil content which stimulates short-term absorption to deliver the medication; however, aromatic herbs relax in the long-term. One cannot use just the essential oil for body rubs; instead, a ratio of 4 ounces of fatty oil (sweet almond, olive, safflower, sesame or avocado) to 1 ounce of essential oil. For babies, this 4:1 ratio may be tried for 24 hours to see if there is a skin reaction, since babies' skin is extremely sensitive.

Herbs useful for Body Rubs:
- For muscles aches: wintergreen
- For coughs: thyme
- For colic: black haw, meadowsweet, lobelia, fennel

Oils for body rubs may be made by heating or by a no-cook method. I prefer the cooking method as there is less chance of growing bacteria than in the no-cook method.

Body Rub (Herbal Oil) Preparation:
- Choose one of the above fatty oils.
- Prepare the herbs (chop or grind, if dried) and cover with adequate oil.
- Let cook in low oven 100-150 degrees F. for 12 to 15 hours or use slow-cooking crock pot for 12 hours.
- Strain and bottle; store in a cool place up to one year for best results.

Creams and Ointments

Creams penetrate the deep layer of skin and are cooling to the body. Creams are made from an oil and water mix that is emulsified and stabilized. Creams are especially useful for the musculoskeletal system, vagina, nose, head and ears.

Ointments are created from a lipid (fat) base. Ointments are useful for surface wounds to insulate the skin and are easy to prepare at home.

Preparation:

- Use 2 ounces beeswax to 1 pint of oil for ointments.
- Grate beeswax while gently heating the prepared herbal oil in a double boiler; add the grated beeswax and melt. When the beeswax has melted, pour or ladle the hot mixture into small 1-oz. containers before it hardens. 10 to 20 drops of essential herbal oils may be added to make the salve more pleasant to the senses - ADD ESSENTIAL OILS WHEN MIXTURE HAS JUST BEEN TAKEN OFF THE HEAT.
- Store in tightly closed containers in a cool, dark place. Refrigeration is ideal for storage.
- Use within one year for best results.

Fomentations and Poultices

Fomentation and poultices are used for swelling and inflammation, particularly glandular swelling and inflammation. A fomentation is a compress of tea (an infusion or decoction) that is placed on the body. Fomentations are excellent for wrapping around the neck for swollen glands in illnesses such as strep throat. In strep throat, an excellent fomentation recipe is: 1 part mullein, 1/4 part lobelia and 1/4 t cayenne. The mullein and lobelia herbs are infused in 1 part vinegar (1 c.) and 1 part water (1 c). Steep for 10 minutes, then add the capsicum. Soak cloth in infusion. Wrap around neck. Hold heat in by covering the moist cloth with plastic wrap, then a towel for insulation. Leave on for 15 to 20 minutes.

A poultice utilizes herbal material directly on the body. An example of this would be an onion poultice for deep lung congestion. Onions are sauteed, then cooled to a temperature that will not burn the chest skin. After cooling somewhat, the onions are placed on the chest (perhaps cheesecloth could be placed beneath the onions) and covered with plastic wrap. Fresh herbs may simply be mashed and ground up (macerated) and the resulting pulp applied to the skin. The herb may be macerated by using a mortar and pestle, a blender or finely chopping the herb with a knife. Dried herbs can be used if reconstituted with water until moist and soft. Fresh roots may be grated and applied to the skin. Herbal powders may be used if mixed with enough warm water to make a paste, then applied to the affected area.

Powders

An herbal powder may be made for the skin. Powders are good for skin folds for soothing and antifungal purposes or on the umbilicus for drying and aid removal. A good multipurpose herbal powder is: slippery elm, calendula, green clay and lavender. A good umbilical powder may be made from goldenseal root or myrrh gum.

Powder Preparation (Body)
- Grind dried leaves, flowers, roots and barks in a coffee grinder or sift through a fine sieve several times.
- Place powder in a shaker or in a container to be applied with a powder puff.

Glycerites and TincTracts

Glycerites utilize vegetable glycerin and usually involve a one-stage high heat process. Straight glycerites may be unstable for non-refrigerated storage if less than 50% glycerin is used to preserve the herbs. Some herbs, the alkaloids, do not extract well in just a high-heat process using glycerin. Mold may occur in glycerites because of the high sugar content of glycerin. Herbs with glycosides extract extremely well in glycerin.

Glycerite Preparation:
- Chop fresh herbs into small pieces.
- Place the chopped herbs into a clean jar
- Mix the glycerin and water together.
- Cover the herbs completely with a mixture of 75% U.S.P. vegetable glycerin and 25% water. (If the plant matter is not completely covered with the glycerin, mold can occur)
- Place in a dark, cool place and shake every few days. After 10 days, press out the herb material, and bottle. Dark, amber bottles are best for homemade glycerites' storage.

TincTracts also utilize a base of vegetable glycerin; however, the TincTract process involves 3 stages: 1st stage - Cold process stage to extract vitamins, enzymes and mineral electrolytes; 2nd stage - Sealed process to obtain aromatic, volatile and fixed oils, resins, phenols and phenolic glycosides; 3rd stage - Extraction step which derives the naturally-occurring organic trace minerals and the remaining nutritional components, resulting in a rich, more potent herbal product. TincTracts remain nutritionally and medicinally superior to simple glycerites since cold-pressing helps to extract more of the active constituents of the herb. I purchase my TincTracts from Tri-Light Company, brand names: Liquid LightTM and Mother's ChoiceTM. See Resource section for contact numbers.

Both TincTracts and glycerites may be used as a tea by placing drops of the liquid herb into a cup of water or made into a popsicle by freezing the "tea."

Tinctures and Elixirs

Tinctures are made by extracting the herbs into alcohol or apple-cider vinegar basically by covering the herbs with alcohol (or vinegar) and water and allowing the mixture to sit (digest) for 14 days to six weeks (longer if desired). Fresh or dried herbs may be used. Tinctures preserve the medicinal properties of herbs for very long periods as long as you do not skimp on the quality of the alcohol used.

Tinctures are not appropriate for alcoholics or those adverse to ingesting alcohol (liquor). While medicinally strong and good for long-term storage, alcohol tinctures are difficult to administer to children because the alcohol is "hot" in the mouth and down the throat. I personally prefer not to use alcohol tinctures with my children since a quality and long-lasting alternative is available in the TincTracts.

Some parents like the aspect of being able to administer a small amount of alcohol with the medicinals to help the child sleep and lessen pain perception. My disagreement with this practice is that while alcohol does tend to make one nod off, the amount of tincture given may not accomplish this goal, and even if it does, alcohol causes a fitful sleep, not a quality sleep which is essential to healing. I prefer instead to administer nervine or sedative herbs with my medicinals if I need the child to calm down and sleep.

Tincture Preparation:

- Prepare 1 part herb to 5 parts, 100% alcohol/water mixture by weight. 100% grain alcohol is best, but a good quality vodka will work for home preparation. If using vodka, use a 50% proof and no dilution with water will be necessary. If using 100% grain alcohol, dilute to desired strength. A 50% alcohol/50% water solution will extract most medicinal constituents from common medicinal herbs.
- Pack a jar with the herb and cover with the alcohol/water solution so that no herb matter is exposed to the air.
- Let stand for 14 days to 6 weeks; press or strain out the herb and bottle in amber bottles.

Elixirs are made by combining tinctures and glycerin-based products to form a syrup. This is sometimes helpful for a cough if the parent decides alcohol is a necessary part of the healing regimen. Herbal syrups can easily be made and stored in the refrigerator for several months. A useful herbal syrup for sore throats and coughs would be Onion Syrup: Stack layers of a baseball-sized onion with granulated raw sugar. Let this alternately-layered mixture sit for 24 hours; then drain the syrup into a container to be kept in the refrigerator. This syrup base has antibacterial properties. One-fourth ounce her tinctures, such as garlic, thyme, elecampane, echinacea, yarrow, mullein and hyssop, may be added to 1/2 oz. onion syrup to form a medicinal respiratory syrup.

Elixer, or Syrup, Preparation:

- Prepare a syrup base by dissolving 2 1/2 lbs. of raw sugar in 1 pint of water over a gentle heat. When all the sugar has dissolved, cook for 1 minute, then remove from the heat. The base syrup can then be mixed with a tincture to make a medicated syrup (1 part tincture to 3 parts syrup).
- Add one cup of raw sugar to one pint of an herbal infusion or decoction.
- Bring the whole mixture to a boil; remove from heat, cool and bottle.
- If using honey instead of sugar, use equal parts honey and infusion or decoction and heat slowly to a simmer. Continue simmering until thick; remove from the heat and bottle. DO NOT USE HONEY ELIXERS WITH CHILDREN UNDER 1 YEAR OF AGE.
- Syrups made with tinctures may be stored at room temperature. Syrups made without sugar are best stored in the refrigerator.

Steams

Steams are warming, decongesting and soothing to the upper respiratory system. An aromatic herb, or its volatile oil, should be used. Chamomile is particularly effective since steam distillation makes it active against *staphylococcus* and *streptococcus* organisms. Chamomile has the added benefit of being pleasing to the olfactory senses.

Steam Preparation:

- If using a volatile oil, add 5 to 8 drops of oil in a large bowl of steaming water.
- If using an herb, add 1 to 2 tablespoons to a quart of boiling water.
- Create a tent over the bowl by draping a towel over the head and breathe the steam for 3 to 5 minutes.

Suppositories and Enemas

The intestinal mucosa absorbs well making enemas excellent for fevers. A good enema solution would be catnip and/or marshmallow. The bulb syringe found in most birth kits is perfect for an infant or child enema. The tip should be lubricated (butter is a great lubricant; petroleum products should never be used to lubricate because they clog the absorption sites). Lay the child, gently, abdomen down. Air should be squirted out of the syringe. The bulb syringe should be inserted 1/2 to 1cm into the rectum, and 1 tablespoon of solution per hour administered, until some comes back. The child will expel the liquid, and the fever will be reduced. If the child is dehydrated, expulsion may not occur due to the enema solution aiding rehydration. Do not overfill the child's bowel with solution, or the child will excrete everything back, causing further dehydration.

During a fever, care should be taken to make the enema solution 1 degree lower than the rectal temperature. Enemas should always be performed with reverse osmosis water.

Distilled water, for drinking and enemas, will leach minerals from the body, which could make matters worse. If distilled water is used for the enema solution, a pinch of salt should be added (or a pinch of baking soda for an adult) to retain minerals. Tap water contains too many chemical and possible microbial contaminants to make it a viable enema solution.

Suppositories are made with a cocoa butter base. Most suppository trays are adult size. Mom should somewhat melt the adult-sized suppository down and reshape for the child's anal opening or halve the adult-sized suppository for the child.

Breastfeeding

We nursing mothers must not forget the ease of administering medicine to our infants through our breastmilk. Breastmilk is a wonderful and powerful medicine alone. Mother can take her medicinals, and 6 to 8 hours later, baby will get reduced amounts of that medicinal in the breastmilk. Aromatic herbs pass extremely well through breast-milk.

HERBAL IMMUNOSUPPORT

Several herbs are used for immunosupport. Those that have been shown in research studies to be most effective are: aloe vera (acemannan); astragalus, echinacea, garlic, shiitake mushroom, panax ginseng, siberian ginseng and milk thistle (silymarin).

Aloe vera has proved to be quite an effective immunostimulant. The leaves must not be ingested by children or pregnant women due to their strong laxative effect. The juice from the inner part of the leaves is acceptable.

Astragalus seems to function best as an immunostimulant when used for viral infections. The herb increases alpha-and gamma-interferon levels in the body. May be taken for long periods without toxicity risk.

Echinacea has the double effect of protecting the cell membrane from pathogens while at the same time increasing the white cell response of the body. This immune-enhancing effect can occur at a 30% increase and lasts approximately 2 hours after herb administration. Echinacea, ideally, should not be used for more than 8 weeks without giving a 1 to 2 week break to prevent a build-up of tolerance to the herb's activity.

Garlic has fared well in research studies for a variety of pathogens: viruses, fungi, protozoa, parasites and bacteria. Dosages need to be at least 3 times daily at an equivalent of 1-2 cloves of garlic at each administration.

Shiitake mushroom increases both T-cell activity and increases macrophage response.

Panax ginseng was studied and found to enhance the immune response with clinical improvement observed beginning in the 4th week of usage.

Siberian ginseng was found to produce a greater number than average immuno-competent cells with enhancement of the broad range of immune functions. Like the Panax ginseng variety, improvement began to be most noticeable after 4 weeks of use. Both of the ginsengs would be long-term (over winter or weakened time) immunosupport.

Milk thistle's active component, silymarin, shows marked liver protective properties as well as general immune enhancement. Adult dosage is 3 tablets daily of standardized (at least 70% silymarin) product.

INDIVIDUALIZING DOSAGES FOR FAMILY MEMBERS

Most herbal preparations sold in health food stores and co-ops have a general recommended amount on the bottle that is usually an adult dosage. Parents can easily become confused by the numerous methods of calculating dosage for children.

The easiest method I've found of calculating individualized dosages is based on the assumption that most dosage amounts on purchased herbal preparations are geared to a 150 lb. person. Thus to figure the amount needed for a 75 lb. person, we would only need to halve the recommended amount. For a 37 lb. child, we would give 1/4 the recommended amount and so on. For a 300 lb. person, the recommended amount would be doubled. I do feel that giving a dose based on the individual's body weight is important to make certain an adequate amount of the medicinal is in the body.

One thing we, as parents, do well to remember is that the above method of dosing relies more heavily upon individual needs (body weight) rather than an age as do some of the other botanical dosing methods. The recommended body weight method is one that may be utilized for those herbs generally considered "safe" for children to use. If a parent is choosing to use an herb that may be toxic in large quantities, a qualified professional herbalist or physician, trained in herbal care, should be consulted before herb administration.

In dosing with botanicals, I find it helpful to remember: Small amounts of herbs given frequently during a crisis are far more beneficial than mega-doses given infrequently and irregularly. Some herbs perform quite well if a steady amount is maintained in the body during an illness.

Part Four

BUILDING KNOWLEDGE

UTILIZING HERBAL TEXTS

The nutritional supplement industry has fairly exploded in growth over the past few years. This has led to a vast number of herb books being written. The confusion for most consumers is: Which book is "right" and worth my investment? Although my husband and I purchase many of the books available due to our Institute for Family Herbal Care needing to review these books for our members, we find that we could get along just fine with only a few of the books of exceptional quality.

How Do We Define Quality in Herbal Texts?

An herbal book worth my monetary and time investment is one that meets the following criteria:

- The book will supply information about historical usage of herbs, pharmacological components of the herb, toxicity data, therapeutic dosages and clinical applications;
- The book will not enter into a discussion of the spirit of the herbs, rather the author will concentrate on the herb's physiological actions on the body;
- The book will either provide footnotes, endnotes or extensive bibliography that directs the reader to their sources so further individual research may be accomplished;
- The book will not function simply as a tool for selling a particular nutritional supplement line (although all authors have favorites, is the author merely trying to sell a line of products?), although these types of books function well as a guide for using that particular supplement line;
- A major bonus for us is when we find books written from a distinctly Christian perspective (this does not occur often enough in this industry as of yet).

Using Herbal Texts for Family Health

The key to using herbal texts successfully in family health is to read them before family members become ill. If we wait until family members are ill, our risk of reading wrongly, interpreting inappropriately and applying wrongly increases due to fatigue and worry. Parents who desire to utilize herbal and nutritional medicine are best served by texts when they provide a regular budget category for the purchase of these home health tools until enough texts have been added to the home library for successfully treating those self-limiting illnesses at home.

My favorite books on nutritional and botanical medicine are as follows:

- *Herbal Prescriptions for Better Health* by Donald J. Brown, N.D.
- *Natural Alternatives to Over-the-Counter and Prescription Drugs* by Michael T. Murray, N.D.
- *The Healing Power of Herbs* by Michael T. Murray, N.D.
- *Food-Your Miracle Medicine* by Jean Carper.

Other books that have served me well in the past years are:

- *Understanding Diagnostic Tests in the Childbearing Years* by Anne Frye.
- *The Toxicology of Botanical Medicine* by Francis Brinker, N.D.
- *Botanical Influences on Illness* by Melvyn Werbach and Michael T. Murray, N.D.
- *The Green Pharmacy* by James Duke, Ph.D.
- *Encyclopedia of Nutritional Supplements* by Michael T. Murray, N.D.
- *The Complete Botanical Prescriber* by John A. Sherman, N.D.
- *Herbs for Health and Healing* by Kathi Keville.

A magazine that I've found incredibly helpful is *The Protocol Journal of Botanical Medicine* published by Herbal Research Publications, P.O. Box 721, Ayer, MA 01432, phone number (800) 466-5422. Although this periodical is fairly expensive, I've found it to be the greatest help in establishing treatment protocols for my family and clients. One must be able to translate (with a botanical name/common name listing) the Latin botanical names into common names to use this magazine. I highly recommend this for those who are ministering to others in herbal medicine as well as those families desiring to further a child's interest in becoming a professional herbalist.

Cross-Referencing

When reading my herb books about specific illnesses, I tend to consult several different books. After reading about the specific illness I am researching, I then cross-reference the herbs that are recommended for that illness to find any toxicity information and exact therapeutic dosage information on those particular herbs.

If I find any disagreement in terms of toxicity or dosage, then I generally will choose to try the lowest therapeutic dosage to begin and increase if I find I need to with the illness, watching for any signs of toxicity. If the herbs recommended are considered to be toxic in large amounts, I usually consult with a professional herbalist or licensed naturopath before proceeding with treatment, particularly when treating my children or my pregnant self.

Always check for toxicity. Do not simply rely on those herbals that do not list toxicity amounts or symptoms, and never use herbs that may be toxic for young children or pregnant women.

RESEARCHING SAFETY & TOXICITY CONCERNS

The safety of certain herbs has been questioned, particularly in the past few years as more consumers choose to employ herbal medicine as part of their health care program. It never ceases to amaze me when television news shows or newspapers and magazines vilify herbal medicine because of a limited number of herbs that may have contributed to pre-existing health problems. Many time, these same medical media sources ignore the overwhelming confirmed and documented evidence of health problems created by over-the-counter and prescription drugs.

The concern about herb safety appears to arise from several different reasons: the inherent toxicity of certain herbs, the presence of potentially toxic chemical constituents in certain herbs, and the potential for adulteration in the herb industry. These are valid concerns that should warrant our investigation into the herbs we plan to consume; however, we need not toss the baby out with bathwater. All of these concerns can be addressed and our risks limited through wise and prudent use.

Inherent Toxicity

There are definitely certain herbs that have toxic effects; most of us would call them poisonous plants. These plants, while certainly herbs, would not be present in the category of commonly-used, medicinal herbal preparations. These herbs primarily function as the basis for pharmaceutical preparations. One example of an inherently toxic plant is belladonna or deadly nightshade. Belladonna toxicity depends largely on the presence of the alkaloids Hyoscyamine and Atropine, with some scopolamine present in the leaves. Belladona is not an herb to be used as part of home health care because it is classified as a poison. Belladonna instead performs as the basis for pharmaceutical preparations because of its narcotic, diuretic, sedative, antispasmodic and mydriatic effects. Other examples of poisonous or inherently toxic herbs that should not be used without professional preparation and guidance would be: poke root, mandrake, ipecac, opium, rauwolfia, foxglove, ergot. This list is by no means exhaustive; rather, it is a sampling of toxic herbs some of us may be familiar with because of their pharmaceutical preparations.

Potentially Toxic Constituents

Many herbs and foods have chemical constituents (chemical parts of their make-up) that are toxic if that chemical alone is administered. This concern has created the most debate. Even some professional herbalists differ in their opinions as to whether an herb with potentially toxic constituents should be consumed in any quantity. While it would certainly not be prudent to ingest these isolated chemicals, does it necessarily follow that these chemicals, when found in the whole herb or portion of the plant that is generally used, constitute a direct threat to the general public? The answer to this question appears to be simple, yet because each of us is unique in design by our Creator, each individual must weigh the risk versus benefit for ourselves and seek the counsel of others with wisdom, in order to come to a decision regarding usage.

Several herbs have come under fire from the FDA because of their pyrollizidine alkaloid (PA)-content, namely, comfrey, borage, coltsfoot and life root. Pyrollizidine alkaloids have been linked as a contributing factor in several individuals who developed a disorder called hepatic veno-occlusive disease (HVOD), also known as Budd-Chiari syndrome. This condition occurs when blood flow from the liver becomes obstructed which then impairs liver function. HVOD can lead to liver damage of varying degrees and, still later, can lead to cancerous liver tumors. This is a serious disorder that might, at first glance, convince anyone that any use of herbs containing pyrollizidine alkaloids would mean certain disease. The problem with this assumption is that these herbs have been used for several thousand years by a great number of people without the end result of all of them contracting HVOD. Why did only these people contract the disease and not all or even most of the world's other comfrey users? I am not trying to minimize the ill effects of pyrollizidine alkaloids. They can be destructive to the body.

Comfrey

The first point to consider when evaluating PA-containing herbs for safety is that we must recognize that some of those who contracted HVOD appeared to already have liver or digestive system problems. Another point to consider is that PA-containing herbs were not definitely identified as the cause; they were linked to the disease because a few of the people who contracted HVOD had consumed comfrey in the form of comfrey/pepsin tablets. Lastly, the people who were using comfrey were ingesting large quantities above the standard recommended dosage. One boy had Crohn's disease, a chronic intestinal disorder. This young boy drank comfrey tea daily for two years before he developed HVOD. Another woman developed HVOD after four months of taking six comfrey/pepsin capsules daily in addition to drinking comfrey tea each day.[1] All of these factors make the case against any use of PA-containing herbs less clear. In point of fact, there has never been reported a case of HVOD in people taking recommended amounts of herbs containing pyrollizidine alkaloids for brief periods.

Since these herbs do have beneficial properties as well as the PA content, a cautious approach would make sense until some definitive research combined with the long history of use clears up this PA/HVOD relationship.

The following people should avoid the internal use of herbs containing pyrollizidine alkaloids (comfrey, borage, coltsfoot, life root):
  • Persons with a history of liver disease, alcoholism, or general digestive problems;

- Children under two because their immature digestive systems might possibly be unable to process any absorbed alkaloid;
- Pregnant women, because pregnancy places a greater burden on the liver's detoxifying process;
- Nursing mothers because whatever mom eats or drinks, baby absorbs while nursing.

History and some herbalists believe that even these individuals could consume small amounts for very short periods, less than 10 days.

Comfrey has also been accused of being carcinogenic. What a bad reputation this once highly-regarded herb is now gaining! A different picture is painted once again with a little investigation into the experiments upon which this ill repute is based. The experiment that deemed comfrey carcinogenic was one in which lab rats or mice were fed very large doses of comfrey roots for 600 days. After 130 days, they began to show liver toxicity. By the end of the study, liver cancer appeared in even the rats fed the lowest dosage of comfrey. Comfrey roots contain 10 times the pyrollizidine alkaloids that the leaves contain, and these rats were (as usual for toxicity studies) being fed doses many times greater than the human equivalent daily dosage. The result extrapolated from this study cannot be equated to human consumption or application of comfrey since we do not exist solely on a diet of mega-doses of comfrey roots for almost two years (at least we certainly should not be existing in this manner).

Tons of comfrey are grown each year to be used as fodder for horses, cattle and pigs with no ill effects observed. Our human history of comfrey use has no reports of harm to the average person. In a 1987 study published in *Science*, Dr. Bruce Ames, Ph.D., chairman of the Biochemistry Department at the University of California at Berkeley, estimated the lifetime cancer risk from exposure to typical man-made and naturally occurring carcinogens. His estimations concluded that one cup of comfrey tea posed:

- about the same risk as one peanut butter sandwich, which contains traces of the natural carcinogen aflatoxin;
- about half the risk of eating one raw mushroom, which contains traces of the natural carcinogen, hydrazine;
- half the risk of one diet soda containing saccharin;
- and about one one-hundredth the risk of a standard beer or glass of wine, which contains the natural carcinogen ethyl alcohol.

He did conclude that comfrey-pepsin tablets carry 4 to 200 times the risk of comfrey tea.[2] The tablets can be avoided because there are so many other herbs that may be used to supplement the digestive process with lesser risk.

Chapparal

Another herb that came under attack and was banned by the FDA a couple of years ago was chapparal. The FDA banned it until it could be proven that it did not cause kidney and liver failure in four cancer patients undergoing extensive chemotherapy treatments. Chapparal contains the chemical NDGA (nordihydroguaiaretic acid) which is approved by the U.S. Department of Agriculture as a preservative in lard and animal shortenings. NDGA has an antiseptic and antioxidant action that kills bacteria and microorganisms that turn fat and oils rancid. This antiseptic action also reduces cavities by 75%, according to a study done on chaparral mouthwash published in the *Journal of Dental Research*.[3] Medical literature has several case reports of tumor shrinkage in people who used chappparal.

The FDA removed NDGA from the list of substances generally regarded as safe (GRAS) in 1968 because experimental animals fed large amounts for long periods developed kidney and lymph-system problems. No human kidney or lymphatic disease has ever been documented in chaparral users until this recent questioning of its safety.[4] The most baffling aspect is that over the long history of chaparral use, this problem has not appeared before even when being used by other cancer patients. All four of the individuals who experienced kidney and liver failure while taking chaparral were also taking extremely toxic drugs known to cause failure of the body's systems. These pharmaceuticals were not blamed, nor were they banned or even investigated; their toxicity was already established in their clinical drug trials. Chaparral seems to have been in the wrong body at the wrong time.

Lobelia

Yet another herb has a lingering cloud of controversy over its name, Lobelia. I read in one book on pregnancy and childbirth that lobelia was a very dangerous herb to be avoided by all. The book claimed that lobelia can cause convulsion, coma and even death due to the toxic alkaloid, lobeline. As I looked up the research done on the herb, lobelia, I found these danger claims were made on drug provings for the isolated constituent, lobeline, of the herb, not on the whole herb, lobelia. As already mentioned, the toxic alkaloid, lobeline, can cause convulsion, coma and even death. Well, this toxic alkaloid, lobeline, is the active ingredient in some over-the-counter (OTC) drugs used as nicotine deterrents.

I phoned a Poison Control Center to inquire about common effects of the herb lobelia. I was told common effects are: vomiting, transient slowing of the heart rate, increase in blood pressure, and an increase in the respiratory or breathing rate.[5] These effects are most often associated with large doses of the herb, not standard recommended dosages. In the history of lobelia use, the emetic (vomiting-inducive) effect is clearly noted and actually honored. This emetic effect makes overdose (with recommended amounts) extremely impossible. The OTC preparations containing lobeline do not have this built-in protective device (emetic property); therefore, lobeline-containing OTCs *do* represent an overdose risk. They have not been banned; instead, they have the FDA stamp of approval.

St. John's Wort

St. John's Wort, an herb with increasingly recognized beneficial effects was included in a March 1977 USFDA "unsafe herb list" due to toxic reactions in cattle. These reactions were not in humans, just in cattle. St. John's Wort may have phototoxic activity (increases sunburn risk) in humans when used in large quantities. There has never been any report that this is the case; however, we might choose to follow the lead of our Eastern neighbors. European consumers who have long used this herb confine their use to moderate dosages and restrict their exposure to sunlight while medicinally using the herb.[6]

Sassafras

Sassafras is another herb with unsavory reputation due to its content of the chemical compound safrole. Safrole was isolated from the whole plant sassafras and fed to mice in the 1960s. A high percentage of the mice had liver damage and liver cancer by the end of the study. This is why the FDA banned the whole herb's internal use. It has been found since that time that safrole itself does not cause cancer in animals; it first must be converted to another compound that is known to be carcinogenic. We do not have adequate research to show that safrole does or does not pose a significant cancer risk in humans. We do know that sassafras has long been popular and is still in use despite its ban with no ill effects being reported.[7]

After all this investigation, it seems that beyond the issue of potentially toxic constituents, the issue really is one of prudent use in recommended amounts for limited periods of time when dealing with those herbs whose safety has been called into question.

Adulteration and Contamination in the Herb Industry

Adulteration of herbal products (accidentally or deliberately substituting one herb for another or processing in such a way as to allow contaminants into the product) is a problem that has plagued the herb industry as long as there has been herb use. The situation is certainly getting better in that there are quite a few reputable companies processing herbs that have a definite commitment to ascertaining that the herb they are processing and labeling as herb X is indeed herb X. The problem with adulteration is that an herb may be given a bad name because the effects of the herb taken were not the effects expected or wanted. In the worst case scenario, the adulterating or contaminating agent can actually cause disease, as in the case of the l-trytophan controversy.

One quite excellent herb, ginseng, is still characterized in some herbals as causing an abuse syndrome. This accusation began with a 1979 study published in the *Journal of the American Medical Association* that linked ginseng to a "ginseng abuse syndrome" which supposedly included symptoms such as nervousness, sleeplessness, and raised blood pressure. The researcher also stated that his subjects (psychiatric patients) used caffeine regularly during the study. Caffeine is well known for the symptoms described in the "ginseng abuse syndrome."[8] In addition to the caffeine consumption, the subject's methods of consuming the herb were rather bizarre when compared to traditional ginseng use: they inhaled and injected it. This strongly suggests that the patients could also have been abusing illicit drugs during the two-year study, which could certainly skew the results.

"Morning diarrhea" was another of the symptoms of GAS. This could possibly be due to adulteration of the herb. The researcher admitted that he made no attempt to verify that his "ginseng" was, indeed, the herb ginseng. It certainly was fact that adulteration was rampant in the health food industry in the 1970s.[9] During the '70s, Wild Red American Ginseng or "desert ginseng" became popular. "Desert" ginseng is an impossibility because ginseng is a shade-loving, moisture-demanding plant. The phony ginseng was actually red dock, a laxative plant that contains anthraquinones (chemicals that stimulate intestinal peristalsis).[10]

As mentioned before, the worst of the adulteration/contamination cases was the l-tryptophan contamination that occurred between October 1988 to June of 1989 resulting in cases of EMS (eosinophilia-myalgia syndrome) in a number of individuals taking l-tryptophan products. The cases of EMS were not a result of taking l-tryptophan per se; rather, they were a result of taking contaminated l-tryptophan from Japanese supplier, Showa Denko.[11] The FDA removed products containing more than 100mg of l-tryptophan from the market due to the cases of EMS in November of 1989 before it became widely known that Showa Denko's contaminated l-tryptophan was the problem. Despite the findings of contamination, the FDA has continued to refuse to lift the ban on uncontaminated l-tryptophan. This situation is a tragic one both for those who developed EMS and their families as well as for those for whom uncontaminated l-tryptophan had been effectively treating their insomnia and depression.[12] The irony and greater tragedy in this is research reported in 1990 that showed uncontaminated l-tryptophan to be one of the most effective treatments for EMS.[13]

As we have looked at the safety issues surrounding herbal products, our directives for safe, responsible use become clear:

- Avoid known toxic (poison) herbs or use only under a professional health care provider's guidance, completely avoid during pregnancy and lactation;
- Use herbs in medicinal amounts only in recommended dosages for limited periods of time, consult with a professional herbalist regarding use during pregnancy and lactation;

- Purchase herbal products only from reputable sources, look for companies with a proven track record for delivering quality assurance to their customers;
- Gather and process herbal medicines at home only after receiving instruction and education regarding identification of herbs in the wild. Before wildcrafting any herb, please check with the endangered plant species list to ensure that we continue to have herbal products to purchase when needed. Better yet, start an herb garden in your backyard with some of those species in it to use for yourself and your neighbors.

SCHOOLS FOR ADVANCED STUDY

There are several schools that offer advanced herbal study. I know of very few that are entirely from a Christian perspective. Keith and I now are able to offer a professional certification through the Institute for Family Herbal Care, allowing those who complete the *Naturally Healthy Family*™ course plus advanced training to teach our course materials in their own locations as well as provide consultations for others.

These are the schools that offer advanced herbal study:

On-Site Learning

The Ojai College of Phytotherapy
Amanda McQuade-Crawford, Director
PO Box 66
Ojai, CA 93024
Brochure: Free

Southwest School of Botanical Medicine
Michael Moore, Director
122 Tulare S.E.
Albuqeurque, NM 87106
(505) 255-9215
Brochure: Free
A 4-month, 500 hour program offering professional training in wildcrafting, pharmacy and a constitutional evaluation system. One month of field work. Feb.-June. $1700.

Christian Homesteading Movement
Richard and Anne Marie Fahey, Directors
Oxford, NY 13830-0523.
Brochure: Send 2 stamps.
This program teaches self-sufficiency including gathering and using herbs medicinally. The Faheys also have a midwifery program as well.
Herbal Correspondence Courses

The Australasian College of Herbal Studies
PO Box 57
Lake Oswego, OR 97034
(503) 697-5992
Catalog or brochure: Free

Australian Horticultural Correspondence School
264 Sansea Rd. Lilydale
Victoria, Australia 3140
61-3-736-1882
Catalog or brochure: Free

Institute for Family Herbal Care
Keith Parker, CEO, and Shonda Parker, Program Director
85 Tunnel Rd., Suite 12-A 287
Asheville, North Carolina 28805
(888) HERB-101, leave name and address for information
Catalog: Free
This self-paced study program includes an initial correspondence course in the basics of nutritional and botanical medicine with an emphasis on Mommy DiagnosticsTM. Professional Family Herbalist certification may be pursued upon completion of the Naturally Healthy Family course through further study and a weekend study intensive, which will allow others to teach the Naturally HealthyTM materials. For those interested in also studying midwifery, we recommend…

The Midwifery Institute of America
RR #2, Box 409, Rome PA 18837, (717) 395-3192.
Offers a Basic Christian Midwifery Course (resident training or correspondence). Their program does not teach the use of medicinal herbs for pregnancy and childbirth in great depth; therefore, we feel our program complements theirs wonderfully.

School of Herbal Medicine
PO Box 168-K
Suquamish, WA 98392
(206) 598-3556
Catalog: SASE
The School of Herbal Medicine (American Branch, National Institute of Medical Herbalists, England) offers a correspondence course covering anatomy and physiology, herbal medicine philosophy, pathology, diagnosis and materia medica.

Therapeutic Herbalism
David Hoffman, Director
2068 Ludwig Ave.
Santa Rosa, CA 95407
Brochure: Free

A correspondence course exploring western herbal medicine written by David Hoffmann, British Medical Herbalist, internationally known teacher and author of *The Holistic Herbal.* The course is intended for both the professional health care practitioner and student of holistic medicine, designed to lay the foundations for the skilled use of herbal medicines within a holistic practice. It is structured so that it may be used in a number of different, yet compatible ways: as the cornerstone of developing a practice as a medical herbalist; as a component within the practice of a therapist whose primary healing modality is another therapy, such as a chiropractor or nurse practitioner; as training for the specialist in the herb industry; may also be used as a herbal foundation for self-help for the nonprofessional.

Naturopathic Medicine Schools

Bastyr College
144-AH N.E. 54th St.
Seattle, WA 98105
(206) 523-9585
Catalog: $5, Brochure: Free

A Naturopathic medicine program leading to a degree as a licensed naturopathic physician, N.D., also has a program in midwifery.

The National College of Naturopathic Medicine
11231 S.E. Market
Portland, OR 97216
(503) 225-4860
Catalog: Free

A Naturopathic medicine program leading to a degree as a licensed naturopathic physician, N.D., also program in midwifery.

Southwest College of Naturopathic Medicine & Health Sciences
6535 East Osborn
Scottsdale, AZ 85251
(602) 858-9100
Brochure: Free

Offers same programs as above schools.

Part Five

REPAIR AND MAINTENANCE

NATURAL HEALING
USING HERBS AND FOOD

This section, dealing with specific illnesses and the dietary, lifestyle and nutritional supplement recommendations for each, is divided into three parts to make mom's life easier as she seeks to care for those in her household of different age groups. We didn't separate these sections because Grandma is not allowed to have a carrot poultice around her neck for a sore throat, as suggested in the Little Sprout section; rather, we separated the information to customize the care for each age group's particular needs and safety issues.

The *When You're a Little Sprout* section is designed for children from birth to 12 years of age.

The *In the Fullness of Your Days* section may be used by those 12 years of age into adulthood.

And the *As We Acquire Wisdom… And Gray Hairs* section is primarily for adults moving into elder and older women status.

When You're a Little Sprout

CREATING HEALTHY CELLS

Cell health is essential to whole health. If our cells are not healthy, our body will begin to send us signals to alert us to make a change for the better. These signals are commonly called symptoms of disease. Cell health is particularly important in allergic conditions. I recently listened to a seminar in which the speaker, Molly Linton, N.D., said that we have two choices in allergic conditions. We can either avoid the allergen, or we can strengthen the cell so that it does not inappropriately open and release histamine that makes us miserable.

The three keys to cell health are: Vitamin C (Buffered), Bioflavonoids (Rosehips syrup is a good source for children) and Omega-3 oils (cod liver oil, fish oils or flax seed oil). Since these three supplements are the key, they need to be taken daily. A child should have a minimum of 500mg of buffered vitamin C daily. Buffered vitamin C powder, if given immediately, can help avoid the constriction of the larynx that occurs in allergic reactions. One teaspoon of rosehips syrup daily and one teaspoon of cod liver oil or flax seed oil daily is a maintenance dose for a child.

Our liver is our second largest organ. The liver performs a multitude of tasks and can become overburdened with its detoxifying mission. Liver support is a necessary part of cell health. Milk thistle is a wonderful liver-supportive herb. For adults, a tablet or capsule of milk thistle should be standardized to contain at least 70% silymarin. Dark, green vegetables are excellent for dietary liver support.

Five Dietary Components For a Healthy Child

1. Caloric intake - Assess by growth chart. Children usually grow in one direction at a time, up or out. As long as something is growing, that's generally a good sign.

2. Protein intake - Children should have 4 to 6 servings of protein each day. Under age 3, 6 servings daily; over 3, 4 servings daily. This protein does not have to come from dairy or meat. A peanut butter sandwich or peanut butter crackers are a protein serving. In an under age 1 population, if the child is nursing six times daily, food is still an experiment. Their nourishment is coming from the breast milk, an excellent source of nutrients.

3. General vitamins - After weaning, a soy formula provides needed vitamins for the child. Soy milk still needs supplemental vitamins. Children can get their vitamins daily from fresh vegetable juice made from beets, carrots and parsley. Do not introduce fruit juice as the first food. Besides possibly causing allergies, this creates a sweet tooth in the child. After the molars come in, the child can take chewable vitamins.

4. Calcium - Calcium is very important to growing children. If your child is experiencing growing pains, he/she has a calcium deficiency. The newest research shows

that the degree to which little girls' bones are calcified prior to the beginning of menses reflects her risk of osteoporosis later in life. The more calcium consumed early in life reduces her osteoporosis risk later. Cow's milk is not the ideal calcium source; it is in a soap-y form. Seeds and soy products are excellent sources. In fact, soybean products provide a very absorbable form of calcium. Green, crunchy (like bones) vegetables are calcium-rich. A liquid calcium/magnesium supplement may be necessary for most growing girls (and boys).

5. Omega-3 (flax and fish) and 6 (evening primrose, black currant) oils - Many of us are deficient in these oils today. In turn-of-the-century England, a flax man would go door-to-door in winter giving flax oil for women to use daily with their family. Ever wonder why our skin gets chicken-y during the winter?

IMMUNOSUPPORT

Healthy Pregnancy

Immunosupport begins with a healthful pregnancy. Health prior to pregnancy is important since baby takes nutrients first, and mom is left with what baby doesn't need. The essential vitamins for pregnancy include: folic acid, biotin, calcium and trace minerals. A good prenatal can be evaluated by its calcium source: bottom of the line - calcium from oyster shell; middle - calcium carbonate; top quality - calcium citrate/maleate.

Natural Birth

A natural birth assists in a strong beginning for the immune system. Babies who birth vaginally have their neurological functions stimulated to develop as their head is "squished," as some children may phrase it, during their passage through the vagina. The good bacteria present in the vagina is "gobbled up" by the baby as he/she passes through which begins their own bowel colonization. Respiratory function is assisted by lung compression during contractions and in the vagina so that adequate respiratory expansion occurs once baby is out. If mom has had to have a cesarean section (necessary in only 3 - 4% of births), mom should consider giving baby some bifidus probiotic bacteria in the postpartum period. Cranio-sacral work may also be considered for c-sec babies. Chest rubs (no oils) stimulates respirations in baby as do feet rubs. Epidural anesthesia presents several problems for babies: babies whose mothers receive epidural anesthesia during labor have more trouble breastfeeding, and although epidural anesthesia does not show up in the blood of infants, it has been found in their spinal fluid.

Breastfeeding

Breastfeeding is essential to a healthy immune system. Baby's first food, colostrum, contains antibodies and bifidus. Colostrum is a bowel stimulant which helps baby clear the meconium from the bowels. Breastfeeding moms should take in 500 extra calories per day over the prenatal amount.

If mothers need to give their breastfed baby a bottle, mom should keep in mind that breastfed babies bottle-feed twice the amount they would have taken at the breast. Breastfed babies have fewer ear infections, less allergies, higher IQ's and are generally more secure. Soyalac by Loma Linda (LaLoma) used to be available and was a good formula for after weaning. Goat's milk makes a good base for children who are allergic both to cow's milk and soy.

Individualized Food Introduction

Rather than following a general rule about the ideal age for food introduction, we should strive to follow our child's physiological development and cue in to the right time to begin food introduction. The first sign that a child is ready to experiment with food is the appearance of teeth and/or a weight of 17 pounds. The average for this is 9 months. If baby can sit and push food away as well as swallow back instead of tonguing the food out, he/she is probably ready to experiment with food. Food introduction should not be thought of as the sole source of nutrition. Food introduction is just that, introduction. Pears squished through the fingers and on the face is food introduction.

Water introduction is important. Tap water is full of chemical and possible microbial contaminants. Distilled water may leach minerals from the body. Reverse osmosis water with carbon block filtration is an excellent method of drinking water filtration. Flouridated water should be avoided. Fluoride is a cockroach poison, not a food. Fluoride binds to the same receptor sites as calcium creating a calcium-deficiency in the body, not something we want for our children.

The first foods to introduce to babies are root vegetables: beets, carrots, yams, sweet potatoes. We follow these root vegetables with fruits: apples, pears, banana, mashed blueberries. Basmati rice can follow vegetables and fruits. Foods should be introduced one at a time and tried for three days to check for food allergies.

Babies should not have cow's milk, chocolate or caffeine until they are at least two years old. After dairy is introduced in the form of yogurt at 2 years of age, meat can then be introduced. Soy or rice milk makes a healthful drink for a baby after weaning.

The foods most likely to cause allergy are: dairy (cow's milk), eggs (immunized children are often allergic to egg because the immune system attacks the albumin that the immunizations are based in), tomato, eggplant. Formal testing for food allergies are not accurate until the child is over 3 years old. Under 3, allergies change constantly due to the maturing of the intestinal tract.

Sweets

Refined sugar should be avoided. Studies show that refined sugar reduces the white cell count for 4 hours after consumption. This reduction can be up to 30%. Even natural sugars from honey and fruit juice can have a white cell lowering effect, so sweets of any kind should be avoided during an illness.

The Basics
Daily Nutritional Supplements:
Babies - A well-nourished mother providing abundant breastmilk!

Toddlers - The juice of carrots, beets and parsley. When introduced with first foods, children really do like freshly-made juices.

Children 3-11 - A chewable multiple vitamin/mineral or a liquid, if preferred by the child. One possibility for those wanting a very natural vitamin/mineral source is Blue-Green Minerals by Mother's ChoiceTM. The Blue-Green Minerals also provides calcium in a completely herbal base for maximum absorbability. Liquid calcium/magnesium in some form should be given separately from a multiple for better absorption.

Young Ladies 12-18 - A multiple vitamin/mineral supplement that supplies sufficient iron to offset the reduction in hemoglobin due to the onset of menses. Liquid calcium/magnesium intake should be continued.

Young Men 12-18 - A multiple vitamin/mineral supplement that does not have unnecessary iron levels. Young men typically have greater caloric requirements during this "growing season."

Women of Childbearing Age - Prenatal formula may be taken throughout the childbearing years. Add additional supplements as family history and health concerns indicate.

Post-Menopausal Women - A good multi-vitamin/mineral/herbal supplement that does not have high amounts of iron and does have sufficient antioxidant activity to prevent aging diseases. High levels of iron in an aging population has been associated with higher cancer risk.

Men - A good multi-vitamin/mineral/herbal supplement that provides circulatory support, prostate support and plenty of antioxidant activity for prevention of men's common health problems.

MOMMY DIAGNOSTICS™

The following chart is one I use when my children are ill. Writing the symptoms down allows me to "rule out" many disorders or diseases so that I may concentrate on a couple of tentative diagnoses.

Primary Symptoms: _____

Fever:
a.m. _____
p.m. _____
throughout day _____
controllable with anti-pyretic herbs? _____
controllable with acetominophen or ibuprophen? _____
nuchal rigidity? _____
bruising? _____

Mucous:
clear? _____
runny or thick? _____
opaque? _____
colored? green or yellow? _____
blood? _____

Cough:
Dry? _____
Raspy voice? _____
Tight-sounding? _____
Wet or gurgly? _____
Deep? _____
Spasmodic? _____
Chest tightness? _____
Chest pain? _____

Gastrointestinal:
Nausea? _____
Vomiting: Food from last meal? Recent meal or last night's? Bile? Repeated episodes?

_____
Gas? _____

Stomach cramps?
Diarrhea: Profuse? Watery? Explosive? Bloody? Mucous? Formed-stool?

_____

_____

Progression of above symptoms? _____

Evaluate previous two days meals: _____

_____

General Body:
Aches and Pains? _____
History of Recent Contact with Sick Persons or Contaminated Objects: _____

_____

Fever

Normal body temperature is 98.6 F. Axillary temperature is 1 degree less, and rectal temperature is .7 degrees more than oral temperature. Temperature fluctuates throughout the day. The lowest temperature of the day occurs between 4:00 a.m. and 6:00 a.m. Body temperature climbs until the peak at 10:00 p.m. Body temperature, in infants, is more vulnerable to external factors than adults. If baby feels too hot, undress him/her. An accurate and extremely gentle way of ascertaining body temperature is through the use of an otothermometer. An otothermometer, such as Thermascan, utilizes fiber optics, which bounce off the tympanic membrane to "read" the body temperature. TIP FOR ACCURATE USE: Hold the thermometer in the ear longer than package insert directs to allow the fiber optic time to do its work.

During a fever, respiration speeds up and the face flushes. A raised body temperature increases the white blood cell count; therefore, a fever is a good infection-fighter. Bacterial infections are usually quite susceptible to raised body temperature. Viral infections are not as affected by fevers as bacterial infections. Fevers tend to make some children nauseated as the fever rises, especially if mucus drainage is present. Liquid calcium/magnesium can settle the stomach and relax the muscles lessening the anxiety of the child. Appropriate dosage can be figured from the recommended amount on the bottle. I really like NF Formulas, Botanical Liquid Cal/Mag that is Peppermint-flavored. The children like the taste.

General guidelines for children with fevers are:
- Under 3 months of age - If the fever is over 101° F. and the child is breastfed, something significant may be going on. The only course of action is to go to the hospital. The baby will have a spinal tap performed on him/her and given 3 days of prophylactic antibiotics. Sometimes all that is actually needed is IV solution; however, 1 out of 4 babies will have a possibly fatal problem that may be avoided by this medical intervention. If mom has to take baby to the hospital for IV antibiotics, she can and should protect baby's intestinal flora by continuing to breastfeed and by giving the baby *bifidus* by licking her finger, dipping the wet finger in *bifidus* powder and letting baby suck the powder off her finger. There is no natural alternative to this practice because the illnesses that cause such a high fever in such a small baby are so abrupt in onset and progression that waiting is not prudent.
- 3 months to 18 months of age - Can tolerate fevers up to 103° F. Over 103° F., the fever should be managed by one of the therapies listed in the Fever Management section, because a child this young will usually experience convulsions at 105° F.

The key to preventing problems with a fever is to keep the child hydrated. A dehydrated child will "bake" if the internal environment of the child's body is dry and hot. Baths, while thought of as a great way of hydrating, are actually dehydrating if not done appropriately. Enemas are an effective way of lowering a fever and rehydrating a feverish child if done properly. "Cleansing"-type enemas will put the child in a riskier position than she was in before the enema due to loss of more water than given and loss of minerals and electrolytes.

In a child who wakes fever-free and spikes a temperature in the evening (which is common with a viral infection), mom must hydrate in the morning—water, water, water. Fruit juices are to be avoided except to administer medicine that cannot be gotten in with any other method. The reason even fruit juices can be a problem is that a fruit juice is a concentrated source of fruit sugar. The fiber is missing which "buffers" the sugar in the whole fruit; therefore, the child only gets the fruit sugar and liquid. *Any type of sugar, even natural, lowers the immune response for four hours after ingestion.*

This lowering of immune response can be up to 30%, a significant decrease. I believe freshly-juiced fruit juice to cause the same problem even though at least the fresh juice contains vitamins, minerals and enzymes for the body to utilize. The only time I would consider giving juice would be if my child were becoming dehydrated, and fruit juice was the only liquid I could get down the child. Fresh vegetable juice (carrot, beet and parsley) is excellent for an illness, as this juice blend supplies all the vitamins and minerals a child needs each day. I do sometimes add fresh lemon to my child's water if I feel the kidneys need some "clearance" help.

One aspect of abrupt onset fevers that every parent should immediately evaluate is to see if the child can move the neck. One of the signs of certain forms of meningitis is nuchal ridigity (very stiff neck). Children with nuchal rigidity will move their entire body to turn their head rather than simply turning their neck. Parents can check this by having the child touch the chin to the chest or by creating a loud (surprise) noise in a room near the child to see if the child turns the neck toward the sound. If nuchal rigidity is present, an emergency room visit is imperative. Another sign of another type of meningitis is an abrupt fever onset combined with a purplish rash appearing on the body rapidly. One mother whose child experienced this form of meningitis said her child suddenly came down with a fever and before the mother's and grandparent's eyes, purplish bruises began to appear on the child's legs. The mother had her child to the hospital within thirty minutes of the onset of fever and rash, and the child is healthy and happy today.

Fever Management

Enemas

An enema can be lifesaving in a child who will not drink any liquids and is becoming dehydrated due to fever. The instructions for enemas in children are important to follow as more damage can come from an improperly performed enema than from the fever itself.

Mom can use a 2-3 ounce bulb syringe (commonly supplied in birth kits to suction baby's mouth at the birth - do not re-use a bulb syringe used for enemas for birth suctioning!). An enema solution of purified water with a pinch of salt, to prevent leaching of minerals, may be used or purified water with a drop of garlic oil or an herbal infusion of catnip, red raspberry or garlic may be used. The solution should be 1 degree less than the rectal temperature. Cooler water will chill the child. Hot water should never be used, or the child could be burned internally. The purified water should be reverse osmosis filtered with an additional carbon filtration. Distilled water should never be used because it may leach minerals from the body (young children should not drink distilled water for the same reason).

Mom can lovingly and gently place her child on his/her abdomen over mom's knees or on a waterproof sheet. The tip of the bulb syringe should be lubricated (butter is a great lubricant). Excess air in the bulb syringe should be squeezed out, then the enema solution can be slowly added. Only one (1) tablespoon per hour of the solution should be used during fevers until something comes back. DO NOT OVERFILL THE BOWEL, or the child will dump everything given back as well as his/her own vital fluid.

Baths

Baths will *de*hydrate a child unless certain measures are taken to seal in the moisture. A bath to hydrate a child follows the same rule as an enema: ideally, the water will be filtered water, not chlorinated tap water and not distilled water. For a bath to be therapeutic, the child must stay in the tub at least 20 minutes. The first 10 minutes of the bath, the skin is hydrating, the next 10-15 minutes, the child will absorb any therapeutic agents in the bath water such as herbs, etc.

Tepid water baths are a good way to lower a high fever; however, the child must be oiled after the bath to seal in the moisture. If the child wants to take a hot bath to relieve body or muscle aches during colds or flu, mom must oil the child *before* getting into the hot tub. Epsom salts should be added to hot baths with the purpose of relaxation and pain relief. Castor oil is the oil of choice for a bath during fever.

Castor oil is anti-inflammatory and analgesic. Castor oil works as a hammer to "drive in" the Epsom salts (magnesium sulfate, which relaxes sore muscles). A castor oil body rub after a tepid bath seals the skin to prevent moisture loss as well as makes the child more comfortable. The body will only absorb what it needs in the tub, so a magnesium or castor oil overdose through the skin is highly unlikely.

Body Rubs

Castor oil also makes an excellent body rub when mixed with very soupy oatmeal. This castor oil and oatmeal mixture may be rubbed all over the body to lower fever. Herbal liquids may also be mixed with castor oil for body rubs.

Body Wraps

Some parents find wrapping the child to increase a temperature hanging around the 101 degree F. mark to be beneficial, particularly in a bacterial illness. Some guidelines for knowing whether a wrap is appropriate are: How high is the temperature (do not increase a 105 degree F. temp.); Is the child pale and chilled; Is the child hot and cherry-cheeked (do not wrap in this situation); Does the child want to be bundled up in "covers?"

A body wrap is accomplished simply by placing a blanket(s) or quilt(s) over the child's body (do not cover the child's head) and letting the warmth created by the wrap increase the temperature in an attempt to "burn-off" the bacteria or virus. As stated before, body wraps work best with bacterial infections. Viruses do not tend to be as affected by body temperature as do bacteria.

TincTracts

When our children have fevers, we immediately begin oral administration of *Yummy Yarrow & Elderberry TincTract*™: 1/8 teaspoon for my babies under 25 pounds, 1/4 teaspoon for my toddlers under 50 pounds, 1/2 teaspoon for my children under 100 pounds, 3/4 teaspoon for those of us over 100 pounds given every 2 hours. This may be given every thirty minutes for 2-3 hours at the beginning of administration to attain body saturation with the herbal medicine. We also give some type of echinacea product for infection-fighting. When we are not sure what type of infection we are dealing with at the onset of fever, we usually choose to give *Echinacea & Thyme w/Elderberry or ViraMune*™ (if any lymph nodes are swollen).

RESPIRATORY ILLNESS

An upper respiratory infection (URI) or cold is the most common disease process in children. Many colds are caused by *Haemophilus influenzae, type B*, which is what most children are routinely immunized for to prevent meningitis. The HIB immunization does not prevent colds or flu from the *Haemophilus* organism. In fact, those immunized usually have the worst case of HIB flu or colds. Antibiotics are of no use in a cold or flu because they do not have antiviral action. Some herbs do exhibit antiviral action such as echinacea and elder flowers and berries. Mom can usually distinguish between a cold and the flu due to the difference in onset. A flu attacks suddenly and debilitates for a couple of days (in a healthy immune system; longer in an unhealthy person), while a cold drags its symptoms out over several days one at a time, scratchy throat, sneezing, runny nose, cough. Adults do not usually run a fever with colds, but children sometimes will.

If there is no dietary or botanical intervention for an upper respiratory infection, flu or teething, bronchitis or pneumonia may develop in susceptible individuals. The word, pneumonia, is a frightening word. Most of us can remember our grandparents speaking of those in their circle of acquaintances who died of pneumonia. Pneumonia simply means fluid in the lungs. I certainly do not mean to make light of what can be quite serious, particularly in infants, the elderly and pulmonary-compromised individuals; however, all pneumonias are not bacterial and fatal.

There are three main types of pneumonia: bacterial, mycoplasma, and viral (often termed "walking" pneumonia). Viral pneumonia in older children and adults is not usually treated with antibiotics, yet most allopaths do treat even viral pneumonia in young children and infants with antibiotics on the assumption that babies and young children cannot clear their lungs as efficiently as adults. This assumption is correct; however, a preventive approach is still superior health-wise to antibiotics. The respiratory and immune systems can be supported with natural medicine unless the illness is already well-established and the child needs respiratory support. Let me insert here that I do believe antibiotics are the only choice once the child has become extremely weakened by the illness. A child will recover quicker without antibiotics in many cases; however, early intervention is the key to success without antibiotics. Once the child is in distress, antibiotics should be employed. If bacterial pneumonia is suspected, a visit to your healthcare provider is necessary.

Prevention through dietary changes include eliminating, during the illness, dairy products, sugar, fruit juice, alcohol, caffeine. Mom will need to add spicy food such as: Thai food, Cajun seasoning, cayenne pepper, Wasabi, etc. to the diet to thin the mucus. Water should be taken in each hour.

Physical medicinal measures would include use of an ultrasonic humidifier consistently throughout the day and night. A humidifier should be cleaned every three days with distilled vinegar or grapefruit seed extract. A vaporizer is not the best idea in a child's room due to a burn risk for the child. One way of pleasantly providing steam inhalation for a child is to purchase a clear bubble umbrella. Break off the cane of the umbrella, put the child under the umbrella with a steam and let the child be in her own "rain forest." Umbrella steam inhalation should only be done with an adult present. The umbrella should not be flush with the floor or bed so that air can circulate in to the child.

Fever Patterns

A high fever with cold symptoms signals a possible bacterial infection. This possible diagnosis can be confirmed by watching for the color of mucus draining from the child's nose during the day (further information regarding mucus below).

A high fever with no cold symptoms may signal a childhood infection. The best thing to do is to wait for three days to see if a rash occurs while applying the dietary and physical medicine appropriate for the symptoms and giving botanicals for immune support.

A fever that comes in the afternoon, peaks in the evening and is gone by morning only to return the next afternoon is common in viral infections. A temperature that is consistent throughout the day may signal a bacterial infection; however, some viruses can cause consistent fever patterns for three to five days. If the fever lingers past three to five days or is combined with other clues signaling a bacterial infection, professional medical counsel should be sought.

Good immune systems allow the body to spike a high fever that produces wellness quickly, while depressed immune systems produce low fevers and slow healing.

Mucus Messages

Mucus is a great clue for home diagnosis. Clear mucus is most commonly associated with colds, flu or allergies. White opaque mucus means that the mucus is thickening and ripe for growth of bacteria, so intervention should definitely begin if not started already. Green or yellow mucus is associated with bacterial infections, especially combined with fevers, even low-grade fevers.

Mucus that is yellow or green upon waking does not necessarily mean a bacterial infection. Any mucus sitting in the nose or in the back of the throat overnight will likely "grow" something; however, the bacteria may not have progressed beyond the nasal passage. The time to begin checking mucus for clues is after the child has been awake several hours. Stronger herbs are necessary for bacterial infections. This is the time I bring out the Oregon grape and goldenseal.

Bacterial respiratory infections, viral infections also, often cause gastrointestinal problems due to "booger-belly" (term coined by Molly Linton, N.D., source of much of this information). Mucus draining into the tummy is hard for some children. These children can sip on ginger tea or black tea (like Lipton or Luzianne, etc.) and take acidophilus. I personally have found acidophilus to be a great tummy-calmer when something is in my stomach that is making me uncomfortable.

TincTract™ Choices

For those infections that we consider viral, I usually choose to administer ViraMune,™ which contains Red root, Echinacea purpurea, Yarrow flower, Myrrh, Red clover and Oregon grape root: 1/8 teaspoon for my babies under 25 lbs., 1/4 teaspoon for my toddlers under 50 lbs., 1/2 teaspoon for my children under 100 lbs., 3/4 teaspoon for those of us under 150lbs. every 2 hours. For those infections we consider bacterial infections, we usually choose either BactaMune,™ which contains Oregon grape root, Echinacea angultifolia, Licorice root and Thyme, or Scout Out,™ which contains Echinacea Angustifolia, Goldenseal root, St. John's Wort, Mullein, Yellow Dock, Red Clover, Honeysuckle flowers, Myrrh, Yucca root, Rosemary and Cloves in the same dosages as with the ViraMune.™

Cough Clues

A cough is a very important diagnostic tool. We need to learn to appreciate the cough. In an upper respiratory infection or a sinus infection, a cough will only be present while lying down, upon awaking and exertion. In a lower lobe infection (pneumonia or bronchitis), a cough will be present throughout the day. Lower lobe infections will cause much fatigue due to a lack of oxygen in the blood. Adult bronchitis is a pool for pertussis (whooping cough) because many doctors fail to diagnose pertussis when an adult comes in with what they believe to be a lingering case of bronchitis. Any cough lasting more than two weeks should indicate to the parent or individual that a sputum culture should be performed if there has been no definitive diagnosis. I am not saying that all adult bronchitis is pertussis. There are many pathogens that cause inflammation of the bronchioles (bronchitis), and pertussis is one of those pathogens. We should not ignore the need for a culture if a cough lasts over two weeks (recommendation supplied by the Centers for Disease Control in Atlanta, GA). Pertussis coughs begin at night, have no other cold symptoms, other than a possible fever. The cough progresses to daytime within a couple of weeks. Not all children "whoop" with pertussis. I've heard the "whoop," and I've heard just a very wet, yuck-y cough with pertussis.

A cough should be wet. A dry cough means that the body is trying to "peel" something (dried mucus) off the mucous membrane. Measures should be taken to create a wet cough from a dry one by drinking water, eating spicy food, keeping the air humidified.

Supplement with expectorant and demulcent herbs such as Elecampane, Licorice, Mullein, and Osha root (for pneumonia or bronchitis for clearing the lungs - not to be used by pregnant women or children under 3 without professional supervision).

TincTract™ Choices:

When I'm dealing primarily with a dry, hacking cough, I choose to give my children 1/2 to 1 teaspoon of *Wild Cherry Coffaway,*™ which contains White Pine bark, Wild Cherry bark, Spikenard root, Whole Elderberries, Cinnamon chips and Licorice root. If their cough is loose or "wet," I prefer to give Lungs Plus,™ containing Mullein, Wild Cherry bark, Chestnut, Astragalus root, Peppermint, Coltsfoot, Plantain, Chickweed, Pleurisy root, Elecampane and Horehound, 1/2 to 1 teaspoon every 2-3 hours. There is another formula that is similar to Lungs Plus,™ without the coltsfoot, called Lung Tonic.™

Other measures to loosen a cough

Chest rubs - Mix equal portions (20 drops) of lobelia with lavender, peppermint, eucalyptus, black haw or thyme (pick one of these to mix with lobelia or all, whatever you prefer). If you use essential oils, use less essential oils of the other herbs than the lobelia.

Marshmallow Syrup - Good for dry coughs and sore throats; herbal tinctures may be added to the syrup.

> 2 oz. marshmallow root, sliced or cut
> 1 1/2 cups sugar
> 1 cup reverse osmosis or distilled water
> Soak marshmallow root in water for 12 hours. Add sugar and heat to a boil; cool and strain through cheesecloth. Bottle and store in the refrigerator.

Onion poultice - Saute onions, place them on cheesecloth, cover with plastic wrap and a towel. Replace with freshly sauteed onions when the first poultice cools. Repeat until cough begins to break up.

Mustard packs - Take 1 tablespoon of dry mustard (less if freshly bought). Combine with 1 cup of white flour (do not use whole wheat). Add water to make a paste. Place a cheesecloth on the chest AVOIDING THE NIPPLES. Add the mustard paste. Cover with plastic wrap. Put hot water bottle over wrap for heat. Check in five minutes. Leave on for NO MORE THAN 10 TO 15 MINUTES. Mustard causes the mucus to break off the chest wall because mustard acts as a counter-irritant. Mustard packs will cause a chemical burn if left on too long. ONLY DO THIS ONCE.

Percussion - Cup hand. Pound lightly, yet firmly, over chest to loosen mucus.

Ephedra - I do not recommend the use of ephedra with small children; however, I have used it with my own child during an asthma attack due to a respiratory illness. Care has to be taken not to give the child so much that she becomes "wired." "A little dab will do ya." I monitor her heart rate after administration very carefully. Ephedra should only be used in family home healthcare under the supervision of a Professional Healthcare Provider.

Otitis Media (Ear Infections)

Otitis media is caused by a blockage of the eustachian tube. Generally, a cold or flu causes thick mucus that stops up the eustachian tube. The tonsils swell; fever occurs and dehydrates the child; nausea may occur because of mucus drainage; and ear pain ensues.

In 1994, the American Academy of Pediatrics put out a report stating that allopaths should stop prescribing antibiotics for otitis media. Children who go completely untreated resolve as quickly as those treated with antibiotics. Antibiotics do not relieve the pain of an ear infection. There seems to be no good reason for using antibiotics for ear infections. For further reading on treating ear infections in the home, please read *Treating Respiratory and Ear Infections in the Home*, formerly titled, *No More Amoxicillin!* By Dr. Mary Ann Block.

Many times the first ear infection coincides with weaning, teething and winter. Weaning increases protein digestion and decreases antibodies that baby has been getting from mother. Teething, in and of itself, can cause mucus drainage leading to an ear infection. Longstanding allergies may play a role in chronic ear infections. The key to treating an ear infection is to prevent it from occurring in the first place.

There are three levels of cure: Suppression, Palliation (make comfortable), and Cure (use of antimicrobial herbs). Since we know that ear infections usually appear 48 hours after a viral infection due to dehydration during the fever-phase, we can treat preventively as follows:

1. Water. Keep the purified water coming at all times.
2. Botanicals. Echinacea has been shown to increase immune response by up to 30% and is specifically indicated for colds, flu and ear infections. Goldenseal should be held back for a really tough infection, such as a sinus infection or serious bacterial infection, as the alkaloids in goldenseal are difficult for a child under 3 to process. Beta-carotene may be given regularly throughout the day unless a fever is present. Beta-carotene will not convert to vitamin A in the body in the presence of fever. Vitamin A must be taken instead if a fever is present. Elder flower, boneset, and thyme may also be used during a respiratory or ear infection for immune support.
3. Diet. No sugars, even fruit juice. No cow's milk or cheese. Soy milk or goat's milk acceptable. No meat, as meat may cause more mucus production.
4. Physical medicine. If the eardrum is intact (look in the ear with otoscope to ascertain), an herbal oil of mullein, St. John's Wort, garlic and other antimicrobial herbs may be given by one to two drops in the ear (warmed to body temperature) once per day. This treatment is best done at night when the child will be sleeping so the

oil can stay in the ear for a prolonged period. Let the child know that she will not be able to hear very well or have good balance after the oil has been applied. If this is done more than once per day, the tympanic membrane will have to struggle to move. The morning after this treatment, mom can drop hydrogen peroxide in the ear to clean out the wax and oil from the night before. As an alternative to using an oil which drives the herbs in, mom may elect to use glycerin or a glycerin-based product which draws the fluid out. For **chronic catarrh (mucous) and fluid,** you may use a plantain glycerite or TincTract for drops in the ear. **For narrowing of the eustachian tube,** you may use Ephedra or lobelia drops in the ear. For severe pain, you may use lobelia drops in the ear. **For acute bacterial infection,** you may add goldenseal glycerite or TincTract to the above oil for drops in the ear.

5. Lymphatic drainage. Oil finger with herbal oil such as Lemon Rub. Place finger behind ear lobe. Begin to rub firmly down the front of the neck muscle to the clavicle bone, one side at a time (doing both sides may cause the child to pass out). Do this several times to stimulate the lymph to drain.

6. Heat or ice. Mom can apply either heat or ice to the ear, whatever the child prefers, to relieve the pain. If heat is chosen, a baked onion is excellent for temporarily easing ear pain. Slice an onion in half. Place on cookie sheet and bake until translucent. Take out of oven and cool to a temperature the child can tolerate over the ear. Place onion over ear like an ear muff until pain subsides.

7. Carrot poultice. Wrap 2 large, grated carrots in a cheesecloth poultice. Tie (not too tightly) or wrap around throat. For a cold poultice, ice may be combined with the carrot, or for a warm poultice, place carrot in hot water, squeeze out excess moisture before applying to the neck.

8. Castor oil pack. Soak cotton flannel or wool in castor oil. Bake in oven on low for 10 to 15 minutes. Wrap around throat. Cover with plastic wrap. Leave on for 20 minutes. Put the pack in a Ziploc bag, in the refrigerator, where it can be pulled out, reheated and used again and again for several months. End a castor oil pack with a 20 minute icing.

TincTract™ Choices

I usually alternate between *ViraMune*™ and *Triple Echinacea & Goldenseal*™ or *Scout Out.*™ I usually choose to only use products with goldenseal when there is a condition with an over-abundance of mucous as goldenseal helps dry up the mucous membrane. Goldenseal administered too early in a respiratory infection can cause over-drying of the mucous membrane resulting in nosebleeds, for some children. Goldenseal is an excellent choice for conditions with an over-abundance of mucous. Tri-Light Herbs, the company that makes these TincTractTMs, only use organically-grown goldenseal so as not to deplete our supplies in the wild.

SINUS INFECTIONS

A sinus infection can usually be distinguished by the headache or face ache that is worse upon bending over. Many times there is an irritating drainage down the back of the throat that may cause a night or morning cough as well as some gastrointestinal discomfort, nausea and gassiness.

The difficulty in treating a sinus infection botanically is that the sinuses are hard for herbs to penetrate. The only botanical that penetrates with much success is goldenseal, which should not be used in high doses in children under three, due to the alkaloids being difficult for the liver to process. The alkaloids in goldenseal, hydrastine and berberine, make this herb inappropriate for a pregnant woman or very young children unless specifically indicated and used with professional counsel.

The herbs most successfully used for sinus infections are: eyebright, ginger, goldenseal and myrrh. Essential oils may be applied to the affected areas of the face (avoiding the eyes) in a child old enough to understand "Don't touch or rub your face." If the child cannot follow this direction, do not apply essential oils to the face because of the risk of getting them in the eyes.

An herbal inhaler may be used by filling a 1 oz. bottle with cotton and adding 5 to 10 drop of an essential oil. Sniff from the bottle gently into each nostril several times a day to decongest the nose and sinuses. Essential oils to choose from: lavender, eucalyptus, peppermint or rosemary.

TincTract™ *Choice:*

Smell No Evil may be used for an herbal inhaler as it contains mullein, goldenseal root, bayberry and peppermint leaf combined with the essential oils of eucalytus and tea tree. For internal use, *Sinus Minus*, containing yerba santa, mullein, green stevia, fennel, echinacea angustifolia, usnea, goldenseal root and ginger root, may be used several times daily. 1/4 teaspoon for my children under 50 pounds, 1/2 teaspoon for those under 100 lbs., and 3/4 teaspoon for those of us under 150 lbs. To avoid aversion to the strong taste of yerba santa, mom may find it helpful to mix the dose in a cup of water with the fresh-squeezed juice of half a lemon added. The lemon will add more vitamin C and bioflavonoids to the tea which will aid in immune response and antiinflammatory effects.

PHARYNGITIS OR TONSILLITIS

Pharyngitis or tonsillitis (sore or inflamed throat or tonsils) may result from infection, or in chronic cases, inflammation may result from food, environmental or airborne allergies. The purpose for mom is to relieve the discomfort and treat the underlying infection.

Gargles help to provide both pain relief as well as bringing botanical medicines directly into contact with the inflamed or infected area. Gargles should not be attempted in anyone under 4 or 5 years of age since those younger than 4 generally do not understand that they should not swallow the gargle or even *how* to gargle. An older child or adult can gargle with salt water or with an herbal tea or preparation such as Throat Coat.™ Herbs well-suited to gargles are: myrrh (excellent for absesses, shrink tonsils, sore throat), yarrow, Oregon grape, goldenseal. These herbs are all bitter; therefore, the child should be warned that the rinse or gargle will taste unpleasant.

A throat swab may be done with Bitter Orange Oil, Calendula or Lympha Rub.™ A long, sterile "Q-Tip"-type swab may be used to "paint" the oil on the tonsils and back of throat. The gag reflex may be averted by tapping temporal points on the child's head before swabbing. One application is generally all that is necessary except in strep throat. Most sore throats will be gone in two hours after swabbing. If throat tissue is raw and irritated, a second swab with calendula should be done twenty minutes after the first. The child should not drink for twenty minutes after each swab. Spritzers are helpful but not as effective as a swab. Since my children do not tolerate the throat swabs very well. I usually drop one to two drops, depending on their age, of Lympha Rub™ on the back of their tongue and have them rub, with their tongue, their tonsils, roof of mouth, and back of throat areas.

Strep throat can be diagnosed with a throat culture done at a physician's office. A culture should be performed, not simply a quick strep which is somewhat unreliable. While waiting for culture, treat with botanicals. When the culture comes back and it is positive, if the treatment is working, continue on with what is working and draw ASO titres, to determine if the child is at risk for rheumatic fever. The new medical literature says that it may not be necessary to medicate those children who are not extremely sick with strep. If the child is extremely sick, the herbal therapy is not working, and the culture is positive for strep, the need for antibiotics should be evaluated with the child's health care provider. The risk with untreated strep is the development of rheumatic fever which can damage a child's heart for life. Botanical treatment includes: high doses of vitamin A (beta-carotene will not be converted to vitamin A in the presence of fever) - up to 50,000 IU's for a very short period; high doses of vitamin C, up to bowel tolerance; goldenseal and Oregon grape.

TincTract™ *Choices:*

I usually choose to spritz my children's throats with *Throat Coat,*™ which contains honey, lemon, wild cherry bark, lime and molasses with essential oils of thyme, wintergreen peppermint and tea tree, several times daily as well as giving them oral administration of *ViraMune*™ at dosages of 1/8 teaspoon for my babies under 25 lbs., 1/4 teaspoon for my children under 50 lbs., 1/2 teaspoon for the big kids under 100 lbs., and 3/4 teaspoon for those of us under 150 lbs. I may choose *Scout Out* or *Triple Echinacea and Goldenseal* if I feel a bacterial infection may be a risk factor at the same dosages as *ViraMune.*™ For those of my children who have shown a tendency to strep infections, I may immediately begin alternating one dose of ViraMune with a dose of a product containing a larger amount of oregon grape or goldenseal such as *BactaMune,*™ Scout Out or *Triple Echinacea and Goldenseal.* When alternating my herbal medicine, I give one at one dosing, then two hours later, I give the other herb formula, switching back and forth between them to allow my child the benefit of both.

Gastrointestinal Difficulties

Constipation

Constipation is the most common gastrointestinal complaint of our entire country, I believe, and the solution is many times extremely simple: water. Most of us simply are not drinking enough water to enable our body to function efficiently. We should be drinking one-third of our body weight in water ounces daily. A 90-lb. person needs 30-ounces of water to stay healthy. Another 8-oz. glass of water should be added for each bad habit we take part in each day. Example: Eat a candy bar, drink a glass of water; drink a soft drink, drink a glass of water, smoke a cigarette, drink a glass of water. All of this water will not prevent the health consequences of these bad habits, but extra water will allow the body to try to keep up with the regular functions such as bowel movements.

Acidophilus or *bifidus* can be taken in powdered form each day to restore normal intestinal flora which solves many constipation problems. Those plagued with irritable bowel syndrome will definitely benefit from this supplementation.

In a child, the introduction of solid food will sometimes cause constipation. Water or prune juice is an effective antidote to this type of constipation. Two ounces of prune juice every two hours should yield a result. Steamed beets are a good food for constipation. Remember, though, beets are red, and they will still be as red out-going as in-going.

Castor oil packs (directions in Otitis Media Section) are sometimes helpful, as is rubbing castor oil on the abdomen in a clockwise motion.

LiquiLax TincTract™ is excellent for children. 1/4 t every two hours until results are seen is my usual dose for my children. For adults, a cascara sagrada product will yield definite results (take care with this if the bowel is sensitive to cramps) if taken at night before bedtime with a large glass of water. Four capsules of cascara should yield a morning b.m. These products are not intended for long-term use or "lazy bowel syndrome" will result.

As a last resort, glycerin suppositories or an enema may be employed. These should be the absolute last resort and not used for more than three days in a row, or the bowel will develop "lazy bowel syndrome."

Diarrhea

In children under the age of 3, diarrhea should not be allowed to last for more than 24 hours. The diarrhea MUST be stopped at 24 hours or severe dehydration or death can result. An older child can understand to "Stop eating." The foods and supplements that are beneficial for halting diarrhea are:

- Fresh applesauce without the peels (the peel stimulates the bowel) with carob powder mixed in (carob is excellent for stopping diarrhea);
- Barley broth - cook the barley in too much water and drink the broth;
- *Acidophilus* and/or *bifidus*;
- One (1) teaspoon of Bentonite Clay per cup of water = 1 dose. Mix and give the dose after the last bout of diarrhea not to exceed four (4) doses;
- *AntiDiatribe* TincTract™ - 1/4 to 1/2 teaspoon given after each bout of diarrhea.

Diarrhea that lasts for more than a couple of days or does not respond to the above measures should be checked for parasites through a stool culture. Diarrhea that occurs after excessive fruit consumption or fiber consumption is easily remedied by not repeating the overeating of that particular food. Parasites are botanically treated with nutritional supplements such as garlic, goldenseal, wormwood, papaya enzymes, grapefruit seed extract (careful, this can burn the mouth if not diluted). Prepared products such as Worm-Out™ TincTract™ and Phytofuge are excellent, if combined with large doses of garlic. Strict hand-washing precautions should be observed as fecal-oral contact is a very common way of spreading pathogens that cause diarrhea.

Nausea and Vomiting

A gastrointestinal virus can be home diagnosed by observing a 12-14 hour period of nausea and/or vomiting followed by diarrhea. Viruses have to travel through the gastrointestinal tract first causing nausea and/or vomiting with diarrhea following with in 1 to 2 days or sooner. Food poisoning differs from a virus in that both vomiting and diarrhea occur simultaneously in an abrupt onset, or diarrhea only occurs. In food poisoning, the vomiting and diarrhea together is the body's attempt to rid the system of toxic bacteria, such as *salmonella, campylobacter, listeria, E-coli, stapholococcus aureus,* and *shigella*; protozoa, such as *giardia* or *crytosporidium*; or a poison. Most people realize that a GI virus is contagious but do not consider food poisoning to be contagious, yet it is. Those pathogens that cause gastrointestinal illness tend to become active in warm weather. Most physicians, like the majority of consumers, always blame vomiting and diarrhea on a "virus" or "stomach flu." The statistics point to a different picture, food or water contamination by bacteria or protozoa. The currents stats indicate that most (up to 20-30%) of children are carrying *giardia*, a protozoa, by the time they reach school-age. Carriers can and do pass this "bug" on to others. *Giardia* can also cause a syndrome marked by infrequent stomach and bowel complaints. A stool culture is indicated if your GI symptoms are lasting longer than a few days or frequently recurring. *Giardia* infection is primarily intestinal with gas, cramps and diarrhea that tends to cause illness, resolve, then recur within weeks or a couple of months.

Whatever the causative agent, care must be taken with other family members not to pass the pathogen by washing hands often and cleaning house surfaces (light switches, counters, door knobs and handles, etc.). Before resuming daily activities among friends and family, keep in mind the incubation period of the illness (usually 24-48 hours for a GI virus) and consider that some family member may be incubating the virus (most contagious time). I find it best to stay home until no one in the family has been sick for over 48 hours.

The biggest mistake we make as parents when trying to make our children feel better when they are down with a "tummy bug" is that we try to make them eat and/or drink normal amounts of food or liquid. The stomach becomes very sensitive after a virus and actually shrinks after ejecting everything out. Instead of offering a glass of juice or water after a vomiting episode, we should offer 1/8 teaspoon sips of black tea every hour until the stomach stretches back out and can handle more liquid. NO GULPING for several hours after the last bout of vomiting.

Everyone experiences a brief period of lactose intolerance due to a change in enzymes in the stomach after a gastrointestinal illness with vomiting and diarrhea. This means that all dairy products should be avoided for several days after GI illness.

Specific herbs that help curb nausea and vomiting:
- **Ginger** - Take enough to get a ginger taste in the mouth or feel a burning in the chest. Capsules are best, but ginger TincTract, or minced ginger root will suffice.
- **Combine** equal part TincTracts of black horehound, meadowsweet, chamomile, anise in a 1 oz. bottle then add 25 drops of ginger. Take 5 - 8 drops (adult dosage) in the mouth or in 1-oz. of water as needed. I usually purchase these as single TincTracts and mix them myself in an amber bottle.
- **Tummy Plus** - A TincTract™ combination that combines herbs that are soothing to the stomach as well as antimicrobials for fighting the infection.
- **Bentonite Clay** as directed previously for diarrhea.

Bites, Burns and Stings

Bites, burns and stings rarely give us time to prepare our home remedies; therefore, we must prepare ahead for these acute conditions. Bentonite clay can be applied to bites and stings to draw out the toxins. The bentonite clay mixture as follows should be made up and kept in the kitchen for occasions of need: 1/2 Bentonite clay to 1/2 Water. Mixing this will take approximately 2 hours, due to the time needed for the water to penetrate the clay.

St. John's Wort oil is indicated as a first line of remedy in the treatment of burns, even sunburn. After the affected area has been cooled with water, pat the skin dry and apply St. John's Wort either directly or using sterile gauze soaked in the oil. The oil dressing may be renewed after 10 hours. St. John's Wort not only causes the wound to heal rapidly, but it actually prevents unsightly scars from developing.[14] Comfrey, too, is beneficial for external wounds.

Aloe vera gel directly from a mature aloe vera leaf is excellent for soothing a burn. Open the leaf with a fingernail; spread the leaf open and apply the gel directly to the affected area.

A healing ointment may be made from calendula, chamomile and echinacea. These three herbs are beneficial for wound healing when applied locally to the affected site. For those wanting a ready-made salve, we really like *Soothing Salve*™ drops that we apply locally to the burn or lesion.

Vitamin C, in large doses, can help avert allergic reactions from stings if begun immediately. Do not delay medical treatment in severe allergic reactions.

BRUISES

Bruising results from broken capillaries under the skin, in addition to a build-up of lymphatic fluid due to the inflammation of the wound. Nutritional supplements to build capillary integrity are bioflavonoids, vitamin C and Omega-3 oils (fish and flax). The daily dose for children from the middle of September through March is 500 - 1,500mg daily. The adult dose is 2,500 - 3,000mg daily for maintenance. Vitamin C from ascerola is more a candy than a medicine for children. A buffered form of vitamin C that contains calcium or magnesium is preferred for medicinal purposes.

I have found that physical medicine works extremely well when my children bump into something or fall down and get a "boo-boo." I immediately begin to lightly rub the "boo-boo" area for several minutes. This prevents the lymph fluid from pooling; therefore, no swelling occurs. The rubbing does not need to be firm, lightly will do nicely.

BROKEN BONES

Broken bones need medical attention so that they may be properly "set." To aid in the healing of a broken bone, the following supplements may be used:

- Calcium/Magnesium, liquid form is preferable for maximum absorption,
- Comfrey: Some herbalists choose to use comfrey for the short period that the bone is in a cast as long as the dosage does not exceed 1 tablespoon per day. The cast may need to be removed earlier if comfrey is used. Please be aware that comfrey is not recommended for internal use due to pyrollizidine alkaloids present in the plant which can cause liver damage and increase cancer risk if taken by susceptible individuals.

Chiropractic or Osteopathic care may be indicated after one has been carrying around a heavy cast for several weeks or months.

ALLERGIC REACTIONS

Allergic reactions result from a histamine-release from a white blood cell. This process is mediated by prostaglandin production. Alka-seltzer Gold used to be good for halting an allergic reaction, but it no longer has this effect. If buffered vitamin C powder is given prior to the constriction of the larynx, the allergic reaction may be avoided. The measures outlined in Bites, Burns and Stings may be followed if the reaction is caused by a bite or sting.

In all allergic reactions, the health of the liver must be addressed. Milk thistle is an excellent protector of our liver. I prefer milk thistle products that contain a standardized amount of silymarin (at least 70%), the protective factor in milk thistle. The Sarsaparilla & Dandelion TincTract™ from Tri-Light is excellent for helping the liver to eliminate toxins and aid its daily functions.

Allergens should be avoided as much as possible. In a child over 4 years of age, allergy testing may prove helpful in identifying allergens. We have installed a HEPA air purifier in the bedroom of our child who has the most severe allergies in the family. I carefully choose cleaners and detergents for our home, bedding specifically for blocking allergens and have a vacuum cleaner that sucks up most of the "yuckies" in the carpet. There is much more we could do. The Mothers of Asthmatics Network has an excellent newsletter about prevention. This newsletter is not from a natural medicine viewpoint; however, the technical information on prevention and medications is the best I have seen.

If allergies progress into asthmatic-reactions, intervention must begin before the allergen triggers a response. We have started giving our daughter a daily dose of ginkgo biloba because it has shown promise as a preventive for asthma. In times of crisis, we do use pharmaceuticals if the herbs we are working with have not begun to work within thirty minutes. Ephedra may be used; however, in children, there is a risk of over-stimulating them which can tire them to the point of making them worse as well as putting more exertion on the heart. Ephedra is not recommended for use in children. We have also begun giving Allerplex by Standard Process Labs (2-3 capsules) and Antronex, also by Standard Process Labs, (2-3 tablets) as soon as allergy symptoms with the asthma cough or wheezing begin. We've found this to be quite helpful in controlling an asthma episode.

If the problem continues, I would consult with a licensed naturopathic physician who had graduated from one of the following naturopathic colleges: Bastyr College in Portland, Oregon; Naturopathic College of Medicine in Seattle, Washington; or the Southwest College of Naturopathic Medicine in Arizona.

URINARY SUPPORT

Urinary tract infections are not often considered in young children, yet they do occur. I recall an instance in which my daughter had fever and cried while urinating, and the doctor told me it was highly unlikely that she had a bladder infection even though she was still in diapers (b.m.s coming in contact with urethra). I treated her for a bladder infection anyway, and she recovered quickly. The symptoms of a bladder infection include: fever, increased urination, painful urination.

Many bladder infections are fungal in origin, yeast or candida being a primary offender. Antibiotics make fungal bladder infections worse since they further destroy the beneficial flora that needs to outnumber the pathogenic bacteria. In these cases, re-population of "friendly" flora has to occur simultaneously with treatment for the infection. *Acidophilus* and *bifidus* may be taken liberally. Herbs that have antifungal action and are helpful for bladder infections are: thyme or rosemary.

The most important factor in preventing and treating bladder infections is to increase the water intake. Unsweetened cranberry juice (high fructose corn syrup types are unacceptable) given right before bedtime helps to acidify the urine and keep it acidic overnight when most bacteria thrive and grow (for mothers, please note that Interstitial cystitis is made worse by cranberry juice). Squeezing the juice from a wedge of lemon into a cup of water helps to keep the urine acidic during the day and helps alleviate the burning of urination.

Botanicals that have been shown to be beneficial for bladder infections include: marshmallow root, cornsilk, juniper berry, buchu, and uva ursi. Uva ursi is an irritant that can make kidney problems worse if used in large amounts. Uva ursi is a uterine stimulant thus should be avoided during pregnancy unless mom is under care of professional health care provider. Sitz baths with comfrey can provide symptomatic relief.

Bedwetting is a concern for many parents. I have seen two effective therapeutic approaches regarding nutritional and botanical medicine: correcting blood sugar imbalance by eliminating refined sugar, particularly before bedtime (even fruit juices) and giving 1 teaspoon of Original Herbal Minerals™ TincTract™ with 1/2 teaspoon of Licorice root TincTract™ before bedtime, or testing for and eliminating food allergens. An undiagnosed bladder infection can cause bed-wetting. A urine test may easily be done to test for bacteria in the urine.

TincTract™ Choice: *UriCare,*™ containing dandelion root, marshmallow root, cornsilk and cleavers herb, may be given 3-4 times daily.

CHILDHOOD ILLNESSES

The mere thought of our children contracting one of the more complicated, thus worrisome, childhood diseases is not a pleasant one. Our parents, and perhaps we, remember the polio epidemics, "whooping cough," and diphtheria. Most of us scratched our way through measles, red (Rubeola) and 3-Day (Rubella) and chicken pox, and we went chubby-jawed through mumps. None of us want to think about our children being uncomfortable with any illness, much less risk permanent injury or death due to a disease we are told we can prevent.

The conventional medical community and government officials warn repeatedly of the dangers of walking around un-immunized. Anti-immunization advocates repeatedly warn of the dangers of receiving the vaccines. How is a parent supposed to decide which side is right so that our children are put at the least amount of risk? I believe the answer to that lies somewhere in the middle of the debate, rather than at either end of the extreme spectrum.

We, as parents, carefully evaluate each thing we allow our children to eat, drink, participate in, etc., yet we usually end up following dogmatically in the camp of "Immunize or die," or "Immunize and die." Our approach has been to evaluate each of our children's health needs and their health risks that have been handed down through the generations of our family along with our family's lifestyle habits to decide if we need to administer vaccines. We take a very individual approach: Will this individual vaccine work for this individual child's needs and risk factors? If the answer is "'Yes" to tetanus, as we choose to live on land that has long been farm land and definitely know the risk of contracting tetanus, which is difficult to treat once you know you have the disease, we allow the vaccine. If the answer is "No" to hepatitis B since our newborn babies are not health-care workers, sexually promiscuous or intravenous drug users, we don't allow the vaccine. We are very specific about the immunizations we allow and how and when we feel they best fit our child's needs. We always factor in maternal antibodies transferred placentally in the womb as well as antibodies transferred through breastmilk.

Most of all, we try to be open to new evaluation, as in the case of finding that our family was coming into contact with pertussis every few years, usually the years and times when we had new babies in the house. We had to make adjustments in our thinking due to new information. There is plenty of research available about the risks and efficacy of immunizations. The National Vaccine Information Center publishes information on dangerous lot numbers for immunizations. Contact them for more information. The Centers for Disease Control (www.cdc.gov) has a number of articles and information available on vaccines and the spread of infectious disease.

A book I've found helpful is *Childhood Immunizations, What Every Parent Needs to Know,* by Jamie Murphy. Do check with state laws for immunization laws and exemptions. In many states, homeschooled children are exempt from mandatory immunization.

I have chosen not to cover the hepatitis B vaccine in this section. I think it the most ludicrous notion to give newborn infants a vaccine that protects them from a disease known to affect primarily the sexually promiscous, intravenous drug users and the health care workers who must care for them. This immunization was originally slated to be required at age 9, when the authorities felt our children would be at risk for the afore-mentioned behaviors, but not enough parents were actually bringing the children in at that age. Combine that with the fact that if only the at-risk groups were required to be immunized with hepatitis B, there wouldn't be a great enough number for the pharma-ceutical companies to financially justify mass-producing the vaccine. Ask questions when your baby is born and care is being administered. If you, having evaluated your child's risk, have decided to forego the vaccine, prepare yourself to be ridiculed for your decision. Know your reasons why you are choosing to forego the immunization. Be con-fident in your presentation of fact. Don't get angry or defensive, just state the facts and your decision. Confidence and persistence while knowing that the law allows your deci-sion (this is why you must educate yourself as to your state law requirements) will allow you to prevail.

Be prepared to do your own research and pray for wisdom. God has given us parents the responsibility and authority to make this decision for our children. What I choose to do in this area may not be your decision. That's okay. You don't answer to me or any other person, you answer to God. If your decision is based on His wisdom given you for your child's sake, your decision is right.

The Rashes: Measles, Rubella, Roseola, Fifth Disease, Coxsackie Virus, Chicken Pox

The childhood illnesses that cause rashes that I will address here are those your child will be most likely to encounter and possibly contract: chicken pox, measles, rubella, roseola, and coxsackie virus (hand, foot and mouth disease) and fifth disease. All of these childhood diseases have the common characteristics of fever and a rash or swelling. For a detailed description of the symptoms and contagious periods, Anne Frye's *Understanding Diagnostic Tests in the Childbearing Year*, published by Labrys Press, New Haven, CT and the *Merck Manual* published by Merck Research Laboratories, Rahway, NJ are excellent resources.

Anytime a child has an unexplained fever for 1 to 3 days then develops a rash, one of these childhood diseases needs to be ruled out (eliminate each disease as a diagnosis). I find that the best way to "rule out" the individual childhood diseases is to make a list of the common diseases of childhood, then place a check next to the diseases the child's symptoms match. At the end of this process, I generally have an idea of what I am dealing with. Since I find diagnostic tools to be helpful, I appreciate the availability of blood tests. I certainly would not recommend blood tests in every case, but if there *is* a great need to know what the child has, a blood test would be quite helpful. See Anne Frye's book to ascertain which blood test to perform.

These diseases generally do not cause severe problems in those with strong immune response. The MMR vaccine is given primarily out of concern for the complications of measles and the danger to an expectant mother who may contract rubella during her pregnancy. Research indicates a link between the onset of diabetes and the MMR vaccine. There are moral issues at stake with the rubella vaccine: please further research the ingredients involved in culturing the rubella vaccine. Re-infection with rubella virus occurs in 3-10% of those who've actually had the disease. For those immunized, infection rates are 14-18%; therefore, current recommendation is that *all* women, even those who've had the disease as well as those immunized, should avoid exposure to rubella virus.[15]

Disease	Usual Age	Season	Prodrome & Symptoms that may occur during disease	Look of Rash
Measles (rubeola)	Infant - Adult	Winter/ Spring	High fever, symptoms of upper respiratory infection, conjunctivitis (pink eye) Koplik's spots (white spots on inside of mouth near molars), child appears sick, sensitive to light, cough, high fever	Red bumps and spots that begin on the face and move downward over the body; bumps and spots tend to run together looking confluent
Rubella (3-day measles)	Adolescents/ Young Adults	Spring	Absent or low-grade fever, fatigue Swollen lymph nodes behind ears and on back of neck, headache and tiredness	Rose pink spots that begins on face and moves downward; spots do not run together or become confluent; can actually look like the pin-point rash of scarlet fever
Erythema Infectiosum (parvovirus B19 or "Fifth Disease")	5-15 years	Winter/ Spring	Usually none Rash comes and goes for several weeks, occasional arthritis pain (more common in adults who contract the disease), headache and malaise	Slapped cheek "look;" Red splotches or red bumps that usually occur on the arms/legs, but may be more generally distributed
Enteroviral exanthems (coxsackie, echovirus, other enteroviruses)	Young Children	Summer/Fall	Fever (occasional) Low-grade fever, occasional pains in chest (a complication of myocarditis should be ruled out if chest pain occurs)	Extremely variable; can be red bumps, appear as small red spots on roof of mouth near uvula, petechial, purpuric or vesicular; usually generalized distribution, may be acral
Hand-foot-mouth syndrome (several coxsackie viruses)	Children	Summer/Fall	Fever (occasional) or sore mouth Oral ulcers, occasional fever	Grey-white vesicles 3-7mm on normal or red base occurring on hands/feet most commonly, diaper area, general distribution

| Chickenpox (varicella virus) | 1-14 years | Late fall/ Winter/ Spring | Fever, symptoms of upper respiratory infection

Itching, fever, oral lesions, occasional tiredness | Red spots and bumps quickly become vesicles on a red base, then crusts; often begins on scalp or face, more profuse on trunk than extremities. |
| Roseola | 6 mos. - 3 yrs | Spring/Fall | High fever 3-5 days

May be swollen lymph nodes behind ears and in neck. | Small red dots or fine lacy rash that appears *after* the fever is gone that affects the trunk and neck, may be generalized and last for hours or several days. |

Some suggestions for comfort measures and immune support during childhood diseases are as follows:

Itchy rash - Nettles tea or TincTract™ in a bath, or an oatmeal bath. An oatmeal bath may be made by placing rolled oats in a clean sock. Then hang the sock from the bathtub faucet and let the warm water run over it. Rolled oats in the tub would create an awful mess. Powdered oatmeal may be placed directly in the tub. A lavender bath may prove soothing and healing to lesions. Another wash for the itchy spots is 1 oz. dried Rosemary, 1 oz. dried Calendula decocted in 1 qt of water for a tea. Strain the tea and cool, then apply with a washcloth to child's skin once each night (discard tea after 3 days) for duration of spots.

Scar prevention - Zinc in a chewable tablet, not to exceed one week's usage at maximum levels. Topical application of Salve Drops™ after the crusts have fallen off of chicken pox lesions helps speed healing.

Immune support - Echinacea & Thyme for general immune support; for more skin involvement (prominent rash and lesions), BactaMune™; for respiratory symptoms and lymphatic swelling, ViraMune™ may be the better choice. If a secondary infection begins, Scout Out may be started immediately.

Fever - Yummy Yarrow and Peppermint TincTract™ may be taken as often as every 30 minutes.

MUMPS

Mumps is an acute, generalized viral disease, in which painful enlargement of the salivary glands, chiefly the parotid glands, is the usual sign that signals parents as to the type of illness their child has encountered. The mumps virus is spread by direct contact, airborne droplets, objects contaminated by saliva and possibly by urine. The incubation period ranges from 14-24 days, with a peak at 17-18 days. Transmission does not seem to occurlonger than 24 hours before the appearance of swelling or 3 days after the swelling has subsided.

Epidemics may occur in any season; however, cases of mumps are slightly more frequent in late winter and spring. Approximately 30-40% of mumps cases are sub-clinical, meaning the person has the disease without symptoms, thus without knowing they are ill. Lifelong immunity follows mumps infection. Mom's antibodies that she transfers to baby in the womb provide baby with immunity during their first 6-8 months of life. Moms who have mumps during the week prior to delivery may have their babies born with a case of mumps.

Prior to the swelling of the glands, children may have fever, muscular pain (especially in the neck), headache and fatigue, though these occur rarely. Generally, the first sign of illness is the pain and swelling in one or both of the parotid glands. The swelling is distinctive in that first the swelling fills the space between the back of the jaw and the mastoid behind the ear, then extends in a series of crescents downward and forward, being limited to above the clavicle. The swelling pushes the ear lobe upward and outward, and the angle of the jaw is not distinguishable. Swelling may come on quickly within hours and peak in 1-3 days. Swelling slowly subsides within 3-7 days but occasionally lasts longer. The pain usually worsens with introduction of sour liquids such as lemon juice, vinegar or pickles. Fever usually accompanies, although high fevers, above 104° F, are rare.

Complications may occur in a small percentage of patients with mumps. Treatment generally involves bed rest and adjusting diet to meet the painful chewing needs.

Immunization protocol and coverage

Mumps vaccine is a live, attenuated vaccine that does not cause fever, excretion of virus, thus no spread through vaccine of the virus; although rare cases of parotitis can develop 7-10 days after vaccination. Efficacy appears to be around 97% against natural mumps infection; however, in one outbreak of mumps, several children who had been immunized experienced an illness with fever, tiredness, nausea and a red rash on the trunk and extremities that resulted in raised mumps antibody titers.[16]

The primary reasoning for giving mumps vaccine is the possibility of contracting mumps as an adult male, which could possibly result in an infection of the testicles and possibly infertility in a small percentage of males. The mumps vaccine is given in a combination with red measles (rubeola) and 3-day measles (rubella). The primary concern with the measles vaccine is the link that has been suspected between measles vaccination and the later development of diabetes. The link has been established and has yet to be disproven. There is also a link between rubella vaccine and the development of an arthritic syndrome with some receiving the vaccination. Parents would be wise to weigh the possible adverse effects of the vaccination with the risks of possible complications from the diseases.

DIPHTHERIA

Diphtheria is an acute toxicoinfection caused by *Corynebacterium diphtheriae*. Diphtheria, once a major cause of childhood death, now is a medical rarity.[17] Diphtheria's primary focus of infection is the tonsils and throat. The nose and larynx may also be infected. After a 2-4 day incubation period, a low-grade fever may present with sore throat. Fever is only present in half of those with diphtheria, and only a few will experience difficulty swallowing, hoarseness, tiredness and/or headache. These symptoms are followed by an unilateral or bilateral membrane formation over the tonsils that may extend to the uvula, soft palate, posterior oropharynx, hypopharynx, and glottic areas. A "bull-neck" appearance may occur due to underlying soft tissue swelling and enlarged lymph nodes. A parent and physician may differentiate between diphtheria and the sore throat due to *Streptococcus pyogenes* and Epstein-Barr virus by looking for diphtheria's leather-like adherent membrane that extends beyond the tonsil area, relative lack of fever and difficulty swallowing.[18]

Diphtheria is primarily spread by airborne respiratory droplets or direct contact with respiratory secretions of symptomatic individuals or exudate from infected skin lesions. Asymptomatic respiratory carriers (3% - 5% of healthy individuals in areas where diphtheria is endemic) are an important form of transmission. Diphtheria remains viable in dust and on fomites for up to 6 months, although this is not a frequent transmission form.

Although diphtheria used to be common in children under 15 years of age, the 27 sporadic cases of respiratory tract diphtheria in the 1980s occurred primarily (70%) in persons older than 25 years of age. Outbreaks in other areas of our world are showing the same incidence of diphtheria occurring in those older than 14-15. Interestingly, in Sweden, which boasts a 95% immunization rate, 19% of persons younger than 20 years of age and 81% of women and 56% of men older than 60 years of age lacked the protective antibody, suggesting a lack of long-term protective benefit from the immunization.[19]

Eradication of diphtheria as a health threat is slated for the year 2000, although travel in developing countries still requires immunization consideration.

PERTUSSIS

Pertussis, more commonly called "whooping cough," is a disease caused by the bacteria, *bordetella pertussis*. Pertussis causes a fairly distinctive set of symptoms. Even with clear symptoms, the disease often proceeds undiagnosed due to a lack of knowledge in physicians who believe the disease to be primarily conquered by immunization. Actually, immunizations have not conquered the disease's presence in our population. Epidemiologists (those who study how disease affects and spreads through our population) continue to receive data indicating that fully-immunized individuals as well as older children and adults are those who the disease is primarily afflicting in the past decade.[20,21] Pertussis is a cyclical disease occurring generally in 3-5 year intervals in the population. What does pertussis "look like?" Whom does it affect? How do we treat it?

Pertussis has three stages of illness: catarrhal stage, paroxysmal stage and the convalescent stage, each lasting approximately 2 weeks. The incubation period is 3 - 12 days. The beginning of pertussis can look much like a cold in some ways: congestion, runny nose accompanied by the variable symptoms of low-grade fever, sneezing and watery eyes.

The distinctive feature of this disease as it moves into the paroxysmal stage is the beginning of a night-only cough, which may be dry and hacking. The cough, within days to a week, becomes a day cough that is paroxysmal (coughing that occurs at intervals that is uninterrupted, and repetitive to the point of breathlessness or gagging at the end of the cough) and very "wet" sounding. Affected individuals may, or may not, have the characteristic "whoop" sound as they try to take a breath after the coughing paroxysm is over. In fact, most people who contract the disease at this point in time do not have the "whoop" sound due to their immunized status or age (older children and adults). They do not experience the disease as severely as non-immunized, very young individuals. Infants cannot even manage the "whoop" and usually appear to choke, gasp, and flail their extremities, eyes watering and bulging, and face reddened. Often the uninterrupted coughing bursts end in the expulsion of a thick plug of mucous. Adults usually describe a sudden feeling of strangulation followed by uninterrupted coughs, feeling of suffocation, bursting headache, diminished awareness, and then the chest heaves and air rushes into the lungs, without a whoop. Throwing-up after the coughing is common in all ages as is post-tussive exhaustion.

The paroxysmal stage progresses from a few coughs daily to the peak of what may be a paroxysm more than one every hour. As the disease progresses to the convalescent stage, the number of the paroxysms diminish in frequency and severity; however, infants may experience even stronger, louder coughs during the convalescent stage.

Immunized children have each stage shortened, and adults do not truly experience distinct stages. Infants may not exhibit any catarrhal stage at all; the first sign of their illness may be the shortness of breath, choking or gasping cough. Once the disease has been weathered, the discouraging note is that the terrible cough and whoop may recur with subsequent respiratory illnesses up to one year post-disease. These recurrences are not contagious for pertussis any longer, but they make convalescence difficult.

Classic signs to indicate pertussis as a possible diagnosis:

Any cough lasting more than 2 weeks that is predominantly just the cough, especially if the following are absent: fever, general fatigue, rash, sore throat, hoarseness, fast-breathing, wheezes and rales. Clinically, pertussis should be diagnosed with any cough lasting 14 days or more with at least one associated symptom of paroxysms, whoop or post-tussive (post-coughing) vomiting. Obtaining a culture for pertussis is not usually considered necessary as the culturing medium does not "grow out" pertussis. If a culture is performed, and pertussis does "grow out," diagnosis is 100% positive, since pertussis has a high false negative, yet no false positive culturing rate. All professional medical literature as well as CDC information indicates that doctors should not only consider pertussis diagnosis with the above clinical features, but they should definitely diagnose pertussis with the above clinical case definition.[22,23,24]

Prevention of Pertussis:

Obviously, from the information garnered from the world's medical literature and research studies in the spread of this disease, immunization has not effectively conquered this disease, even in highly-immunized populations. So what are we to do? Not immunize? Immunize? At this point, I will share simply some points to consider in the decision-making process of whether to immunize or not. I do believe that childhood immunization decisions have never belonged, nor will they ever belong in the hands of the state governing authorities. The state will never be able to do what is necessary for my children, or yours, to be most effectively aided by immunization measures, and that is to individually weigh the risks versus benefits for each individual child's needs, as they relate to environmental risk and their general health condition.

What the immunization for pertussis can do:

Reduce the severity of the disease. Pertussis can usually be tolerated by older children and adults, though the symptoms are no picnic! Young infants, particularly those under 2 months of age, do not fare as well. Their risk of disease complications or death is higher with the disease. Hospitalization needs to occur in 82% of infants under 2 months for their safety in having help to suction out their airways during the coughing paroxysms. Complications of pneumonia is about 25% in those under 2 months, seizures 4%), encephalopathy (1%) and death (1%). Young children, particularly infants, need round-the-clock care during pertussis. Since infants may not even begin immunizations before their most vulnerable period, the question really becomes one of, "Do I want to reduce the severity of this disease in my babies and toddlers?" The answer to that really depends, for us, on our frequency of exposure and how much we can count on those around us who may contract the disease being loving enough to separate themselves during their families' contagious period of the disease.

What the immunization is not doing at present:

Preventing the disease from occurring. Some epidemiologists are finding that mass-immunization has, in fact, created quite a contagious "pool" of pertussis among older children and adults who are not hit hard enough by the disease to realize what they have and continue to pass it on to those around them. Their current clinical case definition is designed to alert the public to the presence of pertussis in their communities, yet this, alone, does not solve the problem of an ineffective vaccine. The whole-cell pertussis vaccine is completely out of vogue. Even the CDC recommends that parents should not give the whole-cell pertussis vaccine (DTP) to their children. They instead, recommend use of the acellular pertussis vaccine, which is associated with fewer side effects (DTaP). Truly, the non-immunized body of the population is at risk primarily due to the immunized population.

The immunization may not be all that effective during the first six months of a breast-fed baby's life due to maternal antibodies still being passed to the baby inhibiting the baby's full immune response to the vaccine.

Preventing spread of the disease when encountered:

Current guidelines by the CDC and medical textbooks indicate that a prophylactic course of erythromycin is an effective means of preventing the spread through family members. If antibiotics are given during the incubation period of the disease or in the very early catarrhal stage, the disease may be averted. Once the disease has reached the paroxysmal stage, antibiotic treatment is only aimed at possibly reducing symptom severity as well as possibly preventing further passage to family members. The bottom line is that if pertussis occurs in our family, we must be willing for the sake of others we come into contact with to stay home for approximately 6 weeks time from the onset of the disease. Separation is the most effective means of halting the spread of the disease.

A Personal Story by Shelley Treadway

After exposure to undiagnosed pertussis that we all thought was just a weird cold or allergies, my daughter was on my bed one night sleeping and was suddenly awakened by a dry, coughing spell that ended in an intake of breath that sounded like "Whoop." She had been coughing in the night probably two weeks prior to this night. I immediately called a friend whose children had been coughing and asked had any of her children made that sound. She said no, but she called her doctor and asked about the possibility of pertussis. He said, "Oh, maybe. Could be. The only way to find out would be to do a naso-pharyngeal washing to see if pertussis cultures out." He doubted pertussis as a possibility. We both watched our children the next few days while reading everything we could get our hands on about pertussis.

From that point, the cough became more persistent, in the day as well as the night. The paroxysms were more severe. She didn't appear sick between paroxysms, but during a coughing spell, she would drool this egg-white consistency "goo" while coughing so severely and so long that she would lose her breath, turn blue and still be coughing. During the coughing, she would throw up making horrid sounds because she was struggling to throw up in the middle of this severe coughing. The cough never let up enough for her to take a good breath. The coughing spasm would end with her breath inspiration that made the "whoop" sound. My friend, whose children were doing the same thing, without the whoop, and I definitely decided we were dealing with pertussis. Initially, we were "pooh-poohed" by friends and doctors alike.

After four weeks of this coughing, my friend convinced her doctor to check for pertussis as well as other possible pathogens. The culture was positive, to the surprise of the doctor and all our friends. Although no one encouraged us to stay in or isolate ourselves, my husband and I chose to do this as a protection for those we loved. We also decided to give our daughter as well as all the rest of our family members a round of erythromycin. My other children had started coughing some, so that made our decision for antibiotics easier. They never progressed as far in the disease as our Allison.

Since she recovered from pertussis in the fall of 1997, she still struggles with that pertussis-like cough, though never as severe as when she was sick with the disease. It was a terrible experience that I would wish no parent had to endure.

How Do We Treat Pertussis:

- Make the child as comfortable as possible, not allowing rigorous play due to provocation of more coughing paroxysms.
- Increase liquid intake to avoid an even further thickening of the mucous plug due to dehydration.
- Consider the post-tussive vomiting when choosing foods to eat.
- Try to sleep when you can since night sleep may be often interrupted.
- Keep the child near with bucket and towel in hand.
- Herbal medicines are aimed at reducing the severity of the paroxysmal attacks and preventing congestion of the clear, viscid mucus that is thrown-up during the attacks. An herbal tea mixture (or one may mix TincTracts to make a glycerin herbal formula) for whooping cough is as follows:

      Thyme   40g
      Sundew *(Droserae)* 40g
      Anise   15g
      Mullein   5g
      Dosage: 1 cup, made by infusing 1 tablespoonful of the mixture in 150ml of boiling water, several times daily.

  Or

      Sundew TincTract   1 part
      Thyme TincTract   4 parts
      Dosage: 20-30 drops several times daily.[25]

Tetanus

Tetanus is an acute, spastic paralytic illness caused by tetaospasmin, the neurotoxin produced by *Clostridium tetani*. Tetanus is an anaerobic organism (thrives without oxygen) that occurs naturally in soil, dust and the digestive tract of various animals. The most common form of tetanus occurs in newborns through unsanitary conditions with their umbilical cord at and after birth in mothers who were not immunized. The other common form of contracting tetanus is in childbearing women worldwide who are not immunized from postpartum, postabortal or postsurgical wound infection. The majority of the 50 cases occurring in the United States each year are in the 60 years or older population; however, toddler-aged and newborn cases do occur.

The incubation period is 2-14 days, but may be as long as months after the injury. The most noticeable symptom is "lockjaw," masseter muscle spasm. Early symptoms include headache, restlessness, and irritability followed by stiffness, difficulty chewing, difficulty swallowing and neck muscle spasm. The disease progresses from intractable spasm of the face and neck muscles down the body. Many complications may occur from tetanus infection. The typical setting for tetanus is an non-immunized patient (and/or the mother) who was injured or born within the preceding 2 weeks who seeks medical care for the intractable spasms, other rigid muscles and clear senses.

Treatment is done through surgery, by excising the wound, and administration of human tetanus immune globulin (TIG) and antibiotics. Supportive care is given in a quiet, dark secluded setting to avoid any stimulus that may trigger the seizures and spasms. The longer the incubation period, the more favorable the outcome; however, reported fatality rates for generalized tetanus range between 5% and 35%. Neonatal tetanus fatality rates range from <10% with intensive care treatment to >75% without it.

Of all the immunizations, tetanus seems to make the most sense. The vaccine is delivered in the exact same fashion as the disease could be contracted, and the vaccine seems to be most effective in the population that is most likely to contract the disease, the mother and newborn. Women who have not been adequately immunized may be given tetanus toxoid during their third trimester of pregnancy that will confer at least 4 months of protection to their newborn infant.[26]

Objections to tetanus toxoid immunizations neglect to accurately describe the ongoing occurrence in our own country as well as the rest of the world. The side effects of the immunization include localized swelling and redness at the wound site as well as low-grade fever.

I do not wish to minimize any side effects that may occur due to immunization; however, I do think that parents need better information to make their decision with rather than very old data from World War II as to tetanus risk.[27] The risk may be low of actually contracting tetanus; however, knowing that the second most poisonous substance in the world resides in and around my home, makes me, personally, more likely to consider the tetanus immunization for my family members.

While most physicians' offices only keep the DTP, DTaP, or Td on hand, parents may ask for just the straight tetanus toxoid, if they wish to avoid the pertussis and diptheria vaccines.

POLIO

Poliomyelitis is an infection caused by an enterovirus, which enters the body via the mouth by fecal-oral or oral-oral (respiratory) transmission then infects the gastrointestinal system. In temperate climates, enteroviruses may occur in winter and spring but are more common in summer and fall, with peaks from August to October. Immunities passed from mother to baby through the placenta last for the first six months of life. Tonsillectomy and adenoidectomy decrease resistance to poliovirus, which may be due to decreased sectretory antibodies in the nose and throat.

Poliovirus may manifest in one of the following ways:

1. subclinical (no apparent symptoms) infection in 90-95% of those infected,
2. abortive poliomyelitis - brief illness consisting of one or more of the following symptoms: fever that seldom exceeds 103° F, tiredness, lack of appetite, nausea, vomiting, headache, sore throat, constipation and unlocalized abdominal pain. Red eyes, cough, pus in the throat, diarrhea and localized abdominal tenderness and pain are uncommon,
3. nonparalytic poliomyelitis - The same symptoms occur as in abortive poliomyelitis, except that headache, nausea and vomiting are more intense, and there is soreness and stiffness of the muscles in the back of the neck, trunk, arms and legs. Sometimes bladder paralysis may occur, and constipation is frequent. These symptoms characterize the first phase of this illness, then the second phase involves nuchal (neck) and spinal rigidity,
4. paralytic poliomyelitis - The symptom pattern is the same for nonparalytic poliomyelitis plus weakness of one or more muscle groups, either skeletal or cranial. These symptoms may be followed by a symptom-free interlude of several days and then a recurrence culminating in paralysis. Flaccid paralysis is the most obvious clinical feature of neuronal injury which results in paralysis from the poliovirus.[28]

Prevention of poliovirus occurs through good hygiene habits, avoidance of those who have just received the live, attenuated, orally administered polio vaccine (OPV) and vaccination with inactivated polio vaccine (IPV) for those who are at risk.

Infectious disease specialists attribute the fact that the United States has experienced no wild-type poliovirus epidemics post the decline of the disease to widespread immunization protocol. The only source for poliovirus occurrences in the United States is from children who receive the live, attenuated OPV. Countries such as Sweden, Finland and Holland use only IPV in their immunization protocol, while Denmark and Israel use a combined IPV/OPV regimen. The U.S. is finally recognizing the wrong of administering a vaccine that actually is the only cause of the disease by now recommending that parents first administer the IPV to confer immunity to the later administered OPV. Basically, the recommendation is that we give the shot IPV vaccine to protect our children from the oral OPV vaccine. We must also note that immunization of very young infants with either IPV or OPV may not be very effective due to maternal antibodies transferred placentally and through breastmilk. Six months seems to be the age at which the immunization might actually be effective in producing antibody in the child.[29]

Anti-immunization educators point to a decline in the poliovirus disease prior to the introduction of the vaccine. I found it to be a close call. What I find more interesting is the lack of wild-type virus despite many parents choosing not to follow recommended immunization protocol. The lack of polio epidemics in light of less than full immunization coverage points to other factors in preventing the disease rather than just credit given to the vaccine alone. Dr. Salk, who made the IPV vaccine, said repeatedly that he did not approve of giving a live vaccine, and the results of paralytic polio cases in the U.S. due to the live vaccine prove his concerns correct.

Our own thinking about poliovirus vaccines is that we evaluate our need based on the available evidence of immunization effectiveness balanced against the risk of the vaccine itself. We also evaluate our own lifestyle patterns. I've often said that if I were at the neighborhood swimming pool in the summer, with all the children who have just been to the doctor for the orally administered, live poliovirus vaccine, I would probably choose to give my children the IPV to protect them against the less than clean habits of small children in swimming pools who are incubating poliovirus in their gut. Day care and church nursery, or even a day with friends who've just received their OPV, should be evaluated as a possible risk factor for those who are not immunized.

HAEMOPHILUS INFLUENZAE, TYPE B (HIB)

Haemophilus influenzae is a bacterial infection that is commonly carried in the normal respiratory flora of 60 - 90% of healthy children. Mode of transmission is by direct contact or inhalation of respiratory tract droplets; however, the incubation period is variable with the exact period of communicability unknown.[30] Carriage of this organism is a definite problem with continuing disease rates even among immunized populations, although the carriage rate has declined with immunization protocol. Interestingly, those younger than 5 months are at the most risk when contracting the disease, although the under 6 months population have low colonization rates. Carriage rates reach a maximum between the ages of 3 and 5 years. The greater number of siblings in a family actually increase carriage rates.[31] Since carriage tends to persist for many weeks or months, it seems that close contact and generous exchange of respiratory secretions are required for the transmission of Hib. Even when the contact between a known carrier and a susceptible child is intimate, spread of Hib occurs slowly over weeks or months.[32]

Since most patients with Hib disease have not had contact with a person who had invasive disease, and the organism has no known reservoir outside humans, asymptomatic carriers have been recognized as the major source of infection. Studies of at-risk populations have shown low carriage rates in the presence of the spread of infection, and no overt disease in the presence of high carriage rates. What is quite interesting is that organisms collected from the pharynx of individuals appear to lack certain virulence (ability to cause invasive disease) found in organisms isolated from patients with invasive disease. Close, sustained contact with those affected with invasive disease seems to be required for spread of the infection.[33]

At birth, babies are protected by material anti-PRP IbG antibodies. At age 2, children begin to produce their own antibody. Babies that are breast-fed receive their own protection through the breast milk.[34] Those ethnic groups most susceptible to invasive Hi disease are: Alaskan Eskimos, Apaches, Navajos and Blacks.[35]

Even with vaccination, carriage is not rapidly curtailed in those already colonized with Hib. The role of the vaccine appears to be more in preventing colonization, since some studies are indicating up to a 90% reduction in Hib carriage among those vaccinated. Antibodies in secretions may simply not be able to reach organisms "holed up" in cells.[36] There are many subtypes of Hi disease with Hib only being one of the identifiable subtypes.

Hib may occur non-invasively as a throat infection, sinusitis or ear infection (in fact, Hib is the most common cause of sinusitis and ear infections); however, invasive Hib disease may cause peri-orbital cellulitis, cellulitis, meningitis, uvulitis, pneumonia, supraglottitis or acute epiglottitis, septic arthritis, osteomyelitis, percarditis, generalized bacteremia.[37]

A major concern that natural health practitioners are seeing in their clinical practices revolves around the question of whether Hib vaccines are contributing to more severe non-invasive Hib illnesses such as ear infections and sinusitis. Since researchers have yet to tackle this, we simply do not know what time will bear out in terms of this immunization. We, Parkers, have encountered Hib disease in one of our own children at the birth of another of our children. Our Zachary had a respiratory infection that cultured out Hib. This was the first illness that we treated solely with herbs. Some of the reason for that was simple ignorance about the disease itself, and some because we felt that since he was not very ill, we had time to try to treat the illness on our own at home. If he had been very ill, we would definitely have sought medical attention while employing our natural healing measures.

Another interesting phenomenon about Hib outbreaks is that when I looked at the studies on the outbreaks and spread of the disease, urban populations were those most at risk.[38] One more reason for enjoying country life!

If treating an ear infection or sinusitis at home that may be caused by Hib, the same measures given in the preceding section on illnesses may be followed. If a more serious disease process, caused by any disease-causing "bug," is presenting in your family, please do not hesitate to seek immediate medical care. Symptoms such as the abrupt onset of high fever, possible stiff neck (nuchal rigidity), and/or sudden appearance of purplish splotches on the body should be evaluated for possible meningitis. The quicker medical care (intravenous antibiotics) are begun in a life-threatening bacterial infection, the better the outcome.

In the
Fullness of
Our Days

ACNE

There are two types of acne: acne vulgaris which affects the hair follicles and oil-secreting glands and is manifested as blackheads, whiteheads and inflammation and acne conglombata which causes deep cyst formation with scarring. The most common form is acne vulgaris. The male sex hormone testosterone is the major hormonal factor in acne, causing sebaceous (sebum-producing) glands to enlarge and produce more sebum. The skin of patients with acne shows increased activity of an enzyme (5-alpha-reductase) that converts testosterone to dihydrotestosterone (a more potent form of testosterone).

Lifestyle/Dietary Recommendations:
1. Wash pillowcase in a natural, laundry liquid detergent.
2. Switch to a water-based, make-up foundation and other oil-free cosmetics.
3. Wash face twice daily to remove excess oil and sebum with a non-soap cleanser.
4. Follow the whole foods diet. Eliminate sugar, foods containing trans-fatty acids such as milk, milk products, margarine, shortening and synthetically-hydrogenated vegetable oils, fried foods and chocolate. Add anti-acne foods: butternut, sunflower seeds, Brazil nuts, pumpkin, soybeans, cashews, pistachios, avocados, breadfruit, black currant, asparagus, chickpea, black beans, lettuce, strawberries, kale.[39]

Nutritional Supplement Recommendations:
1. Quality vitamin-mineral formula providing: Zinc - 30-45 mg daily, Vitamin A - 10,000 IU's daily, Vitamin E - 200 - 400 IU daily, B 6 - 150mg daily in combination with other B vitamins. If vitamin/mineral formula does not supply all of these nutrients, add single vitamins and minerals to satisfy these requirements.
2. Apply Australian Tea Tree Oil topically. A study conducted at the Royal Prince Hospital in New South Wales, Australia, a 5-percent tea tree oil solution demonstrated beneficial effects similar to those of 5% benzoyl peroxide but with substantially fewer side effects.[40][41]
3. Pantothenic acid supplementation showed complete cure of acne vulgaris if given liberally.[42]
4. A topical extract of Hawthorn was found to be effective in the treatment of acne.[43]
5. Since allopathic treatment commonly employs antibiotics to successfully treat acne, a natural alternative might utilize the herbs Echinacea, 1,000mg daily and Burdock, 1,000-2,000mg daily to stimulate immune activity since they both exhibit actions on the skin as well as showing antibacterial actions.

ALLERGY/ASTHMA

An allergic reaction begins when a foreign substance is attacked and bound by an IgE antibody. The substance bound to the allergic antibody is called an "antigen" or "allergen." This IgE-antigen complex then binds to specialized white cells known as "mast cells" and "basophils." This binding causes the release of substances such as histamine which cause swelling and inflammation. Allergy may manifest as sinus congestion, asthma, hives, eczema, arthritis, intestinal inflammation and headaches.

Asthma is an allergic disorder characterized by spasm of the bronchial tubes and excessive excretion of a viscous mucous in the lungs, which can lead to difficulty in breathing. It can be mild wheezing and/or coughing or a life-threatening inability to breathe. The allergic compounds that trigger asthma are derived from arachidonic acid - a fatty acid found only in animal foods.

A recent study of 706 Japanese factory workers demonstrated that a healthful lifestyle reduced IgE levels while unhealthful lifestyles elevated IgE. Those unhealthful practices which elevated IgE levels were: poor dietary habits, alcohol consumption, cigarette smoking, and increased feelings of stress.[44]

Lifestyle/Dietary Recommendations:
1. Eliminate carpets, rugs, upholstered furniture and other surfaces where allergens can collect. Pets should definitely not be indoors.
2. Encase bed mattress in allergen-proof material; wash sheets, blankets, pillowcases and mattress pads each week; toss pillow into clothes dryer for 10 minutes each week; use bedding made from Ventflex - a special hypoallergenic synthetic material; install air purifier. The best air purifiers utilize HEPA (high-efficiency particulate-arresting) filters, which can be attached to central heating/air-conditioning units. Portable HEPA units may be more effective than whole house systems unless the house system is of very high quality. Electrostatic filters maintain effectiveness only if washed weekly. Air purifiers that create ozone may be used as well. See Resource Section for companies selling allergy control products.
3. If rugs and upholstery are in house, use a vacuum with efficient filtering system (traps dust, bacteria, and some viruses in HEPA filters). See Resources.
4. Eliminate food additives tartrazine (yellow dye #5), colorings (azo dyes), flavorings (salicylates, aspartame), preservatives (benzoates, nitrites, sorbic acid), synthetic antioxidants (hydroxytoluene, sulfite, gallate) and emulsifiers/stabilizers (polysorbates, vegetable gums). All of these have been shown to produce allergies and play a role in asthma.[45]
5. Decrease intake of animal fats while increasing consumption of omega-3 oils found in flaxseed oil and cold water fish such as mackerel, herring, sardines and salmon.

6. A vegan diet, followed for one year, proved helpful in 92% of 25 patients in a long-term trial.[46]

Nutritional Supplement Recommendations:

1. Vitamin C - 1000mg daily47, Vitamin E, Selenium, Flavonoids especially Quercetin which has to be combined with Bromelain to increase absorption - 250 - 500 mg of Quercetin with 1,000mg of Bromelain taken thirty minutes before meals.[48,49]

2. Vitamin B12 supplementation in one clinical trial provided definite improvement in asthmatic patients who took weekly intramuscular (IM) injections of 1,000 micrograms.[50] The B12 injections are particularly effective in sulfite-sensitive individuals by forming sulfite-cobalamin complex which blocks sulfite's effect.[51] According to Michael T. Murray in *Natural Prescriptions to Over-the-Counter and Prescription Drugs*, oral supplementation with 1 - 3 mg B12 may provide similar benefit to the injectable form.

3. Vitamin B6 supplementation of 50mg twice daily has been shown in double-blind clinical studies to benefit asthmatic patients because it corrects the defect in tryptophan metabolism commonly found in asthmatics. Tryptophan is converted to serotonin, a known broncho-constricting agent.[52] Milk and dark turkey meats are natural food sources for tryptophan.

4. See **NOTE** The herb Ephedra, also known as Ma Huang, combined with herbs exhibiting expectorant qualities, such as lobelia, licorice and grindelia, have been found to be helpful for many people with allergies and asthma. Synthetic ephedrine is a common ingredient in over-the-counter and prescription medications for colds, allergies and asthma. The crude plant (the herb) not only contains a natural amount of ephedrine but other antiinflammatory and antiallergy compounds as well.[53]

   * The FDA advisory review panel on nonprescription drugs recommends that ephedrine not be taken by patients with heart disease, high blood pressure, thyroid disease, diabetes or difficulty with urination due to enlargement of the prostate gland, nor should ephedrine be used by patients on antihypertensive or antidepressant drugs.
   For use with allergies, the ephedrine content of ephedra preparations should be 12.5 - 25.0 mg taken two to three times daily. For the crude herb, an equivalent dose would be 500-1000mg taken three times daily. If ephedra is taken alone over a long period of time, the effects may diminish due to overstimulation of the adrenal gland. Combining ephedra with the expectorant herbs that are also adrenal-supporting herbs should prevent this from occurring.
   ** NOTE: An issue of *Herbalgram*, a publication of the Herb Research Foundation, reported that ephedrine may be linked to some birth defects. Because of this and ephedra's stimulant effects (similar to caffeine in tea, cof-

fee and colas), ephedra or ma huang should not be used during pregnancy unless mom does so under the supervision of a professional health provider.

5. Dr. Andrew Weil, M.D., author of *Natural Health, Natural Medicine*, recommends a lobelia - cayenne mixture for asthma attacks:

6. 3 parts tincture lobelia (I prefer the use of TincTract[TM]s by Tri-Light/Mother's Choice[TM]), 1 part capsicum. Take 20 drops of mixture in water at start of bronchial constriction and repeat every thirty minutes for a total of 3 - 4 doses.[54]

7. Ginkgo biloba herb has received scientific attention as well for its anti-allergic, anti-asthma agent, platelet-activating factor (PAF). One study concluded that Ginkgolide B is the most active PAF antagonist found in this class of ginkgolides. It appears that Ginkgo relieves bronchoconstriction because of its PAF antagonist activity. Another randomized, double-blind, placebo-controlled crossover study of 8 atopic asthmatic patients showed that Ginkgo achieved significant inhibition of the bronchial allergen challenge compared to placebo.[55] The therapeutic dose used would be equivalent to 40 mg three times daily of the standardized extract containing 24% ginkgo heterosides.

8. Another herb that may be beneficial is coltsfoot, used extensively in Chinese medicine. Two studies show the leaves of the plant to contain substances that can soothe inflamed mucous membranes and suppress asthma attacks (not relieve acute attacks).[56,57] Coltsfoot, just like comfrey and borage, contains pyrrolizidine alkaloids (PAs). These alkaloids may cause a liver disease known as hepatic veno-occlusive disease (HVOD). Different PAs possess different levels of toxicity, and current studies have concentrated on isolated compounds or extremely large doses on rats. The risk to humans has not been firmly established. Although empirical (historical) use implies safe internal consumption, it would seem wise for the pregnant mom to avoid using these herbs internally until safety is established. I personally use a liquid combination containing coltsfoot for my daughter, Eryn, who has been having difficulties with asthma. We have seen no toxicity problem in Eryn by using this combination and only use it as needed for the cough, not as an every day herb. 1/2 - 1 teaspoon of Lungs Plus TincTract[TM] containing coltsfoot as needed for cough and congestion is what we have personally found to be effective for Eryn. If we allow her to get to the point of attack, this combination does not relieve the attack itself. We have to begin using it prior to the acute stage. Lungs Plus[TM] formula is being changed to exclude coltsfoot for added safety.

9. Mullein and marshmallow root are both herbs with a very high mucilage (protective gel that forms when the herb comes in contact with water) content. This demulcent effect is very soothing for mucous membranes. The herbs are used, not their oils. 500 mg two to three times daily may be helpful for soothing inflamed mucous membranes in the respiratory tract.

ANEMIA

Anemia is a condition in which the blood does not contain an adequate amount of red blood cells or hemoglobin (iron-containing) portion of the red blood cells. The function of the red blood cell (RBC) is to transport oxygen from the lungs to the tissues of the body and to exchange it there for carbon dioxide. There are many different types of anemia with the most common ones associated with a deficiency of iron, folic acid and B12. These are the types we will address.

Iron-deficiency anemia - A person with low hemoglobin levels usually experiences symptoms such as fatigue, pale fingernail beds and eyes (under lids), and pica (the desire to eat ice, corn starch or clay).

Folic acid-deficiency or Megaloblastic anemia - This type of anemia is most common in those who eat few or no fresh green vegetables. It may cause vomiting and loss of appetite. Since folic acid has been found to be instrumental in preventing neural tube defects, supplementation of this nutrient ideally should begin three months before pregnancy.

B12-deficiency, also Megaloblastic anemia - B12 is a water-soluble vitamin. It is the only vitamin produced only by bacteria, and this only occurs when there is adequate cobalt available. B12 is a cobalt-containing substance that is necessary for normal functioning of the nervous system and contributes to protein, fat, and carbohydrate metabolism.

Dietary absorption of B12 is highly dependent on the source and how well an individual body assimilates it. Several factors may contribute to impaired B12 absorption:

- Insufficient hydrochloric acid in the stomach. Corrected by stimulating acid-formation with herbs: peppermint, cayenne, papaya, bromelain or supplementing with hydrochloric acid. Adequate salt intake is necessary for acid production.
- Compromised pancreatic function. Corrected by balanced calcium supplementation.
- Pancreas-related malabsorption problem stemming from inhibition of the proteases (protein digesting enzymes). Corrected with enzyme trypsin.
- High heat in cooking destroys B12.
- Diet high in fat, excess mucous-forming foods, and refined foods.
- Exposure to cigarette smoke, alcohol, birth control pills, nitrous oxide (dental anesthetic gas or auto emissions), mercury amalgam dental fillings, and certain antibiotics (such as Neomycin).
- Pectin and vitamin C can both destroy B12, while cellulose (dietary fiber) enhances absorption.[58]

- Food sources that are low in B12. While it has been assumed that meat-eaters have no risk of B12 deficiency, research, in the past years, has uncovered a decrease in B12 from foods normally rich in B12 (cheese and liver), possibly due to soil low in cobalt creating cobalt-deficient plants that the animals graze on creating B12 deficient animals. They can't give what they don't have. Vegetarians need to insure adequate B12 intake as well since plant sources may be cobalt-deficient.

Lifestyle/Dietary Recommendations:
1. Cook with iron skillets.
2. Follow the whole foods diet.
3. Add the following foods to diet : prunes, apricots, black cherries, dark, leafy greens (particularly organic dandelion greens), sea vegetables, fermented foods (soy sauce, miso, tamari, etc.), molasses, grapes, almonds, beets, organ meats (absolutely only from certified organic sources - I personally have my doubts about eating even organic liver!). If you do eat liver, make certain it is certified organic calf liver and eat no more than 4 ounces per week.

Nutritional Supplement Recommendations:
1. Nettle leaf, Red Raspberry and Oatstraw infusion - Make by steeping one ounce of each herb in two quarts of boiled water for at least four hours (This makes a strong infusion). Drink 1/2 to 1 cup several times daily. For those who do not wish to drink an infusion, these herbs may be purchased in capsules singly or in a combination and taken 300 - 500 mg 2 to 3 times daily. All of these herbs are high in iron and vitamin C which aids the absorption of iron. They are also a good source of chlorophyll. For those who like anise, 1 teaspoon of seeds may be added to the infusion. A 1990 study showed that anise enhances iron absorption.[59]
2. Taking a vitamin C and bioflavonoid supplement when taking iron supplements aids absorption.
3. Vitamin E supplementation at 600 IU daily for 30 days may reverse anemia due to vitamin E's ability to reduce the fragility of red blood cells.[60]
4. Alfalfa leaves, Kelp powder and Dandelion herb are also high in iron and chlorophyll as well as a wealth of other minerals. Alfalfa is an excellent source of vitamins A and D as well as a rich source of K. It has been used in medicine for blood clotting.
5. Spirulina and chlorella both contain high amounts of protein and B vitamins, especially folic acid. Spirulina is the best vegetable source of B12. The powder, although not the tastiest thing in the world, is the best way of taking these nutritive foods. Nutritive amount: 2 - 4 T daily of the powder or 6 - 12 tablets or capsules daily.
6. The liquid TincTract™ called **Tri-Iron by Mother's Choice**™ contains the herbs: Yellow Dock, Dandelion, Raspberry, Nettles and Anise. These herbs both supply excellent levels of iron with herbs added to enhance absorption.

7. Yellow Dock in combination with other herbs mentioned above or alone can be helpful for anemia that is unresponsive to other measures. The dock plant family does contain anthraquinones (chemical constituents that stimulate intestinal peristalsis), just as cascara sagrada does, so one would not want to overdo the dosage. One 450 mg capsule may be taken two to three times daily. If loose stool occurs, reduce dosage by one capsule.

8. Chlorophyll, in capsule or liquid form, has been used by herbalists to encourage a quick hemoglobin rise. 2 - 3 capsules daily or 1/2 to 1 cup of the liquid daily.

9. The vitamin/mineral supplement should contain adequate iron, folic acid and B12 levels in absorbable forms (Iron - citrate, gluconate or fumarate, Folic acid - folacin, B12 - cobalamin).

10. Herbal combination in capsules I have used personally to prevent anemia: Red beet root, yellow dock root, red raspberry leaves, chickweed herb, burdock root, nettle herb and mullein leaves.

11. The supplement called Floridix with iron or Liquid Herbal Iron, a mix of fruit and herb concentrates, is beneficial in reversing anemia.

12. Exercising daily or at least three time per week helps increase the oxygen supply to the body which will help raise hemoglobin levels.

13. For those with very low B12 levels, one 1000mcg injection may make all the difference in the world.

ANXIETY AND DEPRESSION

New treatment for anxiety and depression is emerging in herbal medicine as more research is accomplished which confirms the validity of botanical medicine for the treatment of these disorders. The herbal protocols are below:

Nutritional Supplement Recommendations:

1. Kava root (peper methysticum) contains substances called kavalactones that exhibit sedative, analgesic, anticonvulsant and muscle-relaxant effects in laboratory animals. Clinical studies confirm the benefit of using kava extracts for anxiety without having the negative effect of decreasing cognitive function. Actually kava improves mental function. Standardized extracts are best to accurately measure the amount of kavalactones needed for anxiolytic effects, 45-70mg of kavalactones three times daily are needed. For sedative effects, the same daily quantity may be taken all at once one hour before bedtime. Higher dosages are not recommended as side effects may be noted over a prolonged period.

2. St. John's Wort, which contains hypericin and pseudohypericin, may be used as a mild to moderate antidepressant. St. John's Wort inhibits both A and B monoamine oxidases (MAO). As a result of this inhibition, there is an increase in the level of nerve impulse transmitters within the brain that maintain normal mood and emotional stability. St. John's Wort is virtually free of side effects at the standard dosage of 300mg three times daily.

3. Valerian has been widely used in herbal medicine as a sedative. Valerian both improves sleep quality and relieves insomnia. As a mild sedative, valerian extract (0.8% valeric acid) can be taken 30 - 45 minutes before bedtime at a dosage of 150-300mg. Water-soluble extracts standardized for valeric acid content is the best choice for supplements.

Resource book: *1995 Gaia Symposium Proceedings Book*, Michael T. Murray, N.D.'s article on Anxiety and Depression.

ATTENTION DEFICIT DISORDER (ADD)/ HYPERACTIVITY

This is one of the most frequent diagnoses for school-age children in our country at present. Schools are full of children regularly being drugged because of this diagnosis. Because early evidence suggests that ADHD children are at higher risk for depression, restlessness, alcoholism and antisocial behavior as adults, we must intervene early with successful treatment of this disorder. For an alternative viewpoint on ADHD, I highly recommend the reading of *The Home School Digest*, volume 7, number 4. Samuel Blumenfeld's article "Are Schools Causing Attention-Deficit Disorder?" is an excellent read and quite thought-provoking. Write to: Wisdom's Gate, PO Box 374, Covert, MI 49043. The read you won't want to miss regarding ADHD is *No More Ritalin!* by Dr. Mary Ann Block. This is an excellent book for parents to know how to further direct the health care of their child with ADHD.

Dietary and Lifestyle Recommendations:

1. Consider withdrawing child from structured classroom into the home for education that is more one-on-one and "structured" with the child's learning style capabilities.
2. Consume a whole-foods diet, high in protein and complex carbohydrates.
3. Eliminate refined sugar and simple carbohydrates.
4. Eliminate processed foods high in additives and food colorings such as:

Tartrazine	Quinoline Yellow	Carmel
Sunset Yellow	FCF	Cochineal
Benzoic Acid	Carmoiic acid	Sodium benzoate
Amaranth	Sulfur dioxide	Sodium nitrate
Red 2G	Potassium nitrate	BHA
Brilliant Blue FCF	BHT	Indigo

   Carmine as well as foods with high salicylate content:

Plums (canned)	Prunes (canned)
Raspberries (fresh)	Strawberries (Fresh)
Peppers	Tomatoes
Almonds	Peanuts
Peppermint tea	Honey

   Many spices: cardamom, cinnamon, cloves, curry, oregano, paprika, pepper, rosemary, sage, turmeric.

5. Lower intake of possible food allergens: cow's milk, eggs, soy, wheat and citrus.
6. Limit television watching and video games.
7. Consider testing for possible lead poisoning

Nutritional Supplement Recommendations:

1. Make certain the child is receiving the following amounts of: Vitamin B6 - 50-100mg daily; Zinc - 5-10mg daily; Copper - 0.5-1mg daily; Chromium - 200mcg daily.

2. Eleuthero (Siberian ginseng) - 150-200mg of a standardized, concentrated extract or 4-5ml of liquid TincTract™ in two to three divided doses daily to help correct blood sugar metabolism and adrenal function.

3. Evening primrose oil - 2-3grams daily to correct the essential fatty acid deficiency noted in some ADHD children.

4. Peace Treaty TincTract™ by Liquid Light™ at a dosage of 4-5ml daily in three divided doses because of the nervine herb content that helps calm the child without causing a lack of alertness.

Resource book: *Herbal Prescriptions for Better Health* by Donald J. Brown, N.D. Prima Publishing: Rocklin, CA, 1996.

BRONCHITIS

B ronchitis is the term used for inflammation of the bronchial tubes. When these tubes become irritated, they produce mucous which stimulates a cough in an effort to clear the air passages. The main symptom is a cough that hasn't gone away after an illness (eliminate allergies as the source of the cough) that produces thick yellow or green sputum. A low-grade fever (below 101 degrees F) may also be present.

If bronchitis does not improve within 48 hours, the cough is bloody or temperature rises above 101 degrees F, medical attention should be sought immediately.

Lifestyle/Dietary Recommendations:
1. Keep air in the home moist with a humidifier as necessary. If a humidifier is used, it must be disinfected regularly to prevent mold and mildew from growing which could create a worse environment than dry air.
2. Stay away from cigarette smoke - personal and second-hand.
3. Garnish foods liberally with garlic.
4. Identify food allergies and avoid those foods.
5. Eliminate dairy products until condition has resolved and cut down on meat while increasing complex carbohydrates.

Nutritional Supplement Recommendations:
1. Treat colds, flu, sinusitis, chronic post-nasal drip with immuno-stimulant and demulcent herbs such as: Echinacea, Garlic, Myrrh, Thyme, Mullein, and Licorice.[61]
2. Common plantain showed a quick turn-around on subjective complaints and offered objective benefits to 80% of patients with bronchitis in a 1982 study. Treatment lasted for 25-30 days.[62]
3. The bioflavonoid quercitin combined with bromelain is used because of quercitin's ability to aid the immune system's response to respiratory viruses and bromelain's antiinflammatory actions. This combination must be taken 30 minutes before meals for the antiinflammatory effect.

CARPAL TUNNEL SYNDROME

Carpal tunnel syndrome is a disorder caused by compression of the median nerve as it passes between the bones and ligaments of the wrist. Common symptoms are: weakness in the hand, pain, numbness, tingling and aching that can radiate up into the arm and shoulder and is particularly troublesome at night.

Lifestyle/Dietary Recommendations:

1. If one works at a computer keyboard often, one should stop at regular intervals to give the wrists a break. Make small circles in the air with hands to help restore circulation and ease pressure.
2. Warm, moist heat may help relieve pain.
3. Tartrazine (FD&C yellow #5) and excessive protein both are B6 antagonists thus should be avoided.
4. Fresh pineapple juice, which contains the anti-inflammatory enzyme bromelain, can be added to the diet.

Nutritional Supplement Recommendations:

1. A curcumin (from tumeric) preparation can be rubbed on wrist during painful episodes. Curcumin is nature's most potent anti-inflammatory agent.[63] Enzymatic Therapy has some excellent ointments and preparations designed for anti-inflammatory effect. See resource section for more information.
2. Bromelain tablets are antiinflammatory and should have at least 1200 clotting units and may be taken 200 - 500 mg thirty minutes before meals for an antiinflammatory effect.
3. Vitamin B6: 100-200 mg daily has been demonstrated in several clinical studies to relieve all symptoms of carpal tunnel syndrome in patients with low B6 levels.[64][65][66][67][68] Pregnant women should limit their intake to no more than 100mg daily.

CHOLESTEROL

Cholesterol, carried in blood plasma by lipoproteins, is certainly a "buzz" word these days. Cholesterol is often referred to in terms of "good" or "bad." The "good" cholesterol is the high-density lipoprotein (HDL). HDL transports cholesterol to the liver for metabolism and excretion and actually protects against heart disease. Low-density lipoprotein (LDL) transports cholesterol to tissue and is the "bad" cholesterol, which increases a person's risk of heart disease. The table below shows recommended values for cholesterol in pregnant and non-pregnant moms.

Type	Normal Levels
Total Cholesterol	less than 200mg/dl
LDL	less than 130mg/dl
HDL	greater than 35 mg/dl
Triglycerides	50 - 150 mg/dl

Adapted from: Murray, Michael T., N.D. *The Healing Power of Foods*. Rocklin, CA: Prima Publishing, 1993.

Lifestyle/Dietary Recommendations:
1. Saturated fats (milk and other animal fats) must be reduced. They tell the liver (which manufactures the majority of cholesterol in the body) to produce more cholesterol. Unsaturated fats tell the liver to produce less.
2. Not all fats are bad. In fact, essential fatty acids (EFAs) are great for us. EFAs are found in marine fish oils (Omega-3), cold-pressed safflower, sunflower, canola, Evening Primrose, Black Currant and Borage oils. These EFAs actually provide the building blocks for the chemical regulators known as prostaglandins.
3. Nuts and seeds should be eaten. They do have a high oil content; however, a study of 26, 473 Americans found that the people who consumed the most nuts were the least obese. This study also demonstrated higher nut consumption was associated with protective effects against heart attacks.[69] Nuts are best purchased in shells free from splits, cracks, stains, holes or other surface problems. They should be stored in a cool, dry environment. Hulled nuts and seeds should be stored in airtight containers in the refrigerator or freezer.
4. Margarines have "gotta" go because of the negative efforts of polyunsaturated oils causing free radical damage. Butter may be used in limited quantities. Oils for cooking should be canola and olive oils.

5. A whole food diet is essential for lowering cholesterol levels: high in fruits, veggies, whole grains and legumes. A whole food diet is naturally a high-fiber diet. Fiber absorbs bile which contains cholesterol and moves it along the intestines for excretion. Lack of fiber means the bile and cholesterol will be reabsorbed.

Nutritional Supplement Recommendations:

1. Gugulipid, from guggal or mukul myrrh tree, extracts standardized to contain 25mg of gugulipid per tablet taken three times daily have been shown in clinical studies to be effective in lowering cholesterol or triglyceride levels.[70][71]

2. Garlic and onions, those wonderfully odiferous vegetables, have been shown in numerous studies to lower LDL cholesterol and triglycerides while raising HDL cholesterol. The equivalent of 1 clove of garlic and/or half an onion per day is necessary to get a 10 - 15% reduction in total cholesterol.[72][73][74]

3. Another nutrient that has been evaluated for effectiveness in lowering cholesterol and triglycerides is pantethine, the active form of pantothenic acid; however, it is a fairly expensive nutritional supplement. The standard dosage for efficacy is 900mg daily. This should be saved for elevated triglyceride levels.[75][76]

4. Other nutrients recommended for elevated cholesterol and triglyceride levels are chromium and vitamin C.[77]

CHRONIC FATIGUE SYNDROME

Chronic fatigue syndrome, once called the "yuppie flu," and once believed to caused by the Epstein-Barr virus, now has an official diagnosis of chronic fatigue immunodeficiency syndrome. The origin and cause of this disease is still poorly understood, but emerging evidence points to better treatment protocol.

Three areas are essential to treatment: adrenal function, immune function and adrenal-insuffiency-induced depression.

Dietary and Lifestyle Recommendations:

1. Hypoglycemia is common with the affliction; therefore eating small meals every couple of hours during the day that are high in complex carbohydrates and dietary fiber (vegetables, fruits and legumes) is essential. Protein intake may be supplemented by soy, fish and nuts.
2. Eliminate food allergens by first establishing which foods cause allergic reaction.
3. Rule out low thyroid function. Take basal body temperature by checking temperature before rising from bed between 5 a.m. and 6 a.m. each morning. Temperature consistently below 97.7 is indicative of low thyroid function.
4. Have spouse massage soft tissues of the body if fibromyalgia is present.

Nutritional Supplement Recommendations:

1. High-potency multi-vitamin and mineral supplement providing at least: magnesium, 200-300mg twice daily; vitamin B complex, 50-100mg daily; pantothenic acid, 250mg daily; vitamin C, 2-3 grams daily.
2. Choose one of the following adaptogen herbs: Siberian ginseng (eleutherococcus) - standardized, concentrated extract of the root and rhizomes, 300-400mg daily. Use continuously for 4-6 weeks with a 1-2 week break before resuming; Asian (panax) ginseng - 100mg twice daily of an extract standardized to contain 4-7% ginsenosides; Astragalus - 3-6grams daily.
3. St. John's wort extract at a daily dose that delivers approximately 1mg of hypericin for control of depression.
4. Evening primrose oil - 4-6grams daily with meals.

Resource: *Herbal Prescriptions for Better Health*, Donald J. Brown, N.D. Prima Publishing, Rocklin, CA, 1996.

COLDS

Colds are caused by viruses in the upper respiratory tract. Allergies may decrease resistance and allow the virus to infect. The best course of action is to boost the immune system to prevent secondary infections and reduce length and severity of symptoms. These aggravating symptoms include: stuffy nose; sneezing; dry, sore throat; possible slight temperature with fatigue and headache. Cold symptoms come along one or more per day spread out over a period of 3-10 days with an average duration of 7 days. Adults rarely experience fever with colds. Antihistamines are useless for colds and are actually detrimental as they dry out mucous membranes that need to be kept moist with thin secretions.[78]

Lifestyle/Dietary Recommendations:
1. Rest and wash hands frequently.
2. Increase liquid intake to keep nasal secretions thin. A dry throat and nose allow viruses to attack. Herbal teas and water with lemon juice added are best.

Nutritional Supplement Recommendations:
1. Vitamin C with bioflavonoids - 500 - 1000 mg every 1 - 2 hours.
2. Zinc lozenges containing 23 mg elemental zinc taken every 2 hours have been shown to reduce the duration of the common cold. They should not be taken at this dosage for more than one (1) week. [79]
3. Echinacea (E. purpurea, angustifolia, pallida) taken three times daily in the following amounts have been shown to decrease length of colds and flu: Dried root (or as tea) - 0.5 to 1 g; Freeze-dried plant, 325 - 650 mg; Juice of E. purpurea stabilized in 22% ethanol - 1 - 2 ml (1/4 - 1/2 t); Tincture (1:5) - 2 - 4 ml; Solid (dry, powdered) extract (6.5:1 or 3.5% echinacoside) - 100 - 250 mg. [80]
4. Other beneficial herbs are licorice, especially for scratchy or hoarse throats and astragalus.[81 82]

CONSTIPATION

Constipation is characterized by infrequent bowel movements that often results in a hard-to-pass stool. This condition is caused by an inappropriate diet, inadequate exercise and can even be caused by laxative and/or enema abuse. The ideal frequency of bowel movements is two to three times daily. Elimination should correspond to the number of times one eats a meal each day. Mild, infrequent constipation usually responds well to a high-fiber diet, plenty of fluids and exercise. If the situation has become chronic, a "re-training" of the bowels may need to occur.

Lifestyle/Dietary Recommendations:
1. Eliminate known causes such as certain foods or poor dietary habits.
2. Never repress the urge to defecate. "Go when ya gotta go."
3. Focus on a high-fiber diet - the whole foods diet is naturally high-fiber.
4. Drink at least two quarts of water daily. Some of this can be fresh juices.
5. Begin a bathroom routine. Sit on the toilet at the same time every day (even when the urge is not there). The best times are after breakfast and exercise.
6. Exercise at least 20 minutes three times weekly.

Nutritional Supplement Recommendations:
1. For mild constipation, psyllium hulls provide bulk to make the stool more fibrous and soft, making passage more comfortable and regular.
2. Take no laxatives or enemas except as outlined below in bowel "re-training."
   Week 1: Take Yellow Dock before bed (lowest amount necessary to ensure bowel movement in the morning - probably 2 - 4 capsules).
   Week 2 - 6: Decrease dosage by 1/2 each week. If constipation recurs, take previous week's dosage. Decrease if diarrhea occurs.
   For non-pregnant moms, cascara sagrada may be used instead of yellow dock.

COUGHS

This is one discomfort that needs no explanation. We all have had a cough at one time or another. Coughs may be the result of inhaling irritating substances (cigarette smoke, environmental pollution), allergy, dry air or respiratory infections. If the cough persists more than 2 weeks, medical attention should be sought. Please see "Pertussis" in the previous section as older, immunized children and adults form the majority of pertussis (whooping cough) cases in recent years. Any cough accompanied by high fever, extreme lethargy and/or bloody or rust-colored sputum requires medical attention.

Generally, it is better not to suppress a cough. A cough is the body's way of getting irritating mucous up and out. The exception to the "not suppress" rule would be a dry, irritating cough at night that prevents rest or a spasmodic cough that is painful or leads to gagging.

Lifestyle/Dietary Recommendations:

1. Drink extra amounts of liquids, preferably sipping on warm herbal teas or chicken soup throughout the day to loosen and thin secretions.
2. Eliminate irritating factors such as cigarette smoke, perfumes, dry air, etc.

Nutritional Supplement Recommendations:

1. For dry, irritating coughs, wild cherry bark is well-known for its ability to quiet a harsh cough. I particularly like a combination that contains: White Pine, Wild Cherry, Spikenard Root, Whole Elder Berries, Cinnamon Chips, Licorice Root (Available from Tri-Light and Mother's Choice™).
2. For coughs that sound wet or loose, I like a combination containing: Mullein, Wild Cherry Bark, Chestnut, Astragalus Root, Peppermint, Coltsfoot, Plantain, Chickweed, Pleurisy Root, Elecampane Root, Horehound (Also available from Tri-Light and Mother's Choice™). I understand, from the company, that coltsfoot is being eliminated from the combination. Thank you, Tri-Light/Mother's Choice!
3. Marshmallow root (Althaea officinalis) is very soothing to respiratory membranes because of the high amount of mucilage in the plant. It is best combined with other expectorants and used as a tea. A tea may be made combining licorice, marshmallow and plantain with small amount of thyme.

CRAMPS, MUSCLE

Muscle cramps (a sudden, involuntary, and painful tightening of a muscle) may occur after strenuous work, after sitting or standing uncomfortably for a long period or after a huge meal. All of these may cause muscles to be temporarily nutrient-deprived or prevent the muscles from properly disposing of waste. While most people immediately think of calcium deficiency when experiencing leg cramps at night, magnesium-deficiency is much more likely. Magnesium-deficiency may be the result of ensuring adequate calcium intake without simultaneously getting in adequate magnesium. Severely low calcium intake may also cause muscle cramps.[83]

Lifestyle/Dietary Recommendations:

1. Stretch and massage cramped muscle. Pull foot toward body instead of pointing toes downward. This will relieve most leg cramps immediately.
2. Apply pressure to the upper lip, 2/3 of the way up from the upper lip to the nose. This works very well for any type of cramp.

Nutritional Supplement Recommendations:

1. Make certain vitamin/mineral supplement contains at least 1000mg of Calcium and at least 500mg of Magnesium.
2. An additional 400 - 500mg of Magnesium may be necessary if diet is high in dairy products.
3. ContractEase Formula by Mother's Choice™ can also help relieve muscle cramps. The formula contains: Black Haw, Valerian, Skullcap, Hops, Chamomile, Fennel and Catnip. This is one of the Midwife's Formulas that I gave (I do not receive monies from sales of any of their products) to them for processing. I like the Mother's Choice™ formulas because they are glycerin-based TincTract™s (not standard glycerites) that moms can use without having to be concerned about alcohol like most alcohol-based tinctures.

DIABETES

Diabetes is a chronic disorder of carbohydrate, fat and protein metabolism characterized by elevations of blood sugar (glucose) levels. Diabetes greatly increases the risk of heart disease, stroke, kidney disease, blindness and loss of nerve function. This disease can occur when the pancreas does not secrete enough insulin or if the cells of the body become resistant to insulin. Insulin is a hormone that promotes uptake of blood sugar by the cells of the body.

Type I - Insulin-Dependent Diabetes Mellitus (IDDM) occurs most often in children and adolescents. Complete destruction of beta cells of the pancreas which make insulin is usual with IDDM. Lifelong insulin-therapy is necessary for glucose control. Moms with Type I diabetes need medical supervision in their prenatal care to help them in controlling their insulin/glucose ratio. These moms still need to follow the whole foods diet while adding protein to equal 1 gram of protein for each pound of their body weight. Exercise is extremely important. Mom's weight gain and salt intake do not need to be restricted as this can cause additional problems such as metabolic toxemia of late pregnancy.

Type II - Non-Insulin Dependent Diabetes Mellitus (NIDDM). The onset of this disease is usually after the age of 40. Insulin levels may be low, normal, or elevated. Lack of sensitivity to insulin by cells of the body is a major characteristic. Obesity is a major contributor (90% of all Type II diabetics are obese). In this form of diabetes, diet is of primary importance. Over 75% of Type II diabetics can control their disease by diet alone. Diabetes is very rare in cultures with diets rich in whole plant foods. Our Western diet and life-style is an overwhelming causative factor.[84] Generally, there are few complications during pregnancy in moms with NIDDM if they are diligent to follow a whole foods diet and exercise regularly.

Lifestyle/Dietary Recommendations:

1. The best diet for diabetics is the high-complex-carbohydrate, high-fiber diet (HCF) popularized by Dr. James Anderson and supported by scientific literature.[85] The HCF diet's positive effects are: reduced elevations in blood sugar levels after meals, increased tissue sensitivity to insulin, reduced cholesterol and triglyceride levels with increased HDL levels, and progressive weight reduction. If the conventional American Diabetic Association (ADA) diet is resumed, insulin requirements return. The HCF diet is as follows: Carbohydrate calories - 70 to 75%; Protein calories - 15 to 20%; Fat calories - 5 to 10%.

2. Legumes should be encouraged in addition to other factors in diet as they have been shown to be helpful in diabetes control.[86 87] Fiber supplements only reduce

insulin dosages by 2/3 whereas dietary changes led to total discontinuation of insulin in 60% of type II diabetics and reduced doses in the other 40% in one study.[88]

3. Maintain ideal body weight.

4. Exercise enhances insulin sensitivity, improves glucose tolerance and reduces total serum cholesterol and triglycerides.[89]

Nutritional Supplement Recommendations:

1. There is an increased need for nutrients in addition to a healthful diet. These additional nutrients may help prevent or improve major diabetic complications. The supplement recommendations that follow are adapted from Michael T. Murray, N.D.'s book *Natural Alternatives to Over-the Counter & Prescription Drugs*.[90] These are the most well-researched (and clinically experienced in natural medicine) recommendations I have found. This book is a must for the family bookshelf. Dr. Murray also has a book called *Diabetes* that is essential for diabetics wishing to incorporate herbal health care into their treatment protocol.

2. Chromium picolinate or polynicotinate (bound to several niacin molecules) - 200 - 400 mcg daily.

3. Manganese is a co-factor in key enzymes of glucose metabolism. Diabetics have been shown to have only 1/2 of the manganese of healthy people. 30mg daily.

4. Magnesium is involved in glucose metabolism. It is best derived from the diet: tofu, legumes, seeds, nuts, whole grains and green leafy vegetables. Supplementation needs to be 300 - 500mg daily, with 50mg of B6 needed for the magnesium to get inside of cells.

5. Zinc because diabetics tend to excrete too much zinc in their urine. 30mg daily.

6. Biotin enhances insulin action by increasing enzyme glucokinase which is responsible for the first step in glucose utilization by the liver. One study revealed 16mg of biotin daily resulted in significant improvements in blood glucose control in diabetics.

7. Bitter melon (Momordica charantia) (looks like an ugly cucumber) has been used extensively in folk medicine for diabetes. Studies have confirmed its blood-sugar lowering action. Clinical trials show that 2 oz of the fresh juice result in lower insulin requirements. The juice tastes very bitter. Not recommended for use during pregnancy.

8. Onions & Garlic both lower blood sugar. The active principles are believed to be sulfur-containing compounds, allyl propyl disulphide (APDS) and diallyl disulphide oxide (allicin) respectively. Flavonoids may also play some role. APDS given in doses of 125mg per kg of body weight to fasting humans caused a marked fall in blood glucose levels and increase in serum insulin. Allicin at 100mg per kg of

body weight produced similar effects. Raw & cooked onions are effective in amounts of one to seven ounces.

9. The herbal extract of Gymnema sylvestre, given to 27 patients with type I diabetes on insulin, reduced insulin requirements and fasting blood sugar levels and improved control. It enhances insulin action and may possibly regenerate or revitalize beta cells of pancreas. One study shown that gymnema sylvestre given with oral hypoglycemic drugs improved blood sugar control in Type II diabetics. Twenty-one out of twenty-two reduced drug dosage; five discontinued medications and controlled diabetes with gymnema extract alone. Dosage was 400mg daily of extract. No side effects were reported, and it does not produce hypoglycemic effects in healthy individuals.

10. Other beneficial nutrients: Vitamin C - 3 - 8 g daily, Vitamin E - 400-600 IU daily, B12 - 1000mcg daily, and Selenium - 200mcg daily.

Diarrhea

Diarrhea is characterized by loose, possibly watery, frequent bowel movements. Most people experience some degree of cramping prior to and during bowel movements. Diarrhea may be caused by excessive fruit consumption (we call this "fruit poop"), diet sodas, bacteria-laden food, intestinal "flu" virus or stress. Diarrhea contracted while traveling abroad is called "traveler's diarrhea" and may be caused by a parasitic infection (see Parasites). Chronic diarrhea is most commonly caused by: lactose intolerance, inflammatory bowel disease (IBD), food allergy, gluten sensitivity, parasitic infections or benign/malignant tumors. Any diarrhea that lasts for more than a couple of days or includes pain, rectal bleeding, fever or chills, and/or extreme lethargy should be discussed with your professional health care provider.

Lifestyle/Dietary Recommendations:
1. Stay near the toilet. This means rest.
2. If diarrhea episode came after eating half a cantaloupe by oneself, cut back on cantaloupe consumption.
3. Do not go on clear, sugary liquid diet. "Sugar passes right through you and draws water and salts out of the body, leading to vomiting," says Dr. William B. Greenough, III, M.D., Johns Hopkins University.[91]
4. Do eat starchy foods such as bananas, rice, potatoes, corn, wheat, peas, carrots in thick soup or drink form.
5. Blueberry soup made from 1/3 oz. dried blueberries or black currant extract from dried black currants both have proved effective in human tests to combat gastrointestinal infections especially *Escherichia coli*, a bacteria responsible for many cases of diarrhea (at least half of all cases of traveler's diarrhea).[92] Pour 1 pint cold water over 3 heaping teaspoons of dried blueberries. Bring to a boil; let simmer for 15 minutes. Let cool; strain. Pour into bottle and drink 1 - 2 tablespoons several times daily (up to 10).
6. Avoid milk or clear broth. Add yogurt with live cultures. Research at the University of Minnesota found that various strains of *E. coli* thrived in milk and broth but died or did not grow in yogurt cultures. A special strain of friendly bacteria, *Lactobacillus GG*, in a new yogurt developed by professors Sherwood Gorbach and Barry Goldin of Tufts University produces an antimicrobial substance that acts like an antibiotic.[93] In fact, yogurt eaten daily (6 oz.) can actually prevent diarrhea according to studies at the University of California at Davis.[94]

Nutritional Supplement Recommendations:

1. Two - three capsules of fenugreek seeds with water three times daily often produces quick and "marked" relief, usually after the second dose according to Dr. Krishna C. Srivastava at Odense University in Denmark.[95] While fenugreek does contain saponins and sapogenins which are starters for steroidal hormonal drugs, the use of fenugreek seeds for a short period of time has produced no ill-effect for pregnant women.[96] There is a possibility of uterine stimulation due to the saponin content; however, diarrhea itself produces uterine stimulation. Risk of short-term stimulation versus the benefit of a shortened diarrhea attack must be weighed.

2. Berberine, a chemical constituent of barberry, goldenseal, and oregon grape has been found in studies around the world to kill microorganisms such as *Staphylococci, Streptococci, Salmonella, Shigella, Entamoeba histolytica, Vibrio cholerae, Giardia lamblia, Escherichia coli* and *Candida albicans*.[97] These are impressive results from some potent herbs. Berberine is a uterine stimulant; therefore, pregnant women should exercise caution when using herbs containing this chemical. *Women should not use berberine-containing herbs without consultation with a herbal professional.* 1 - 2, 250mg capsules three times daily for bacterial or protozoan diarrhea.

3. Inner Strength™ (or Probioplex™ available from Ethical Nutrients or Metagenics) is a product containing "Active Immunoglobulin Concentrate" (AIC). It is derived from a raw milk whey product shown to be effective in increasing the production of friendly bacteria. The effect is enhanced when combined with a probiotic supplement such as *Lactobacillus acidophilus* or *Bifidobacterium infantis*. 1/3 t. Inner Strength to 1/8 to 1/4 t. of a probiotic taken three to four times daily can increase beneficial bacteria and decrease pathogenic bacteria.

4. Another product I like is AntiDiaTribe (available from Mother's Choice™). It contains herbs commonly used to support the normalization of bowel movements: Peppermint, Catnip, Nettle, Chamomile, Slippery Elm, Blackberry, Raspberry, Bayberry, Pau D'Arco, Cinnamon, Gentian, White Oak Bark and Clove. 1/2 t. for adults with every bowel movement, or three to four times daily.

DIZZINESS/FAINTING

Dizziness (vertigo) or feeling "faint" may occur upon rising too quickly from a reclining position. This "blacking out" may be due to a change in blood flow to the brain when standing up quickly.

Lifestyle/Dietary Recommendation:
1. Rise slowly from seated position.
2. Do not stand for long periods of time without moving around.
3. Drink adequate (at least 2 qts. daily) amounts of water daily.
4. If feeling faint, put head below the rest of body for several minutes until feeling better.
5. Loosen any restrictive clothing so circulation can be adequately maintained.
6. Inhale the scent of rosemary oil with the essential oil of camphor or just rosemary oil.

Nutritional Supplement Recommendations:
1. Ginger has been shown to relieve dizziness (vertigo).[98] One gram (1000mg) as needed.
2. One study of people with chronic dizziness showed a significant improvement or alleviation of their symptom when treated with ginkgo extract.[99] Ginkgo stimulates a positive circulatory response in the body, which makes it a beneficial herb for improving blood flow. One 450mg capsule 2 - 3 times daily.

EAR INFECTIONS (OTITIS MEDIA)

This condition occurs primarily because of swelling and blockage of the eustachian tube. This swelling allows fluid to accumulate which provides an environment for bacteria and viruses to grow. Common symptoms include: earache, redness or bulging of the eardrum, and fever with chills. Most ear infections may be prevented through adequate hydration (drinking water) during respiratory infections. A lack of good water intake causes the secretions to thicken leading to a prime environment for bacterial overgrowth and increasing pressure.

Lifestyle/Dietary Recommendations:
1. Take steps to open eustachian tubes: yawn and chew gum.
2. Drink warm chamomile tea.
3. Massage area around ear. Pull earlobe down gently, stroke neck and rub temple. These actions encourage drainage and increase blood flow.
4. Eliminate dairy products from diet until condition clears. Dairy products cause the body to produce mucous which further clogs eustachian tube.
5. Raise the head of the bed to help tubes drain.
6. Drink plenty of water to encourage thinning of mucous.
7. Eliminate foods to which mom is allergic. In one study of children with frequent, severe ear infections presented to the American College of Allergy and Immunology, 78% were found to have specific food allergies. After eliminating the offending food from the diet for 11 weeks, 70 out of 81 experienced improvement.
8. Avoid foods with simple sugars: sucrose (white table sugar), candies, cookies, ice cream, sodas, maple syrup, honey, dried fruits, fruit juices. Yes, even the more healthful sweeteners (honey, fruit juice, maple syrup) can provide enough sugar to feed bacteria or viruses during illness.

Nutritional Supplement Recommendations:
1. Apply warm (not hot) drops of herbal ear drops containing Mullein, Echinacea or Goldenseal, Garlic, etc. to ear canal once daily. This is not to be done if the eardrum is perforated. I particularly like a combination called HearDrops™ that contains: Mullein, Skullcap, Goldenseal, Black Cohosh, Blue Cohosh, Yarrow, Rosemary with the essential oils of garlic, tea tree and peppermint in a base of extra virgin olive oil (Mother's Choice™). Before using drops, dry ear first with a few drops of a vinegar/alcohol mixture. This prevents the oil from sealing in excess moisture, which could make the problem worse. Remember that oil "drives in the herbs," while glycerin "draws" fluid out of the ear. Whatever the product used,

flushing the ear with hydrogen peroxide the following morning after treatment will allow the regaining of equilibrium that may be lost due to fluid in the ear canal.

2. German researchers have found the herb Echinacea to kill a broad range of disease-causing bacteria, viruses, fungi and protozoa, through immune-stimulation rather than by direct action. The herb contains a natural antibiotic, echinacoside, that compares to penicillin in its broad-spectrum activity. It also contains echinacein that counteracts germs' tissue-dissolving enzyme, hyluronidase, preventing the germs from getting into body tissues. Other studies show increased macrophage (germ-eaters) activity and increased T-cell (T-lymphocytes) activity up to 30% more than immune-boosting drugs.[100] 500 - 1000mg every 2 hours in the acute crisis stage, tapering off to at least 1,000mg for 7 to 10 days after improvement.

3. ViraMune™(Mother's Choice™) contains Red Root, Echinacea, Yarrow, Myrrh, Red Clover, and Oregon Grape Root. These herbs are immunostimulants that increase lymphatic drainage, which should be encouraged during an ear infection.

4. Essential fatty acids are very important for those who experience repeated ear infections. These may be found in foods such as nuts and seeds, deep-sea fish such as herring or mackerel, and in Evening Primrose Oil, Flax Seed Oil and Black Currant Oil.

5. N-acetylcysteine local application decreases inflammation of the middle-ear mucosa and prevents long-term fibrotic changes in patients suffering from secretory otitis media.[101]

Eczema, Psoriasis

Eczema (atopic dermatitis) and psoriasis are both considered an allergic disease characterized by intense itching and red, dry skin primarily located on the face, wrists, insides of elbow and knees.

Lifestyle/Dietary Recommendations:

1. Since food allergy is a major cause of these conditions, eliminating common allergens to see if improvement occurs would seem a wise move. Most common foods causing dermatitis are: cow's milk, eggs, tomatoes, artificial colors and food preservatives.
2. Those people with eczema and psoriasis appear to have an essential fatty acid (EFA) deficiency. EFAs synthesize anti-inflammatory prostaglandins; therefore, a deficiency would allow inflammation to occur. Foods high in EFAs are: fatty fish (such as mackerel, herring and salmon), nuts and seeds.
3. Be sure to get plenty of sunlight.
4. Eliminate bath oils, lotions, etc.

Nutritional Supplementation Recommendations:

1. Treatment with Evening Primrose Oil has shown a normalizing effect in essential fatty acid abnormalities and relieved eczema in many patients., 500 - 1000 mg three times daily.[102] Borage oil may also be used for beneficial effects.[103]
2. Licorice extracts contain a compound that when applied to skin exerts an effect similar to that of cortisone in treatment of eczema, contact or allergic dermatitis, and psoriasis. The compound 18-beta-glycyrrhetinic acid, acts like cortisone but does not exhibit negative side effects. Several studies show glycyrrhetinic acid to be superior to cortisone especially in chronic cases. One study showed 93% of eczema patients treated with glycyrrhetinic acid improved, compared with 83% of those treated with cortisone.[104]
3. Chamomile extracts. The flavonoid and essential-oil components of chamomile possess significant anti-inflammatory and anti-allergy activity.[105]
4. Allantoin-compounds isolated from comfrey root, which has a long history of use in skin care, has been shown to soften, protect and stimulate normal cell growth.[106] It is particularly useful in eczema and psoriasis. It is safe, non-allergenic and non-irritating for external use. The roots have twice the allantoin content as the leaves.[107]
5. Zinc is important in fatty acid metabolism in which eczema and psoriasis sufferers are deficient. 30 mg daily.[108]

6. Another supplement, which has been recommended for psoriasis, is milk thistle extract which improves liver function, inhibits inflammation and reduces excessive cellular proliferation. 70 - 210mg three times daily.[109]

EPSTEIN-BARR VIRUS

The Epstein-Barr Virus is a member of the herpes family of viruses. It replicates in the B-lymphocytes and remains for life. Like other herpes viruses, it lies dormant until something triggers an outbreak. Incubation in primary infection is 30 to 50 days. The symptoms are fatigue, swollen glands, fever, sore throat and increased white blood count.[110] The virus is transmitted by saliva/respiratory droplet secretions contact. Clinical episodes are generally expressed as infectious mononucleosis. The virus if reactivated during pregnancy does not seem to correlate with congenital birth defects.[111] Any initial episode of infectious mononucleosis should have lab tests to rule out Cytomegalovirus or Toxoplasmosis infection, both of which could have detrimental effects on a developing baby in the womb.

Lifestyle/Dietary Recommendations:
1. During the episode, Dr. Richard S. Griffith, M.D., professor emeritus of medicine at Indiana School of Medicine and an infectious disease specialist, recommends avoiding high arginine foods such as: almonds, Brazil nuts, cashews, hazelnuts, peanuts, pecans, walnuts, chocolate and gelatin; restricting coconut, barley, oats, corn, wheat, pasta and brussel sprouts; and adding 1 - 2, 500mg, lysine tablets daily during infection.[112]
2. Eating foods high in Quercetin and other bioflavonoids such as: buckwheat, onions, green peppers and tomatoes may decrease the infectiousness of RNA and DNA viruses, such as herpes, polio and Epstein-Barr, by inhibiting their replication.[113]
3. As always with any infection, limit or eliminate sugar intake, stick to simple foods: fruits and veggies, and rest.

Nutritional Supplement Recommendations:
1. Glycyrrhizin, a saponin present in licorice root demonstrated inhibition of Epstein-Barr Virus (EBV), cytomegalovirus (CMV) and hepatitis B virus in a 1979 study.[114]
2. Organo-germanium sesquioxide (marketed primarily as Ge-132) appears to be helpful in the treatment of viral diseases such as Epstein-Barr. 50 - 100 mg daily minimum for treatment. To induce interferon synthesis in humans, a daily intake of 50 - 75 mg/kg of body weight is necessary. It seems to be without any significant toxic effects.[115]
3. Lapacho or Pau D'Arco may be effective against Epstein-Barr virus due to its inhibiting effects on the synthesis of DNA and RNA of the virus in the cell. No significant toxicity in humans is apparent,[116] although use during pregnancy is not advised.

EXCESS MUCOUS (PHLEGM)

Signs of excess mucous in the body are: increased vaginal discharge, oily hair, shiny nose, possibly a blocked nose, postnasal drip, or phlegm collecting in the throat. These may be occurring due to a respiratory illness, allergies, pregnancy or food intolerance.

Lifestyle/Dietary Recommendations:

Certain foods tend to increase the formation of mucous in the body. The table below lists those that are mucous-forming and those that are mucous-reducing.

Mucous-Forming Foods:	Mucous-Reducing Foods:
All meat, milk, cheese	Fruits and vegetables especially raw (exceptions on other list)
Chocolate, cocoa	Whole grains - oats, wheat, rice, barley, rye, etc.
Tofu (soybean curd)	Whole grain bread (except for sensitive people)
Eggs	Onions
Most nuts, especially peanuts	Garlic
Yams	Watercress, mustard greens and seeds
Bananas, oranges (in excess)	Horseradish
Oily or greasy foods	Hot peppers
Alcohol	

Most people can cope with the mucous-forming foods because of strong digestive systems. It would be prudent to avoid those foods during periods of illness, weak digestion (first months of pregnancy) or if having a problem with postnasal drip and phlegm in the throat during the night or upon waking.

Nutritional Supplement Recommendations:
1. Elder berries and flowers reduce phlegm as well as act as an anti-inflammatory and expectorant. A very useful combination is one of elder, yarrow and peppermint (Yummy Yarrow & Elderberry by Mother's Choice™). These are best taken in a liquid so that the herbs come in contact with the mucous membranes and phlegm.
2. A combination containing herbs such as Horseradish root, Mullein leaves, Fenugreek seeds, Fennel, and Boneset herb is helpful in liquefying and moving mucous secretions out of the body.

3. Freeze-dried Nettle leaves (available from Eclectic Institute) have been shown to be effective in reducing hay-fever symptoms in allergic persons. I personally have found these to be quite helpful during those times when I wake up with phlegm in my throat. I take 2 capsules before bedtime and 2 upon rising.

4. Quercitin with bromelain, 200-500 mg taken 30 minutes before each meal.

FEVER

An elevated body temperature, fever, is the body's mechanism for mobilizing the immune system to defend against invading organisms. Most of the time, we want to allow the fever to do its work in the body; however, in pregnancy an elevated temperature of 101° F, or above, in mom can cause developmental problems for baby (mostly in early pregnancy). It is advisable to work to lower the temperature naturally and, if the temperature continues to rise even while utilizing natural measures, to consult with a maternal care provider about other treatment options. In our own family, we tend to let fevers "ride" unless they are accompanied by severe pain. At the point of pain and fever, we evaluate whether we should lower the fever using pharmaceuticals or seek outside healthcare consultation.

While acetaminophen is the most common pharmaceutical analgesic/antipyretic used, it does carry some risks. Acetaminophen does place a heavier burden on the liver to process this drug. It is my practice to always use the herb milk thistle which contains silymarin while using acetaminophen. One study found that Milk thistle may offer some protection against the toxic side effects of acetaminophen.[117] Herbal extracts or tinctures containing alcohol should not be used in combination with acetaminophen due to possible lethal effects. Acetaminophen has actually been shown to lengthen the duration of illness and increase pain in some studies; therefore, when choosing to use acetaminophen, one should be willing to accept a possible few more days of illness for the temporary relief of pain and fever.

Since acetaminophen may actually increase inflammation, for inflammatory conditions with fever (sinusitis, for example), if we choose to utilize a pharmaceutical medicine, we may choose ibuprofen for its fever-reducing and anti-inflammatory properties. If we do this, we also recognize that we must be drinking adequate amounts of water or ibuprofen's kidney-damaging effects could become a bigger problem than the fever.

Lifestyle/Dietary Recommendations:
1. During a fever, the only foods consumed should be fruits and vegetables which can be easily digested so energy is not diverted from the immune response to digest heavy foods.
2. Liquid intake (water with lemon) should be increased to one cup per hour to keep the body well-hydrated.
3. Rest is an important part of healing. Fever is a symptom of an illness, and when we are ill, we need to be in bed — not doing errands. Call on friends and family for help with other children or household chores, if necessary.
4. Bathing in lukewarm water may help lower the fever. Adding essential oils of chamomile or lavender to bath water is soothing and calming.

5. Fresh star fruit should be eaten twice daily as well as cucumber, cantaloupe and water chestnuts.

6. A tea recommended in *The Healing Power of Foods* by Michael T. Murray, N.D. to promote perspiration thereby lowering temperature is:

   Cinnamon-Ginger Tea
   1 inch slice of fresh ginger
   1/4 t. cinnamon
   1/4 lemon
   1 c. hot water
   Juice or grind ginger - juice lemon - add to water and cinnamon.

Nutritional Supplement Recommendations:

1. The herbs white willow and meadowsweet contain salicin which is converted to salicylic acid in the body. The structural formulas for Acetylsalicylic acid (Aspirin) and salicylic acid are very similar; therefore, a very cautious herbal healing approach should be used when ingesting plant products containing salicin as when using aspirin. Salicin in plants does not cause gastric or intestinal upset or bleeding because it bypasses the stomach or intestine. It does have prostaglandin blocking (PGE2) effects when it reaches the liver where the acetyl-group is metabolically picked up.[118] The plant product containing salicin has not been associated with increased birth defects or Reye's syndrome as aspirin has; however, I do not feel comfortable using these herbs during fever in those younger than 16 years of age.[119]

2. A TincTract™ (glycerin-based liquid herbs processed in 3-stages) of peppermint, yarrow and elder (Mother's Choice™ as Yummy Yarrow & Elderberry) is beneficial in increasing perspiration and lowering the body temperature.

3. Since fever is only a symptom of an infection, immuno-stimulants should be used to combat the underlying infection. Echinacea - 500 - 1000mg every 2 hours; Garlic - Fresh garlic, 1 - 2 cloves, or Garlic tablets - 3 - 6 daily; Oregon grape root (not during pregnancy without consultation with herbal professional) if dealing with a bacterial infection - 500mg three times daily.

4. Keep the bowels open with plenty of fruit, liquids and mild bowel stimulants if necessary - Yellow Dock plant is okay for mild bowel stimulation.

5. Capsaicin, a compound in capsicum or cayenne pepper, has been shown to lower body temperature through stimulation of the cooling center of the hypothalamus in the brain.[120]

FLU (INFLUENZA)

Flu or influenza is a respiratory infection that affects the nose, throat and chest. While colds are upper respiratory infections, influenza infects the lower respiratory tract also. It affects the whole body causing muscle aches, fever and extreme lethargy. Contrary to popular belief, there is no "intestinal or stomach flu." These conditions are gastrointestinal viruses or bacteria unrelated to influenza. Adults very rarely experience gastrointestinal upset during influenza although children may have stomach upset during a bout of the flu.

Flu or Just a Cold?

The flu may be distinguished from a cold by its sudden attack. A cold comes on gradually, beginning with one or two symptoms, with others appearing during the cold's duration. A cold very rarely causes fever in adults. The flu, in the other hand, hits like a freight train: fever, severe headache, extreme tiredness (lethargy) with a cough developing over the course of the illness. With the flu, you can be feeling great one moment, and the next hour finds you in bed, moaning and groaning.

Lifestyle/Dietary Recommendations:

1. Bed rest is a necessity during the flu — most people find themselves unable to do much else besides crawl into the bed and stay there.
2. Appetites generally are not hearty during the flu. Foods should be limited to fruits, vegetables and plenty of liquids.
3. Warm chamomile or lemon balm tea can be very soothing and healing.

Nutritional Supplement Recommendations:

1. Vitamin C (buffered powder or Ester-C powder) should be taken at 1000mg every 2 hours at the beginning of symptoms and continued until symptoms subside. Moms in their first trimester should limit their daily intake of Vitamin C to 3000mg.
2. A product containing ginger root, capsicum fruit, goldenseal root and licorice root may be taken at 2 capsules every 2 - 4 hours. This combination should not be used by pregnant women. This combination is particularly effective in combating the flu virus especially if begun at initial onset of symptoms.[121]
3. A liquid favorite of ours to take at bedtime when fighting the flu is Flew Away (available from Tri-Light) which contains: Boneset, Osha root, Mullein, Shavegrass, St. John's Wort, Peppermint, Capsicum, Clove. The major constituent, boneset, is prescribed currently in Germany by physicians for patients with colds and flu.[122] Pregnant women should avoid this combination due to osha root content.

4. The herb Astragalus has been found in studies to boost macrophage production and induce interferon production which prevents viruses from settling in to "homestead" in the respiratory tract.[123] This is more a preventive-use herb, although it may be used for crisis situations. There are no indications in the professional herbal texts that astragalus is inappropriate for use with fever, contrary to some popular herbalists' opinion.

5. Echinacea is always the herb of choice for any type of infection —especially upper and lower respiratory viruses. Echinacea's effects on boosting immune response is well-documented.[124]

6. Bee Propolis extract given when exposed to influenza may lead to a reduction in HA titer and reduction in mortality and increased survival time.[125]

7. When my husband, Keith, arrived home from work this past year with flu symptoms, I immediately began the above protocol with the addition of Standard Process Lab's "Immuplex" product. Keith was fever-free within 6 hours and only missed one day of work (we always stay home until we are fever and symptom-free 24-48 hours). I began the rest of the family on immunostimulants such as echinacea, elderberry and the Immuplex. No one else contracted the flu. We are thankful for the quick return to health for Keith. Since we began an aggressive approach with herbal medicines in the early stages of flu occurring in our family, we have managed to keep the "sick time" to 2 days or less, compared with most people staying ill for 2 weeks or more.

GALLSTONES

Gallstones are formed in the gallbladder when the bile crystallizes into hard pellets that can be as small as grains of sand or as big as an inch in diameter. Most of the time (80%), the stones are harmless, but sometimes when the gallbladder contracts to release bile, a stone or stones are forced out and plug the opening of the duct leading to the liver and small intestine. This leads to a gallstone attack characterized by pain that may radiate from the upper right chest. Some people describe the pain as extending up over the shoulder and down the back. Attacks can last minutes or hours. Nausea and vomiting sometimes accompany the painful attack.

Diet is an important preventive and treatment measure for gallstones. Gallstones tend to run in families and occur more frequently in women than men. Pregnancy itself is conducive to stone formation. Many women who have gallstone attacks experience them while pregnant or immediately postpartum.[126]

Lifestyle/Dietary Recommendations:

1. Eat more vegetables. A study in England found vegetarian women to be half as likely to form gallstones as meat-eating women.[127] Another recent study at Harvard found that women who ate specifically the most nuts, beans, lentils, peas, lima beans and oranges were resistant to gallbladder attacks.[128]

2. Avoid sugar, white flour and white rice. One British test revealed an increase in cholesterol content in bile (super-saturated bile produces stones) in the test group consuming sugar, white rice and white flour.[129]

3. Avoid coffee. Coffee with *or without* caffeine (and as little as one cup) can stimulate the gallbladder to contract which could lead to a gallbladder attack in those with gallstones according to Bruce R. Douglas and colleagues at the University Hospital in Leiden, the Netherlands.[130]

4. Don't skip breakfast. In a ten-year study by James Everhart, M.D., a scientist at the National Institute of Diabetes and Digestive and Kidney Disease, women who fasted overnight (fourteen hours or more) had the highest rate of gallstones.[131]

Nutritional Supplement Recommendations:

1. For gallstones accompanied by fatigue with sore liver and a tendency toward constipation, Christopher Hobbs in his book, *Foundations of Health - The Liver and Digestive Herbal*, recommends the following combination of herbs: Buplureum (6 parts), scutellaria (3) paeonia (3), ginger (4), unripe orange peel (2), jujube (3), rhubarb (1) and pinellia (3).

2. For gallstones accompanied by gallbladder inflammation and loss of appetite due to intestinal discomfort, Hobbs recommends a combination of: Buplureum (5 parts), pinellia (4), licorice (1.5), paeonia (2.5), jujube (2), and ginger (1).[132]

3. Dandelion has performed well in studies in both humans and laboratory animals to enhance bile flow and improve conditions such as liver congestion, bile duct inflammation, hepatitis, gallstones and jaundice.[133] 1 - 2, 250 - 500mg capsules three times daily.

4. An in vitro study on mice found that curcumin given over a period of 10 weeks significantly decreased incidence of gallstone formation relative to controls as well as a significant reduction in biliary cholesterol concentration.[134]

5. One study showed that N-acetyl cysteine (NAC) accelerated the dissolution of gallstone in vitro significantly.[135]

6. During my pregnancy with my third child, Eryn, I had gallbladder attacks in my second trimester and in the immediate postpartum time. I had experienced tremendous relief by using an herbal combination containing: Buplureum root, peony root, pinellia rhizome, cinnamon twig, dang gui root, rushen plant, zhishi fruit, scute root, atractylodes rhizome, panax ginseng root, ginger rhizome, and licorice root (marketed as LIV-C™ by NSP) and lecithin capsules. As soon as the pain and nausea began, I took 4 LIV-C and 2 - 3 lecithin capsules. Relief came within fifteen (15) minutes usually. I have to admit, too, that I had a strong attraction to fast food during that pregnancy as well. Could there be a correlation?

GAS (FLATULENCE)

We all know what this is: the bloated feeling we have with pain in our abdomen or side (sometimes even in our chests) until we are able to pass the gas without embarrassing ourselves in front of others. The normal, healthy person passes gas approximately 14 times per day. What we eat and how we prepare it can make a big difference in the amount of gas our bodies produce.

Lifestyle/Dietary Recommendations:
1. Watch out for dairy foods - the number 1 cause of gas in our country, says Dr. Michael Levitt of the University of Minnesota, an international authority on flatulence (gas). Many people are not aware that they are somewhat lactose (milk sugar) intolerant. One sign of lactose intolerance is excessive gas after drinking or eating milk products. Yogurt does not produce gas and is acceptable for those with lactose intolerance because it basically comes predigested (those friendly bacteria eat up the milk sugar for you). Plain yogurt has more anti-lactose activity than flavored versions. Frozen yogurt does not have live bacteria so it is an offender.[136]
2. Beans are notorious for causing gas. You can "de-gas" your beans by about 50% by soaking them. The process is as follows: Rinse beans. Add them to boiling water and boil in a covered pot for 3 minutes. Let stand for two hours. Pour off old water and add new water at room temperature just to cover the beans. After two hours, pour this water off. Add more water and let soak overnight. Rinse again with room-temperature water. Add water to cover and cook until done, about 75 - 90 minutes.[137]
3. Add garlic and/or ginger to beans or other gaseous veggies. Both have been traditionally touted to relieve gas. Researchers at India's G.B. Pant University decided the tradition of adding spices to legumes and vegetables was based on "sound principles."[138]
4. Also of note is that when changing to a whole foods - more fiber-diet - many people experience an increase in gas. This usually will pass in two to three weeks and is a great support for the "make changes slowly" way of moving toward a healthier lifestyle.

Nutritional Supplement Recommendations:
1. A small vial of peppermint oil carried along in the purse will make having a cup of peppermint tea while away from home much simpler. Simply place 2 to 3 drops of the oil in a cup of hot herb tea or water. Stir it well and drink.[139]
2. Papaya contains an enzyme, papain, that aids digestion thereby lowering the amount of undigested food in the intestinal tract to ferment and cause gas. Tablets

are available in the health food store. I like the combination of papaya fruit and peppermint tablets.

3. Activated charcoal has shown benefit in absorbing toxins and undigested food in the intestinal tract, which decreases gas production.

HAIR LOSS

Hair loss is very common as we age and occurs most often in women during the first year after giving birth. My hair usually begins falling out "by the handful" when my babies are five or six months old. It usually lasts about six months for me. My vacuum cleaner and bathroom sinks clog up with all my hair. The laundry has my hair in it. Hair everywhere! It's a wonder I've any hair left! Keith doesn't seem to mind cutting my hair off the vacuum cleaner beater bar, but he does seem a bit annoyed at all my hair sticking out of his freshly-laundered socks!

Whether husband loses his hair as he ages depends, not so much on his own father's hairline, as on his mother's father's hairline, sayeth genetics. While nutritional intervention has yet to find the "cure" for hair loss, we do know that the better nourished in our bodies, the more nourished and vital our hair is!

Lifestyle/Dietary Recommendations:
1. Do not brush wet hair. Let hair dry before brushing, or comb gently with a wide-toothed comb.
2. De-stress lifestyle as much as possible. Stress increases hair loss.
3. Massage scalp daily. Increased circulation stimulates new hair growth.

Nutritional Supplement Recommendations:
1. In a double-blind, placebo-controlled study, long-term oral therapy with 18,000 IU of retinol combined with 70mg L-cystine and 700mg gelatin led to an improvement of diffuse hair loss relative to controls.[140] This supplementation is not appropriate for pregnancy.
2. A B-complex vitamin or a high-quality multivitamin may aid the body in adapting to increased stress levels.
3. Adding herbs that increase circulation may help: cayenne, ginkgo biloba, gotu kola. 2 to 6 capsules of one of these herbs daily.
4. There are several hair growth formulas available on the market presently. The *Self Care Catalog* has a supplement plan for stimulating hair growth. Please see the Resource section for the address and phone number.

HEADACHE

An ache in the head, or headache, occurs when pain arises from the outer lining of the brain and scalp and its blood vessels and muscles. There are essentially two types of headaches: migraine, or vascular headache, characterized by throbbing, pounding, sharp pain in the head (can be behind one eye); tension headache characterized by a steady, constant, dull pain that starts at the back of the head or forehead and spreads over the entire head with a sense of pressure applied to skull.

Headaches may also occur due to hypoglycemia. A sudden drop in blood sugar (glucose) levels may cause a headache.

Lifestyle/Dietary Recommendations:
1. Allergy may be a major cause of migraines.[141] The same allergens can cause tension headaches as well. Common allergens: milk, wheat, chocolate, food additives, MSG, artificial sweeteners like aspartame, tomatoes and fish.
2. Chocolate, cheese, beer, wine and aspartame may cause migraines due to "vasoactive amines" which cause blood vessels to expand. Many migraine sufferers are found to have low levels of platelet enzyme that normally breaks down dietary amines.
3. If Hypoglycemia is suspected, the recommendations in the Hypoglycemia section may be followed.

Nutritional Supplement Recommendations:
1. Magnesium deficiency is known to set the stage for migraines and tension headaches.[142] One function of magnesium is to maintain tone of blood vessels. Mom needs 350 - 500mg of magnesium aspartate or citrate daily.
2. Feverfew, while not to be used during pregnancy because of its emmenagogue properties (promotes menstruation; abortifacient), has been used for centuries for headaches. Modern research continues to confirm its historical use. A 1988 survey found 70% of 270 migraine sufferers who ate feverfew daily for prolonged periods claimed that the herb decreased the frequency and/or intensity of the attacks. This prompted clinical trials at the London Migraine Clinic, a double-blind study that used patients reporting help by feverfew. Those receiving placebo significantly increased the frequency and severity of their headaches, nausea and vomiting during the six months of study. Those taking feverfew showed no change. Two patients in the placebo group who had been in complete remission during self-treatment with feverfew said they developed recurrence of incapacitating migraines and had to withdraw from the study. Self-treatment renewed remission in both patients.[143] A second double-blind study at the University of Nottingham showed feverfew to be effective in reducing the number of severity of migraine attacks.[144] Feverfew works

by inhibiting the release of blood-vessel dilating substances from platelets, inhibiting production of inflammatory substances and re-establishing blood vessel tone.[145] Parthenolide is thought to be the active ingredient. To achieve the same results as those in the studies, each capsule should contain at least 0.2% of parthenolide per 25mg freeze-dried pulverized leaves twice daily or 82mg dried powdered leaves once daily. A higher dose (1 - 2 g) is needed during an acute attack. No side effects have been reported as long as the leaves are not chewed. This can result in small ulcerations in the mouth, swelling of the lips and tongue in 10% of users.

3. Nitrites may cause headaches according to neurologists William P. Henderson and Neil H. Raskin, of the University of California at San Francisco. If prone to headaches, watch out for hot dogs, bacon, salami, ham and other meats cured with sodium nitrite or nitrate.[146] These foods are not the best to choose, anyway, since they can be contaminated with *campylobacter* or *listeria* bacteria, which can cause miscarriage or stillbirth.

4. Caffeine has been referred to as the nation's #1 headache instigator, says Dr. David W. Buchholz, director of the Neurological Consultation Clinic at Johns Hopkins University Hospital. Although some tests have shown small amounts of caffeine to be able to relieve headaches by temporarily constricting dilated and swollen blood vessels, the vessels swell up and dilate worse in a rebound action, worsening the headache. The other problem with caffeine is that it is addictive, and most people experience caffeine-withdrawal headaches as well as fatigue, mild depression, nausea and vomiting. Withdrawal symptoms usually start 12 - 24 hours after ceasing caffeine consumption and are usually over in a week.[147] To get off caffeine without feeling "Yuck," mix regular and decaf coffee over a week's period increasing the amount of decaf each day until it is all decaf (Same for tea and soda pops). It is a good idea to wean off the decaf versions after overcoming the caffeine hurdle. The decaf versions have their own health risks.

5. Ginger acts much like aspirin in that it blocks prostaglandin synthesis, which leads to a reduction in inflammation and pain according to Dr. Drishna C. Srivastava at Odense University in Denmark. It is safe to use for adults and children with no side effects reported. The recommended amount is 1 - 2, 500 - 600mg capsules taken with water up to four times daily as needed.[148] In China, birth practitioners caution against using too much ginger (20 - 28 grams = 20,000 - 28,000mg) in the early portion of pregnancy due to its stimulant properties.[149] I could find no scientific documentation of any abortive-aspects of this herb in quantities recommended above, and scientific research on ginger does include studies of pregnant women, particularly those with hyperemesis gravidum, excessive vomiting during pregnancy.

6. Omega-3 fish oils may be a migraine headache preventive. This means moms cannot reach for it as a headache is coming on; rather, the supplement can be taken over the long-term in those who are prone to migraine attacks.[150]

HEARTBURN
(GASTROESOPHAGEAL REFLUX)

Heartburn is a burning sensation or pressure in the chest that extends upward to the back of the throat. Some people have even suspected a heart attack because of a bad case of heartburn. Heartburn occurs when the lower esophageal sphincter muscle relaxes and allows stomach acids, hydrochloric acid and pepsin, to spurt into the esophagus causing pain and a bad taste in the mouth.

Lifestyle/Dietary Recommendations:
1. There are several foods that can cause heartburn by relaxing the sphincter: chocolate, caffeine, fatty foods, alcohol, and possibly onions. Other foods increase stomach acidity making heartburn more painful: coffee, colas, beer and milk.[151] Avoid these foods and drinks if you are having a heartburn problem.
2. Eat slowly and calmly, chewing food well before swallowing. This allows the saliva to begin digesting the food prior to traveling to the stomach, a very important part of the digestive process.
3. Do not overeat. There is a consequence to gluttony, and it just may be heartburn.
4. Do not lie down immediately after a meal. If one does lie down, lie on the left side to prevent pressure on the sphincter muscle.

Nutritional Supplement Recommendations:
1. Marshmallow root has a very high mucilage content that swells when combined with water to form a soft, soothing protective gel.[152] This can provide heartburn relief in 15 to 30 minutes. 2 capsules after meals.
2. Chamomile has been clearly shown in several studies to protect and heal the mucosa of the gastrointestinal tract and prevent ulcers from forming.[153] This is important for those suffering from chronic heartburn, which can damage or ulcerate the esophageal lining. Although chamomile has been claimed, by those afraid of consumer herb use, to cause severe allergic reactions, this is only potentially possible in those who have an anaphylactic reaction to ragweed. In all the world's literature from 1887 to 1982, only 50 reactions were reported: 45 from Roman chamomile and 5 from the German variety, which is the variety most often used in the U.S. This herb would best be used, in this case, as a tea or infusion.
3. For those who anticipate a large or high-fat meal, it would be wise to take a dandelion preparation thirty minutes before the meal. This herb aids the flow of digestive juices and bile, which provides for better digestion of fats and proteins.
4. I have also found Papaya tablets to be helpful in aiding digestion to avoid heartburn after indulging in a large or fatty meal.
5. Peppermint relaxes the stomach including the esophageal sphincter. Use in heartburn may increase problems with reflux.

HEMORRHOIDS/VARICOSE VEINS

Hemorrhoids are actually varicose veins (enlarged blood vessels with weakened valves) of the rectum. This blood vessel distension in the rectal area (hemorrhoids) can cause itching, redness, swelling and outright pain. Most hemorrhoids protrude out of the anus although some are located just inside the anal opening and may bleed during bowel movements with hard stool or vigorous straining. Any bleeding from the rectum should be evaluated by a professional healthcare provider due to the possibility of more serious health concerns associated with rectal bleeding.

Lifestyle/Dietary Recommendations:
1. A diet rich in whole grains has been shown to protect against many chronic degenerative (Western) diseases: cancer, especially colon cancer, heart disease, diabetes, varicose veins, inflammatory bowel disease (IBD), hemorrhoids and diverticulitis.[154]
2. A healthful diet full of fruits, vegetables, legumes and grains lends itself to regular, soft, bulky, easy to pass bowel movements. While many people keep reading material in the bathroom, one should only be spending a couple of minutes on defecation. Reading while on the toilet increases the amount of time of pressure on the rectal and anal area. If you need a quiet place to read, try a nice warm bath!
3. Have a footstool handy in the bathroom to use during bowel movements to reduce pressure on rectum and anus.

Nutritional Supplement Recommendations:
1. Topical treatment can provide temporary relief while changing to healthier dietary habits. A witch hazel bark infusion can be used by soaking gauze in the infusion and applying to hemorrhoids.[155] This is a very effective remedy for swollen, painful hemorrhoids.
2. An ointment or infusion (for gauze compresses) made of Horse chestnut, mullein, white oak bark and yarrow is beneficial to help shrink hemorrhoidal tissue.[156] The cream Cellu-Var by Enzymatic Therapy may be used as well as the capsules per recommendation by Dr. Michael T. Murray, N.D. during a phone conversation.
3. The liquid TincTract™ *Circulatone by Mother's Choice*™ by Liquid Light is a formula containing Bilberry, Rose Hips, Cleavers and Ginkgo to enhance circulation and decrease varicosities.
4. Rutin supplements can help to shrink and tone blood vessels. 500mg daily (NOT for use in the first trimester of pregnancy).[157]
5. Butcher's broom has been termed a "phlebotherapeutic agent" - used to treat circulatory disorders especially varicose veins and hemorrhoids. Studies confirm this

definition with patients improving when treated with Butcher's broom.[158] Butcher's broom raises the blood pressure making it useful for those with low blood pressure. Broom gently raises the blood pressure by constricting the peripheral blood vessels resulting in an overall decreased blood volume. Although there are no safety restrictions on butcher's broom during pregnancy, there may be a safety concern due to decreased blood volume. The standard dosage is 2, 250-500mg capsules two to three times daily.

6. Bilberry has been shown in a study of pregnant women to reduce varices (varicose veins) and various blood problems while exhibiting no side effects in mother or baby.[159] 2 - 450mg capsules three times daily.

7. Topical application of calendula lotion may be beneficial: Place the lotion on a cotton swab and apply to sore tissue around or in the rectum after bowel movements.

HEPATITIS

Hepatitis is an inflammation of the liver. There are several types of hepatitis. Each will be briefly discussed.

Hepatitis A (infectious):

Type A hepatitis (HAV) is termed "infectious" hepatitis because it produces an acute infection that is relatively mild. This virus is transmitted by food and/or water contaminated by oral/fecal contact. It is an RNA virus with all the features of an enterovirus. It is very similar in pathogenesis to the polio virus except HAV infects the hepatocyte and polio targets the neuron.[160]

Different medical texts report an incubation period from 14 to 45 days (2 to 6 weeks).[161] [162] The onset of symptoms is acute consisting of lethargy, loss of appetite with nausea and vomiting, headache, fever, and body aches. Jaundice follows by about one week and may persist for four to six weeks. Virus excretion in the feces may begin 2 - 3 weeks before the onset of symptoms and also last 4 - 6 weeks.

Long-term immunity normally follows recovery from the infection, although there is no cross-immunity between HAV and HBV.[163]

Hepatitis B (serum):

Hepatitis B is a DNA virus. Exposure to Hepatitis B Virus (HBV) could result in one of the following outcomes:

1. An acute, self-limiting infection with or without symptoms of clinical hepatitis (as explained in HAV). This is the most common form of HBV infection. The period of infectivity may be longer than other viral infections, but infectivity is usually lost and antibody (anti-HBc & Hbs) appears in the blood.
2. An acute infection followed by development of an asymptomatic carrier state with the continuing presence of HBsAg.
3. An acute infection followed by chronic active hepatitis and persistent HBsAg and signs of continuing infection.[164]

The virus is transmitted by body fluids: blood, blood by-products, saliva, vaginal secretions and semen. Most medical texts include breastmilk as a means of transfer. Household items that come in contact with HBV-infected blood are also a risk: syringes, razors, toothbrushes, eating utensils, etc.

Vertical transmission (mother to infant) may occur during three periods:

1. Prenatal period through intrauterine or transplacental infection (5 to 6% of baby infections). This is an uncommon mode of transmission.
2. During the third trimester and birth, from contact with currently infected maternal blood and secretions (69 to 85%). This is the most common to infect baby if mother is in an acute condition or a carrier.
3. During the postnatal period (infancy) from breastmilk or bottle-feeding, or overcrowded living conditions (49 - 53%).[165]

Cesareans are not indicated because both delivery methods put baby in contact with maternal fluid. Congenital defects are unlikely. Generally, baby will present with asymptomatic chronic Hepatitis B. Some will be jaundiced by three to four months of age. Immunoglobulin may be administered with hepatitis B vaccine as a preventive measure.[166]

Breastfeeding, while a risk factor, still shows a lower incidence of transmission to baby than bottle-feeding. A firm link between breastfeeding and neonatal infection has yet to be established.[167] Careful prayer and study should take place before decisions are made.

Hepatitis C virus (HCV)/Non-A, non-B Hepatitis (NANB):

Hepatitis C (HCV) is caused by another virus which accounts for 20% to 40% of all viral hepatitis in the U.S. Diagnosis is made by ruling out HAV and HBV. Blood tests are now available to detect the HCV IgG antibody; however, a 15-week delay between the onset of symptoms and a positive titer is common. HCV is most commonly transferred by blood transfusions or improperly sterilized syringes or needles but may also be transmitted by body fluids. Symptoms include: muscle aches, fever, headache, tiredness, loss of appetite, nausea, abdominal pain and joint pain, sometimes followed by dark urine and jaundice. Management and risk is similar to type B infection. Maternal transmission to baby is possible.[168]

D Hepatitis (Delta):

The type D hepatitis requires type B to reproduce. Type D may transform mild, chronic HBV into severe, chronic active hepatitis leading to cirrhosis of the liver. It has been transmitted perinatally at least once,[169] but percentages and risks are unknown at present.

Hepatitis E virus (HEV)

This virus was previously classified in the Non-A/Non-B virus group. Hepatitis E (HEV) is transmitted by oral ingestion of fecal-contaminated water or food. HEV has been found in India, Africa, Asia, Mexico and several Middle Eastern countries. Fatality rates for pregnant women range from 15% to 20%. Blood tests are available which can detect both IgM and IgG antibodies for HEV.[170]

Lifestyle/Dietary Recommendations (For all forms of hepatitis):
1. The need for a high-quality food diet prior to and during the illness has made the greatest difference in mortality. A diet high in carbohydrates, protein, vitamins and minerals as well as adequate liquids is of prime importance.[171] If vomiting is severe, an IV should be discussed with the health care provider.
2. Rest is imperative in an infection of this nature. This is the time for bed, not carpooling.
3. Limit contact with others during the infection so as not to infect those in the household, friends, relatives and strangers who do not need to get sick either.
4. Reduce fat intake - absolutely no alcohol.
5. Water with a wedge of lemon squeezed in is nourishing to the liver and helps to alkalize the rest of the body.
6. Some may find that taking one tablespoon of extra virgin olive oil daily is helpful.
7. During the illness and healing phase, foods should be steamed instead of eating them raw. Plenty of green leafy vegetables should be eaten.
8. Hospital birth for carrier-moms or moms with current infection is a necessity.
9. Mom should handle baby carefully postpartum (gloves if caring for open wounds, wash hands frequently, and watch out for wet kisses).

Nutritional Supplement Recommendations:
1. Liver-supportive herbs, such as milk thistle and dandelion, are definitely helpful to protect and build liver function.[172] [173] Three capsules of each three times daily.
2. Licorice root has been validated in experimental work to be useful in the treatment of hepatitis, cirrhosis and related liver disorders.[174] Three to six capsules daily.
3. Immune-enhancing herbs would be beneficial to support the body in fighting the infection. Echinacea has documented immunostimulant activity.[175] [176] [177] Astragalus, a Chinese herb, has definite positive action on the immune system and glands (liver included). In some Chinese journals, astragalus has been reported to inhibit hepatitis (even chronic HBV).[178] [179]
4. Daily doses of 300 and 600mg of calcium pantothenate and 90mg and 180mg of pantethine taken for 3-4 weeks has positive immunomodulatory action and effects on blood serum levels of immunoglobulins and phagocytic activity of peripheral blood neutrophils in hepatitis patients.[180]
5. Supplementation with coenzyme-B12 or cyanocobalamin at a dosage of 100mcg IV daily may product a normalizing effect on blood enzyme levels during hepatitis.[181] [182]
6. One study showed that Ginkgo biloba arrested the development of liver fibrosis of chronic hepatitis.[183]

HERPES SIMPLEX VIRUSES

Herpes Simplex Viruses both Type I (HSV-1) and Type II (HSV-II) are recurrent viral infections that may remain dormant for short or long periods after initial, primary infection and recur anytime, usually during times of physical or emotional stress.

HSV-I

Type I is the cause of the common fever blister in, on or around the mouth. It may also be found on the fingers of the hand in individuals who touch their fever blisters often.[184] If lesions (fever blisters) are present, oral contact with others should be avoided. Type I may be transmitted to the genitals (10% of genital herpes is Type I). Handwashing should be employed often with warm, soapy water.

HSV-II

Type II herpes is almost always transmitted sexually. Skin to skin contact is necessary to contract herpes.[185] The incubation period from exposure is usually 6 to 10 days, and initial symptoms are intense vulvar itching, burning, tingling and tenderness. There are one or many small or large thin-walled, fluid-filled vesicles that may appear over the vulva, vestibule, perianal area, or inner surfaces of the thigh, inside the vagina and/or on the cervix. Urination may be painful because of lesions. Vesicles rupture forming painful ulcers. At this stage, most moms feel ill and have a low-grade temperature.

Lesions usually regress, with the pain disappearing in 2 to 4 weeks. Lesions recur in 50% of persons infected with the herpes simplex virus. Recurrences are usually less severe and of shorter duration.[186] Prior to recurring outbreaks, some experience a prodromal phase of tingling, neuralgia, sensation of pressure or increased vaginal discharge.[187]

HSV-II may transplacentally infect baby and cause congenital defects, although this is rare. Congenital defects most often occur with a primary infection of mom prenatally. There is an increased risk of miscarriage and prematurity for babies with mothers who are infected during pregnancy.

Babies born to mothers infected at the time of birth have a 40 to 60% chance of infection. Cesareans are indicated if mom has a current outbreak during labor.[188]

Lifestyle/Dietary Recommendations:

1. Avoid foods high in arginine: almonds, Brazil nuts, cashews, hazelnuts, peanuts, pecans, walnuts, chocolate, gelatin. Restrict amounts of: coconut, barley, corn, oats, wheat, pasta, brussel sprouts.[189]

2. Do eat foods high in lysine: milk, soybeans, beef, poultry, sour cream, yogurt, fish, eggs, buckwheat.[190]
3. Icy cloths or ice packs may provide pain relief for lesions.
4. Keep lesions clean and dry - cotton underwear is a must.
5. Wash hands often and do not touch or pick at lesions.

Nutritional Supplement Recommendations:
1. L-Lysine is an amino acid that is highly recommended to combat herpes outbreaks. 1,200mg to 3,000mg of l-lysine daily.[191]
2. *Lactobacillus acidophilus* may help relieve symptoms of outbreaks as well as prevent future recurrences. Three capsules daily or 1/4 to 1/2 teaspoon three times daily of powder. Only purchase refrigerated probiotic supplements.[192]
3. Herbs exhibiting anti-viral activity in current research against herpes are: Uva ursi,[193] 2 capsules three times daily (Use caution during pregnancy due to uterine stimulating properties); Bilberry,[194] 2 capsules three times daily; Buckthorn,[195] 1 capsule three times daily (Use caution during pregnancy due to bowel stimulating properties); Echinacea,[196] 500mg every 2 - 3 hours during outbreak; Red raspberry,[197] 2 capsules three times daily; Blue-green algae,[198] 1,000mg to 3,000mg daily; Licorice,[199] 2 to 4 capsules daily (use caution during pregnancy due to phytosterols in plant). Obviously we would not want to use all of these herbs, at the same time.
4. For herbal topical antiviral herbs, clove oil and tea tree oil have both been found to inhibit the herpes virus.[200]
5. Peppermint has been shown to inhibit and kill the herpes simplex virus, among many other microorganisms.[201]
6. Herpilyn, by Enzymatic Therapy, may be applied topically to lesions for speedier healing.
7. Bee Propolis has been shown in studies to reduce the viral titer of herpes simplex virus and reduce viral synthesis as well as cut recovery time in half for patients with postherpetic trophic keratitis and/or postherpetic nebula.[202 203]
8. Echinacea root and burdock root, in equal amounts, have been reported to prevent outbreaks and eradicate the herpes virus from the body system if taken for six months (10 days on, 10 days off - 500mg to 1,000 mg of each two to three times daily). I have no clinically-documented experience with "eliminating" the herpes virus, but this combination of herbs, at the very least, has proved beneficial in clinical practice in limiting an outbreak and preventing recurrence.

HYPERTHYROIDISM

Symptoms of hyperthyroidism are: emotional fluctuations, intolerance to heat, irritability, increased perspiration, variable appetite, and variable weight gain. Hyperthyroidism causes these symptoms to be pronounced and causes: enlarged thyroid, bulging eyes, an elevated heart rate, and a slightly higher blood pressure and an elevated basal body temperature.[204]

There is a risk of miscarriage, particularly in the first trimester of pregnancy, if the problem is not treated. The other risk of untreated hyperthyroidism is the possible development of thyrotoxicosis (a "thyroid storm" or crisis). This condition can be fatal if left untreated; therefore, professional healthcare should be sought.[205]

Lifestyle/Dietary Recommendations:
1. The increased rate of metabolism means extra calories are needed.

Nutritional Supplement Recommendations:
1. Astragalus is an herb that has been used extensively in Chinese medicine. In recent years, it has been introduced in Western herbal medicine as an important immunostimulant and glandular herb. One particular study published in the *Journal of Chinese Medicine* in 1986 showed the effectiveness of astragalus in treating hyperthyroidism.[206] 2 capsules three times daily.
2. In doing research for plant medicines associated with hyperthyroidism, I found very few substantiated remedies that would be safe for pregnancy. The safest two mentioned (besides astragalus) were balm (Melissa officinalis) and thyme. In animal studies, they did inhibit thyroid-stimulating hormone (TSH).[207] Others mentioned were bugleweed (Lycopus virginicus), gypsywort (Lycopus europaeus) and motherwort (Leonurus cardiaca); however, all three of these have antigonadotropic hormonal action.[208] Since gonadotropin is the pregnancy hormone, it would be ill-advised to take an herb with anti-pregnancy hormone effects on the body.
3. A physician should be consulted, preferably one with extensive knowledge of preventive, natural and dietary medicine.

HYPOGLYCEMIA

Hypoglycemia is often called "low blood sugar." It is caused by faulty carbohydrate metabolism. The pancreas causes too much insulin to be released in response to the ingestion of simple sugars or refined carbohydrates (white foods: flour, sugar, pasta, bread). These simple sugars enter the bloodstream quickly (sometimes within seconds of eating these foods) and overwhelm the body system with glucose. The pancreas responds by releasing too much insulin which causes a dive in blood sugar levels. The adrenal glands then release epinephrine (adrenaline) which causes a headache, sweating, weakness, hunger, heart palpitations, and inward trembling. The liver then releases stored glycogen (sugar) to regulate blood sugar and insulin levels.[209] [210]

Highly processed foods are so lacking in essential nutrients that nutrients are leached from the body system to make up for what is missing. As the entire body becomes nutrient depleted, cravings for sugar and/or fruit are common. This is an attempt to keep up glucose levels. A cycle of up-down blood sugar fluctuations ensues. This physiologic process designed to protect us in emergencies, if abused by regular ingestion of refined carbohydrates, can lead to a "wearing-out" of the pancreas, adrenals and liver.

Common symptoms of hypoglycemia: nausea, lack of appetite, headaches, fatigue, fainting, dizzy spells, ketones in urine (reveals that the liver is depleted of glycogen, stored glucose, can check with urine strips), night-waking (when blood sugar goes "low," waking up is very common).[211]

Lifestyle/Dietary Recommendations:
1. Basically, the same recommendations dietary-wise as for diabetes — high complex carbohydrate, high-fiber diet.
2. Eat often, every one to two hours, in small amounts.
3. At bedtime, have a high-protein snack: peanut butter on whole-wheat bread, cheese, yogurt (plain - add fruit or unsweetened preserves), etc.
4. Have a high-protein snack when a craving for something sweet occurs.
5. All sugars should be eliminated, even naturally-occurring ones such as high-sugar fruits and honey unless combined with or followed by a protein such as yogurt or whole-wheat bread, etc.

Nutritional Supplement Recommendations:
1. Chromium is a mineral that has received a great deal of attention regarding blood sugar regulation. Make certain the daily vitamin/mineral formula contains an adequate amount in an absorbable form - chromium picolinate 100mcg three times daily before meals.[212]

2. Use liver-supportive herbs such as dandelion or milk thistle since the liver regulates how much glucose stays in the system through its storage and release of glycogen. One milk thistle tablet or capsule containing at least 70% silymarin three times daily.

HYPOTHYROIDISM

Hypothyroidism occurs when the thyroid gland is not producing adequate thyroid hormones. This can increase the risk of miscarriage because of the need for increased production of thyroid hormones by six weeks gestation.[213] Hypothyroidism is most often caused by inadequate iodine intake. The thyroid combines iodine with the amino acid tyrosine to create thyroid hormones. This is why iodized salt was introduced into our society. Those people not eating fish and seafood or sea vegetables usually do not get enough iodine in their diet.

Hypothyroidism is usually mild in pregnant moms because infertility is the major side effect of severe cases. Checking basal body temperature is one way of ascertaining if the thyroid is functioning normally. To check basal body temperature (BBT), place a thermometer in the armpit for 10 minutes after waking but before doing anything in the morning and while still reclining in bed. Temperature may also be taken vaginally. This eliminates variances in oral temperature due to respiratory infections.

Normal, axillary (armpit) temperature in a non-pregnant woman ranges from 97.4° to 98.2° F (36.3° to 36.8° C). Consistently lower readings may indicate low thyroid function; higher readings could mean an overactive thyroid. At ovulation, BBT is raised by approximately half a degree (called the "thermal shift") making the normal, pregnant range 97.9° to 98.7° F (36.65° to 37.05° C). A slight drop between weeks 9 and 12 gestation may be due to the influence of HCG (human chorionic gonodotropin).[214]

The most common symptoms of hypothyroidism are: weakness, dry or coarse hair and skin, lethargy, slow speech, edema of the eyelids, feeling cold, minimal perspiration, thick tongue, cool and pallid skin, impaired memory, constipation, weight gain, difficult breathing, headaches, fatigue, susceptibility to infections, poor appetite and heavy periods.[215]

Lifestyle/Dietary Recommendations:
1. Include more iodine-containing foods in the diet: seafish, sea vegetables such as kelp, dulse, spirulina, etc.
2. Decrease the intake of vegetables known as goitrogens (foods that block iodine utilization): turnips, cabbage, mustard, cassava root, soybeans, peanuts, pine nuts and millet. If these foods are a part of the diet, cook them to inactivate the goitrogens.[216]
3. Use iodized sea salt for seasoning to supply extra iodine.

Nutritional Supplement Recommendations:
1. Naturopaths use organic thyroid glandular supplements derived from cattle. Recommended amount: 1 tablet daily while monitoring BBT to check effectiveness.[217]

2. As with hyperthyroidism, Siberian Ginseng improves thyroid responsiveness to changing demands in the body. It has an adaptogenic effect meaning it normalizes glandular function whether high or low.[218]

3. Other herbs that stimulate thyroid function such as ephedra combined with white willow bark or caffeine-containing herbs are not appropriate for pregnancy in the dosages necessary or the methods necessary for positive results. An excellent book to consult: Michael T. Murray, N.D., *Natural Alternatives to Over-the-Counter and Prescription Drugs* published by William Morrow & Co., NY,NY, 1994.

IRRITABLE BOWEL SYNDROME

Irritable bowel syndrome (IBS), sometimes referred to as spastic colon, is very common in the U.S. with as many as 15 to 30% of Americans suffering from this uncomfortable condition. Many of the more current studies point to diet as the major cause of IBS. Food intolerance or allergy is evident in approximately two-thirds of patients with IBS.[219] [220]

Symptoms of IBS include: abdominal pain and distension (bloating); constipation alternating with cramps followed by more frequent bowel movements or diarrhea; pain usually relieved after bowel movements; excessive production of mucous in the colon; flatulence (gas); nausea; loss of appetite; and, commonly, feelings of stress or depression prior to cramp-y bowel movements. Prevention is the key in this disorder as in so many others. A high-fiber, processed-food-free diet is essential.

Foods that may cause IBS from food intolerance or allergy:

- Milk - One study revealed 74% of IBS patients had some degree of milk intolerance.[221]
- Dietetic sugars, particularly sorbitol. One study of healthy adults found almost half of subjects were sorbitol-intolerant. Sorbitol is found in some natural products and supplements as well as dietetic candies. Foods rich in sorbitol are: peaches, apple juice, pears, plums, prunes, sugarless gums, dietetic jams and chocolate.[222] Fructose may cause some individuals a problem.
- Coffee, tea
- Wheat and corn cereals
- Potatoes
- Onions
- Citrus fruits

Dr. John O. Hunter, gastroenterologist at Addenbrookes Hospital in Cambridge, Mass. believes that irritable bowel syndrome induced by food reactions is not caused by the typical allergenic reaction involving the immune system. He believes the problem is an abnormal imbalance of bacteria in the intestines, triggered by eating certain foods or taking antibiotics. Dr. Hunter found excessive numbers of aerobic (require air) bacteria in fecal samples of IBS patients after they ate an offending food. These aerobes wreck normal friendly bacteria activity which triggers colon disturbances leading to constipation, diarrhea, pain and bloating.[223]

Lifestyle/Dietary Recommendations:

1. Eliminate foods to which you may be allergic or intolerant for 2 to 3 weeks then add one back at a time to see if a reaction occurs.
2. Eliminate sugar and dietetic sugars as well as natural sugar additives such as fructose. Sugar adversely affects normal bowel function.[224]
3. Add water-soluble fiber such as that found in vegetables, fruit, oat bran, brown rice, guar gum, psyllium hulls or husks and legumes (beans, peas).

Nutritional Supplement Recommendations:

1. Ginger aids in the elimination of gas and relaxes and soothes the intestinal tract which may offer some relief of IBS-sufferers.[225] Fresh ginger (1/4" slice) added to fresh fruit or vegetable juice may be used or ginger capsules (2 to 3 capsules as needed).
2. Psyllium hulls may be added to daily supplement routine until normal bowel bacteria are back in balance. 4 to 6 capsules daily.
3. A special peppermint oil product (Peppermint Plus - an enteric-coated oil capsule) inhibits intestinal spasms and relieves gas.[226] The enteric-coat does not allow the oil to be released in the tummy, which could cause heartburn. 1 - 2 capsules between meals three times daily.
4. A product containing "Active Immunoglobulin Concentrate" derived from raw milk whey (Inner Strength by EN) has shown a remarkable ability to not only aid repopulation of normal bacteria but to attack the membrane coating of pathogenic (bad) bacteria, viruses and yeast. This attack renders the pathogens unable to infect the body and are then eliminated.[227] Inner Strength is enhanced when taken with probiotics such as *l. acidophilus* or *b. bifidus*.

INDIGESTION

Indigestion is characterized by a feeling of gaseousness or fullness in the abdomen caused by either increased secretion of hydrochloric acid (HCL) or decreased secretion of HCL as well as other digestive juices and enzymes.

Common symptoms of low gastric acidity:

Bloating, belching, burning and flatulence immediately after meals

Sense of "fullness" after eating

Indigestion, diarrhea or constipation

Multiple food allergies

Nausea after taking supplements

Itching around rectum

Common signs of low gastric acidity:

Weak, peeling or cracked fingernails

Dilated blood vessels in the cheeks and nose

Acne

Iron deficiency

Chronic intestinal parasites or abnormal flora

Undigested food in stool

Chronic candida infections

Upper gastrointestinal gassiness[228]

Several studies have shown that the ability to secrete gastric acid decreases with age.[229]

Lifestyle/Dietary Recommendations:

1. To find out if the problem is too much hydrochloric acid (HCL) or too little HCL, the following at home test may be performed: Take 1 tablespoon of apple cider vinegar or lemon juice when experiencing indigestion. If this eliminates the symptoms, too little HCL may be the problem. If it makes the symptoms worse, an overproduction of HCL is the problem. If the vinegar has helped, it can be taken with meals or an HCL supplement could be taken instead. Since HCL supplements make the condition of hiatal hernia, gastritis and duodenal ulcers worse, do the above test before self-treating with the HCL supplements.[230]

2. Foods or substances that stimulate the flow of HCL production are: hot peppers, onions, salsa, peppermint, papaya, pineapple, alcohol, milk, coffee (caffeinated and de-caf), tea with caffeine, 7-up, Coca-Cola, etc.

3. Avoid foods that are known allergens.

4. If excess stomach acid is the problem, 1/2 cup cooked rice ties up excess stomach acid and is very easy on the stomach, says Ava H. Der Mandersoian, Ph.D., professor of pharmacognosy and medicinal chemistry at Philadelphia College of Pharmacy and Science.[231] Other foods that may neutralize or absorb stomach acid: dried white or red beans, bananas, corn, tofu, whole grain bread. The only caution with using food to combat stomach acid is "don't eat too much." Excess food will only cause more acid to be secreted.

Nutritional Supplement Recommendations:
1. Organic peppermint tablets have proven to be quite helpful around the Parker home after meals to stimulate digestion and "freshen the breath."
2. I prefer to use supplements that stimulate the body to produce its own HCL for deficiency conditions. Those I have found to be most helpful are: cayenne pepper (known as the herb capsicum) and papaya mint chewable tablets, 1 to 2 taken 30 minutes before meals or during meals.
3. Two natural enzymes are available from fresh papaya (papain) and fresh pineapple (bromelain), 250 - 500 mg at each meal. These have been shown to aid digestion and prevent/treat indigestion.[232]
4. Pancreatic enzymes can be helpful to aid digestion of fats, proteins and starches; however, those derived from pork are a less than healthy choice.
5. Other herbs known to relieve indigestion are fennel and clove tea.[233]

INSOMNIA

Insomnia is a term used to essentially say "I cannot sleep!" Insomnia may simply be due to factors we all deal with: excess stimulation, exercising before bed, hot baths before bed and/or stress.

Lifestyle/Dietary Recommendations:
1. Eliminate natural stimulants - caffeine, alcohol.
2. Nocturnal hypoglycemia is an important cause of sleep-maintenance insomnia. Nocturnal hypoglycemia causes a release of hormones like adrenaline, glucagon, cortisol and growth hormone which regulates glucose levels. These compounds stimulate the brain signaling "time to eat." Eat a good snack 30-45 minutes before bed - oatmeal, other whole grain cereals, breads, muffins. No sugars.
3. Relax.
4. Exercise in the morning or early evening for 20 minutes.
5. Do not overeat at the dinner meal.
6. Adopt regular bedtime habits - go to bed at the same time and rise at the same time. "Early to bed, early to rise" is a good admonition.

Nutritional Supplement Recommendations:
1. Valerian root in scientific studies has been shown to have the ability to improve sleep quality and relieve insomnia.[234] One large double-blind study revealed the aqueous extract of valerian root improved insomnia and left no "hangover" the next morning. It has been suggested to be as effective in reducing sleep latency (time required to get to sleep) as small doses of benzodiazepines. Valerian also reduced morning sleepiness. Thirty to forty-five minutes before bedtime: 1 - 2g of dried root (or as tea) or 4 - 6mg (1 - 1.5t) of tincture or 1 - 2 mg (0.5 - 1t) of fluid extract or 150 - 300mg capsules of valerian extract containing 0.8% valeric acid.
2. Passionflower and Chamomile are other natural herbal sedatives that may be taken as teas or in capsule form before bedtime.[235]
3. An herbal calcium supplement such as ChamoCalm by Mother's Choice™ makes a good instant, "no-steep" tea before bed.

KIDNEY STONES

Kidney stones is another of those maladies associated with our "Western" diet.[236] Calcium-containing stones are made up of calcium oxalate, calcium oxalate mixed with calcium phosphate, or (rarely) calcium phosphate alone. Dietary patterns that have been shown to be associated with calcium-containing stones (as in kidney stones) are: low fiber, highly refined carbohydrates; high alcohol; large amounts of animal protein; high fat, high calcium foods; high salt; and high vitamin D enriched food.[237 238]

Kidney stones are very common in the U.S. Almost 6% of our U.S. population develop a kidney stone each year. Men are two to three times more likely to experience kidney stones than women. The discouraging note is that if someone has stones once, the chances of recurrence are high (40% in next 5 years; 80% in next 25 years).[239] An encouraging word would be that this problem may be entirely preventable with lifestyle and dietary modifications.

Lifestyle/Dietary Recommendations:
1. An increase of fluid intake is vital. More liquid in — more liquid out. A daily output of 1 1/2 to 2 quarts is recommended. These liquids do not include coffee, tea, colas, sweetened juices or punches. They should be pure water (home purification is the most reliable means of ensuring pure water), fresh fruit and vegetable juices. Lemon juice and cranberry juice are particularly effective.[240]
2. Lower animal protein intake and increase fresh fruits and vegetables. Going completely vegan (no animal products whatsoever) does not seem necessary. Meat eaters who do not focus their meals on meat, rather they make fresh fruits and vegetables the mainstay, have a lower incidence of stones.[241] Animal protein increases the amount of calcium in the urine which when combined with uric acid (also increased with high meat consumption) can lead to stone formation.
3. Eat whole wheat, brown rice or corn. These fiber-rich foods reduce urinary calcium, which results in lowered risk of kidney stone formation.[242]
4. Leave the milk in the cow. Milk (in the supermarket) is fortified with vitamin D, which increases calcium absorption and calcium concentration in the urine. Milk fortified with vitamin D also lowers magnesium levels in the body.[243] This makes vitamin D-fortified milk a risk factor for stone-formers.
5. Include leafy greens in the diet - kale, leafy lettuce, parsley. The high amount of vitamin K may help lower the incidence of kidney stones. Vitamin K is necessary for the synthesis of a natural compound in urine that inhibits crystalline growth of calcium oxalate.[244]

Nutritional Supplement Recommendations:

1. Magnesium supplements combined with Vitamin B6 (pyridoxine) have been shown to be effective in preventing kidney stone recurrence. 400mg magnesium daily with 50mg of B6.[245] [246] Foods rich in magnesium and vitamin B6 include: barley, bran, corn, buckwheat, rye, soy, oats, brown rice, avocado, banana, lima beans and potato.

2. Calcium supplements should be from a chelated form rather than bone meal, oyster shell or calcium carbonate. Calcium chelates such as calcium citrate are more easily absorbable by the body.

3. If one has a history of kidney stones, it would be wise to limit vitamin C intake (daily over long-term) to 2,000mg. High levels of vitamin C over extended periods can contribute in creating stones.[247]

4. Herbs found to be helpful in dissolving and/or eliminating stones are: Cornsilk,[248] Cranberry,[249] Flax,[250] Gravel root, Hydrangea, Marshmallow and Horsetail.[251] [252]

LOW BLOOD PRESSURE

Low blood pressure readings are not a problem unless the reading is very low and associated with symptoms indicating a health problem. In fact, those persons with low blood pressure have been shown to live longer than those with normal blood pressure.[253] Low blood pressure readings are generally found in young people or elderly people who are in good health, vegetarians and women who exercise regularly. In pregnancy, a slight drop in blood pressure around 28 weeks is a healthy sign that mom's blood volume is expanding according to plan.

For those who have low blood pressure combined with other symptoms such as nausea, dizziness upon rising, fainting, visual disturbances and/or breathlessness with exertion, an underlying problem may be present. Anemia and hypoglycemia may be contributing factors in feeling unwell and low blood pressure.[254] The main thrust of any (if any) treatment is nutritional counseling and aiding the circulatory function.

Lifestyle/Dietary Recommendations:
1. Exercise. A nice daily walk is to be encouraged for all for good circulatory health.
2. Slowly rise to a standing position instead of jumping up. A quick rise temporarily will decrease the blood flow to the brain.
3. Be diligent to follow the whole foods diet as outlined in Part 2. Eat often to prevent hypoglycemic reactions.

Nutritional Supplement Recommendations:
1. Herbs to avoid because of their hypotensive effects demonstrated in clinical studies are: Agrimony, Ashwagandha, Black cohosh, and Goldenseal.[255]
2. Siberian ginseng has also been shown to have an ability to raise blood pressure in those with hypotension.[256] 4 capsules daily.
3. Ginkgo may help both blood pressure problems by increasing circulatory function. 2 - 4 capsules each day.
4. Korean (Panax) ginseng helps with low blood pressure by its adaptogenic factor. This basically means that it lowers blood pressure in hypertensive individuals and raises it in hypotensive people.[257 258 259 260] 4 - 6 capsules daily. Panax ginseng is not recommended for use during pregnancy.

MOUTH SORES/INFLAMED GUMS

Mouth sores or ulcers (canker sores) and inflamed gums are painful conditions that fortunately respond well to natural treatment. While these two discomforts are separate entities, I have grouped them together here because the treatment is similar for both.

Canker or mouth sores are generally small, round sores that are white in the center with a red, raised border. Certain foods seem to aggravate them and may even bring them on (food allergy).

Inflamed gums make gums more susceptible to bacteria and plaque. The inflammatory condition does not speak well of the overall health of the mouth.

Lifestyle/Dietary Recommendations:
1. Eliminate foods that are allergens.
2. Brush teeth, tongue, gums, inside of cheeks and palate twice daily to remove build-up.
3. Floss at least once daily.

Nutritional Supplement Recommendations:
1. Allow a 25 - 50mg zinc lozenge to dissolve on the sore or inflamed area up to twice daily until inflammation is gone.[261]
2. Dissolve one teaspoon of acidophilus in water and gargle/swish twice daily. This is okay, even good, to swallow.
3. Vitamin C with bioflavonoids: 1000mg three times daily for 3 days then 1000mg daily on a regular basis. The positive effect of vitamin C on dental health has been scientifically confirmed.[262]
4. Deglycyrrhizinated licorice (DGL) in a gargle or as a lozenge three times daily.
5. John Bastyr, pioneering naturopath, developed an excellent formula: Mix tincture of echinacea with myrrh gum powder to make a paste and apply locally to the inflamed area.
6. Propolis tincture is recommended by herbalist Christopher Hobbs. Put a few drops on the gums or the sore and let sit. A few studies have confirmed antibacterial effects of bee propolis on wounds. NOTE** Propolis may cause allergic reactions.
7. A product I have found helpful is called "Oxyfresh Gel" manufactured by Oxyfresh USA, Inc., P.O. Box 3723, Spokane, WA 99220. It contains OXYGENE(which is stabilized chlorine dioxide as well as purified deionized water, carrageenan, chamomile extract, aloe vera, methylparaben and propylparaben. I rub this gel on my gums or sore spots as needed.

8. Another product I recently have benefited from for better oral care is FoliCare[TM] by Advanced Medical Nutrition, Inc., 2247 National Avenue, Hayward, CA 94545. It is an oral care rinse to be used twice daily that contains folic acid which is recommended by Drs. Murray and Pizzorno, authors of the *Textbook of Naturopathic Medicine*. A dose of 4mg per day for 30 days of folic acid increased resistance of gingiva to local irritants and reduced gum inflammation in a double-blind, placebo-controlled study of human subjects.[263]

NOCTURNAL MYODONUS (NIGHT MUSCLE TWITCHING)

Nocturnal myodonus is an intimidating name for the problem of muscle twitching at night. It is a nerve and muscle disorder characterized by repeated contractions of one or more muscle groups (the legs are a popular spot) during sleep. The twitching lasts less than ten seconds. Most people are not aware they are experiencing this unless their spouse alerts them (like I do with my husband) with a polite elbow reminder to "be still."

Nutritional Supplement Recommendations:
1. Vitamin E at 400 IU daily (a quality prenatal will probably supply this amount) has been shown to benefit "muscle twitchers."[264]

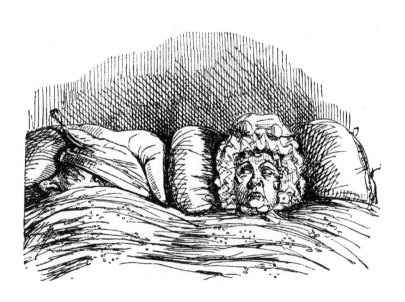

NOSEBLEEDS

Nosebleeds may be due to a lack of vitamin C and bioflavonoids which help decrease capillary fragility. Another cause of "nose-spotting," so to speak, upon waking in the morning is dry air in the home.

Lifestyle/Dietary Recommendations:
1. Eat plenty of dark, leafy green vegetables and citrus fruits.
2. Consider a humidifier or vaporizer for overly-dry indoor air. If mom chooses to use one of these, she should be diligent to keep it clean and free of molds and mildew which can create other problems for the family.

Nutritional Supplement Recommendations:
1. Extra vitamin C and bioflavonoids should be considered until the condition is resolved.
2. If the nose is dry and itchy, one may apply a thin layer of vitamin E oil, comfrey ointment, aloe gel or unpetroleum jelly to moisten nasal membranes.

PALPITATIONS

Heart palpitations are generally painless although very uncomfortable. Palpitations are characterized by a pounding heartbeat that is faster than normal and feels as though the heart is filling the chest cavity. When I have experienced these, I feel as though the blood vessels in my neck and head are bulging, and I have a sense of breathlessness.

Frequent palpitations may be a sign of anemia. The blood deprived of adequate oxygen causes the heart muscle to work faster and harder to supply vital organs with oxygen. Hemoglobin should be checked and anemia treated if this is the root problem. Palpitations may be occurring as a response to stress, caffeine consumption or overexertion of physical activity. Any palpitations occurring with any of the following should be evaluated by a professional healthcare provider: nausea, numbness of tingling in the left arm, chest pain.

Lifestyle/Dietary Recommendations:
1. Follow the whole foods diet with an emphasis on dark, leafy green vegetables.
2. Slow down and relax to relieve stress.
3. If palpitations occur during strenuous physical activity, discontinue that activity.

Nutritional Supplement Recommendations:
1. I have found the most effective supplement for palpitations is a combination of ginkgo and hawthorn in a powdered capsule - 2, 450mg, capsules as soon as the palpitations start. If chronic or frequent, 2 capsules each day, 1 in the morning and 1 thirty minutes before bedtime. This has always stopped my palpitations within 2 - 3 minutes of taking the capsules.

PARASITES (PROTOZOA DISEASE)

Most people do not consider parasites to be a risk for them unless they have been, or are going out of, the country. The unfortunate fact is that parasitic infections are all too common in United States.

Our community or well water supply is often contaminated with the little fellows — some of them resistant to municipal water treatment methods such as chlorine. People who handle our food or the food itself may be infected. The most common means of transfer person-to-person is in day care centers. My own personal thought on another means of picking up one of these nasty infections is from the ever popular kiddie play equipment at restaurants geared to children. Little tots are not known for their meticulous hygiene habits, and where there are lots of little ones, there is to be expected intermingling of germs and parasites.

The three most common parasites causing symptoms are: *Entamoeba histolytica, Giardia lamblia,* and *Blastocystis hominis.* Symptoms for these infections include: diarrhea, gas, bloating, weight loss, loss of appetite, fatigue, nausea, abdominal cramping and/or fever. A physician should be consulted if some or all of these symptoms are present and remain for more than the standard 24 to 48 hours for a gastrointestinal infection. A stool sample test can be performed to identify the infectious agent. Although it may be necessary to follow allopathic treatment for severe cases, natural measures can benefit recovery and help fight the protozoa disease. Some of these parasites, if untreated, can remain in the system causing re-infection when the body is susceptible. While the person may be asymptomatic, they can still transfer the parasite to others; therefore, treatment is a must.

Lifestyle/Dietary Recommendations:

1. Prevent occurrence by drinking only distilled or reverse osmosis water preferably treated at your home (See resource section for water treatment system suppliers).
2. On trips, use only bottled distilled or reverse osmosis water. Do not sip from sparkling streams while camping. Do not eat fresh fruits and vegetables (which may have been rinsed in contaminated water) while out of the country — eat only cooked foods, or peel fruit yourself.
3. Eat bananas that have not fully ripened (slightly green) and basmati rice with plain yogurt containing live cultures.
4. Eat a high-fiber diet if well tolerated.
5. Avoid high-risk settings such as day care centers and indoor playgrounds.
6. Pumpkin seeds are effective in expelling worms or helminths and internal parasites. They may be eaten raw or slightly roasted.[265]
7. Clove tea is also helpful in the recovery from protozoa disease.

Nutritional Supplement Recommendations:

1. The product Inner Strength (EN), containing Active Immunoglobulin Concentrate derived from raw milk whey, may be taken 1/4 to 1/2 teaspoon three to four times daily. If combined with the super strain of *acidophilus* or *bifidus* found in certain brands of *acidophilus* and *bifidus* (EN and UAS Labs), the re-population of beneficial bowel bacteria will be enhanced.

2. Garlic should be eaten freely and taken in supplement form. Garlic was proven superior to antibiotics in a recent test by Egyptian doctors at Ain Shams University in Cairo. Small doses of fresh garlic combined with garlic capsules virtually wiped out symptoms of *Giardia lamblia* in one day. All were protozoan-free after three days.[266] Garlic tablets or capsules (equivalent to 4 - 5 fresh cloves) - 3 to 6 daily or, as the researchers did, whip up thirty peeled fresh garlic cloves with a little water in a blender at short bursts until it is homogenized; chill the mixture. The dosage given to the children was one-third cup of the garlic solution twice a day.

3. Bee Propolis in a concentrated strength from 10%-30% can be an effective treatment for those suffering with giardiasis.[267]

4. Pau D'Arco demonstrated anti-parasitic function in several studies. The most notable study was a carefully controlled animal study at the Naval Medical Research Institute in Bethesda, Maryland that showed lapachol (Pau D'Arco constituent) to be protective against the deadly parasite, *Schistosoma mansoni.*[268] [269] 3 to 6 daily. Pau D'Arco is not recommended for use in pregnancy.

5. Elecampane contains the chemical alantolactone that helps expel intestinal parasites especially pinworms and *Giardia lamblia.*[270] Recommended dosage: 2 to 3 capsules three times daily.

6. WormOut™ may be used, 1 teaspoon several times daily, for two to four weeks combined with garlic.

PLANTAR WARTS

Plantar warts are common on the sole of the foot. They typically are extremely tender, flattened by pressure. Unlike corns or calluses, they tend to pinpoint bleed when the wart surface is pared away. Standard allopathic treatment includes applying 40% salicylic acid tape for several days after which the physician debrides (scrapes away) the wart, finally destroying the wart through freezing or the use of caustic agents such as 30% to 70% trichloroacetic acid.[271] Nutritional and botanical supplementation centers on immune system and liver support, as well as topical application of anti-viral herbs.

Lifestyle/Dietary Recommendations:
1. Eliminate alcohol and sugar (even "natural" sugars from fruit juices, fructose, maple syrup, etc.) since they depress the immune system.
2. Keep socks on around the house to protect other family members from the wart-producing virus.
3. Support the liver with dark, leafy greens and fermented foods such as yogurt, apple cider vinegar, miso, sauerkraut.

Nutritional Supplement Recommendations:
1. Apply the fresh juice of Cheledonium (Greater Celandine) to wart, cover and leave for several days. Cheledonium exhibits anti-viral activity, which explains why it has been used so successfully for warts since they are induced by a virus.[272]
2. Thuja (Tree of Life) oil may be topically applied to the wart(s) two to three times daily. The addition of garlic oil to Thuja oil may enhance the chemical activity of both.[273] Thuja should not be used during pregnancy.
3. The use of Milk Thistle (containing at least 70% silymarin) aids liver function. Assisting the liver is necessary part of botanical protocol for any growth on or in the body. 1 tablet or capsule three times daily.[274]
4. Immunostimulating herbs such as astragalus and echinacea may be taken internally. Echinacea should not be taken for more than three months because a tolerance to the immune-stimulating effects may build. 2,000mg daily of each. Licorice may be beneficial due to the anti-viral activity of the herb (De-glyzirrinated licorice is the best choice for this type of use). 1 to 3 capsules or tablets daily.
5. Vitamin A acid (2% in petrolatum, one time daily, topically) produced good results in 50% of patients with plantar warts after four weeks of treatment. Complete cure occurred in two of the patients.[275]

POISON IVY, OAK, SUMAC

The problem of skin reaction to poison ivy or oak or sumac is that it is extremely uncomfortable. The technical term for the rash is *allergic contact dermatitis*. The reaction occurs as a red, very itchy rash that may swell and leak fluid from the small vesicles.

The sap from the plant contains urushiol, one of the most toxic skin agents known to humanity. Urushiol is not only potent but long lasting. Gloves that crumbled a poison ivy leaf 6 to 12 months ago may still be coated with active oil. The rash is not contagious. The oil, however, may be transferred by hands, fingernails and clothing.

Lifestyle/Dietary Recommendations:
1. Wash with mild soap and running water immediately upon contact with the plant.

Nutritional Supplement Recommendations:
2. Apply Jewelweed (Impatiens biflora). Pick the leaves and juicy stems. Crush them in the hand; put the plant and juice directly on the rash. Jewelweed may be placed in boiling water for five minutes; let steep and strain. Freeze tea into ice cubes and apply to poison ivy rash. Jewelweed relieves the itch and reduces inflammation. Although scientific evidence is scant, at least one study indicated jewelweed was as effective as pharmaceutical cortisone creams in treating poison ivy rash.
3. Grindelia (gumweed/gum plant) has pain-relieving and anti-inflammatory qualities. Christopher Hobbs recommends "Put a few drops of the tincture on the lesions and spread it with your fingers. The drops actually form a bandage-like, resinous, shiny coating over the top of the rash. It can be applied before going to bed, and it helps prevent you from scratching and spreading the rash." Hobbs also recommends taking Echinacea orally to boost the immune system for severe cases of contact dermatitis.
4. Tea tree oil may be applied to lesions.
5. For the camper, the Tecnu Poison Oak-N-Ivy Cleanser made by Tec Labs of Albany, Oregon helps cleanse urushiol form the skin after contact if water is not available.

RESTLESS LEGS

This discomfort makes me crazy! It is the feeling of restlessness in the legs that makes me want to kick or beat my legs against the bed after lying down for a night's sleep. Restless legs feels like all the energy of the entire body is focused in the legs. This is unfortunate since the rest of the body wants to go to sleep.

Lifestyle/Dietary Recommendations:
1. Foods rich in folic acid: Daily - 1 cup of orange juice (.07mg), 1/3 cup whole grain cereal (0.1mg), 1/2 cup cooked spinach (.13mg) and 1/2 cup cooked dry beans (.12mg).

Nutritional Supplement Recommendations:
2. Make certain that the daily vitamin/mineral formula contains at least 400mcg of folic acid, preferably 800 - 1,000mcg.
3. L-Dopamine has been found to be effective in the treatment of restless legs syndrome at a dosage of 100-200mg daily.[276] Please check with health care provider before using during pregnancy.

SALMONELLA/
CAMPYLOBACTER/LISTERIA

Salmonella, Campylobacter and Listeria are bacteria commonly known for causing food-borne illness - gastrointestinal infection actually. These infections have become more prevalent in recent years due to antibiotic usage in our food (meat, most commonly chicken and eggs) supply. Drs. Michael A. Schmidt, Lendon H. Smith and Keith W. Sehnert in their book, *Beyond Antibiotics*, state that "Roughly, 40% of all antibiotics produced are used in animal husbandry. In most cases, antibiotics are used in animals raised for slaughter and eventual sale to consumers."[277] Even though these animals or their by-products are sometimes tested for antibiotic residue, if antibiotic-resistant bacteria have already been created, it is too late for the consumer who purchases bacteria-infected pork, beef, chicken, eggs, shellfish, sushi and dairy products.

There are almost 500,000 reported cases of *salmonella* or *campylobacter* infections each year. The actual number of infections (reported and unreported) may be as many as 20 to 80 million people in the United States.[278] The symptoms which include nausea, abdominal cramps, diarrhea, fever, headache and sometimes vomiting, mimic the "stomach flu" or a gastrointestinal virus. The incubation period is from 6 to 72 hours after eating infected food.

Campylobacter infections are on the rise, numbering two times more than salmonella last year in the U.S. Pregnant women, the elderly and very young babies are at most risk. Pregnant women who contract *campylobacter* during pregnancy are at very high risk for miscarriage or stillbirth. Common sources of *campylobacter* contamination: deli meats, uncooked hot dogs, leftovers, raw milk or pastuerized milk that has not been heated to 145 degrees Fahrenheit for 35 minutes, eggs and raw or undercooked poultry.

Listeria infections are also on the rise, with several widespread sources of contamination occurring in 1999 through packaged deli meats and hot dogs. *Listeria*, while causing only mild gastrointestinal infection in healthy children and adults, can be fatal to developing babes in the womb.

Lifestyle/Dietary Recommendations:
1. To prevent the occurrence, purchase organically-grown meat if possible. This does not totally eliminate the possibility of infection but greatly reduces one's risk.
2. Cook meat, especially chicken and turkey, thoroughly until there are no pink juices running.
3. Keep food preparation area clean. Do not allow raw meat or its juices to touch other food.
4. Wash hands or utensils in hot, soapy water after handling raw meat. The family cook might even want to wear disposable gloves for poultry.

5. Wooden cutting boards may harbor bacteria - plastic ones are supposed to be better.
6. Thaw meat in the refrigerator, not on the kitchen counter or in the microwave.
7. Keep the refrigerator below 40 degrees F and the freezer at or below 0 degrees F.
8. Do not eat raw eggs. Prepare as follows:
   - Scramble 1 minutes at 250 F (121 C).
   - Poach for 5 minutes in boiling water.
   - Fry uncovered sunny-side up for 4 minutes at 250 F.
   - Fry over-easy 3 minutes one side, 2 minutes other side at 250 F.
   - Boil in shell for at least 7 minutes.[279]

Nutritional Supplement Recommendations:

1. Take 1 teaspoon of acidophilus (one of the super-strains) powder every hour until symptoms subside.
2. Take 1/2 teaspoon of Inner Strength (Probioplex - EN) with acidophilus. Mix in lukewarm water and drink.
3. Liberal use of garlic, known to be effective against these microbes would seem appropriate.
4. Goldenseal is known to work on the mucous membranes of the body, of which the intestinal wall is one. Goldenseal also has shown activity against certain bacterial microbes making it a choice for GI illnesses. Purchase only organically-grown goldenseal, rather than wild-crafted as our sources in the wild are diminishing.
5. Seek medical care if no improvement is seen in 24 to 48 hours in small children, pregnant women and the elderly.
6. If numbness, tingling or paralysis follows a meal, seek emergency care immediately. A very serious food poisoning, such as botulism, may have occurred.

SHINGLES

Shingles are caused by varicella-zoster or herpes zoster — the same virus that causes chicken pox. Shingles occurs when the virus which has been lying dormant in the body is activated by fatigue, stress, chicken pox exposure, anticancer drugs, immune system deficiency, Hodgkin's disease or other cancers. The virus travels to the nerve endings near the skin's surface. The result is burning, itching or pain that develops into blisters and a ring of rash on the abdomen or chest area. Shingles sometimes affects the neck, lower back, forehead or eyes. Althought the lesions usually crust over and heal after 1 to 2 weeks, persistent pain may develop due to nerve damage by the virus (postherpetic neuralgia).

The incidence of baby infection in the womb is low with shingles although it is possible. Moms with shingles should definitely avoid contact with pregnant women who have NOT had chicken pox because of the higher incidence of congenital baby infection from the varicella or chicken pox virus.

Allopathic treatment for shingles is Acyclovir (Zovirax). Medical treatment should be considered in those who have asthma and/or those who are on immunosuppressive drug treatment, such as steroids.

Lifestyle/Dietary Recommendations:
1. Eat foods high in lysine and low in arginine: chocolate, peanuts, leeks, cereal grains (see Herpes Simplex).
2. Apply cool or cold wet dressings to the affected area. Some even put the wet cloth into the freezer to make it colder. Avoid heat.
3. Vitamin E capsules can be pricked with a pin and the oil applied directly onto lesions.

Nutritional Supplement Recommendations:
1. Vitamin E - 600 IU daily.
2. Vitamin C - 2 to 3 grams daily until lesions clear.
3. Lysine - 500 - 1,000mg three times daily during outbreak.
4. Vitamin B12 injections has helped with postviral neuralgia.
5. Intramuscular injections of adenosine monophosphate (AMP) should be discussed with physician for safe use during pregnancy. One study showed 88% of patients treated with AMP became free from pain and remained pain-free from 3 to 18 months after treatment.[280]
6. Follow Herpes Simplex herbal regimen.

SINUSITIS

Sinusitis is an infection located in the sinus cavities of the head. Symptoms include swelling, congestion with thick, yellowish-green discharge, pain, headache that is worse upon bending over and all-around feeling unwell. Sinusitis occurs when mucous becomes thick and blocks the single exit out of the sinus cavities. Once blocked, bacteria find a home in which to thrive. The condition can become chronic if preventive measures are not employed.

Lifestyle/Dietary Recommendations:

1. Keep mucous thin by drinking 1 glass (8 oz.) of water every hour during a respiratory infection or allergy. Lemon added to the water supplies extra vitamin C without adding extra sugar.
2. Eat hot, spicy food - Mexican salsa, red peppers, chicken soup loaded with onions and garlic.[281]
3. Keep air moist with humidifier. Be certain to clean humidifier so mold and mildew do not grow.
4. Apply a hot cloth to the face for a few minutes to encourage circulation and mucous flow.
5. Pinch the sides of the upper nose with fingers to relieve pain and stimulate the flow of mucous.
6. Avoid allergens.

Nutritional Supplement Recommendations:

1. Vitamin C with bioflavonoids is always a good supplement to take during any infection. Moms in the first trimester should limit vitamin C intake to 3,000mg daily. Other family members may take up to 1,000mg every 2 hours.
2. Bromelain has clinically-documented efficacy in treating sinusitis[282] by reducing inflammation, promoting drainage and decreasing swelling. 250 - 500mg three times daily taken 30 minutes before meals.
3. Echinacea is always a good choice for immune stimulation, and it has shown antibacterial effectiveness in studies.[283] [284] When I feel pressure in my sinuses, I take 500 - 1,000mg every 2 hours.
4. A product called E.H.B. (NF) was very helpful for our family one Christmas when we developed sinusitis. Although it has goldenseal in it, the amount was not enough to cause me to have a hypoglycemic reaction and was not enough to stimulate contractions in my pregnancy. The caution against using goldenseal during pregnancy still applies, however.

5. Garlic has potent antibacterial properties. The equivalent of 3 to 4 cloves may be taken daily, or if family can stand it, eat 3 to 4 cloves daily. For those resistant infections, 3 to 4 cloves every 3 to 4 hours during the acute stage of the illness.

Skin Infection, Mild

Mild skin infections from wounds or lesions are those not causing a systemic (whole body) response. There is no fever or general feeling of illness with a mild skin infection. This condition can be prevented with good hygiene and immuno-stimulant herbs.

Lifestyle/Dietary Recommendations:
1. Add to diet plenty of foods rich in vitamin C and bioflavonoids to aid healing: peppers, cantaloupe, guava, citrus fruit and their fresh juices, papaya and kiwi.
2. Wash affected area with soap and water several times daily to keep wound clean.
3. Eat onions and garlic which stimulate immune response.

Nutritional Supplement Recommendations:
1. Take 1,000 - 2,000mg Echinacea daily to stimulate immune function.
2. Apply 3 drops Echinacea tincture or tinctract and 1 drop of tea tree oil to inflamed area three times daily. Soothing Salve Drops by Mother's Choice™ may be used instead of trying to combine the drops to apply to the wound oneself. These drops have been very helpful in our family; we even use them on our animal's wounds.
3. Apply aloe vera gel 2 to 3 times daily to aid healing and provide protection for wound.

SMOKING CESSATION

There are several herbal supplements that have been used to help stop smoking. I have listed these below; however, the herbs are not guaranteed to work and are not a substitute for the desire to quit. Try to abstain for six weeks by setting a goal (treat) for yourself or set a punishment (give money to a cause you despise) if you don't achieve the six weeks of non-smoking. Don't worry about weight gain at this point. Worry, instead, about dying of cancer or emphysema or heart disease.

Nutritional Supplement Recommendations:
1. Sweet flag (Acorus calamus) may be taken at a dosage of 1 teaspoon three times daily. This herbs is stimulating and should not be taken in the late evening.
2. Wild oats (avena sativa) - 250-500mg three times daily.
3. Lobelia (Lobelia inflata) may be used at 10 drops three to four times daily. Do not overdose on this herb; it will act as an emetic in larger doses.
4. High-potency multi-vitamin and mineral formula taken daily.

SORE THROAT

A sore throat - does it really need a definition or will "OUCH" do? The throat becomes sore because of inflammation or irritation due to allergies, dry air, viruses or bacteria. It is sometimes difficult to distinguish one cause from another. The most common cause of a sore throat is a virus causing the "common cold" which is responsible for 80% of all sore throats.[285] A cold usually causes a scratchy or sore throat that is gone in a day or two followed by sneezing, coughing and increased mucous production.

Another cause of sore or scratchy throat is allergies or dry, indoor air. This type of sore throat usually is only felt in the morning upon waking and gets better as the day progresses. Eating and drinking usually relieve this type of sore throat.

The third cause of sore throat is a bacterial infection such as the *streptococcus* bacteria. The symptoms that accompany this sore throat are: fever of 102° or higher, fatigue, headache, stomach ache and/or nausea. The throat appears red with white patches on it. If a strep infection is suspected, a throat culture, not just a quick strep test, should be performed to determine if it is indeed bacterial. If antibiotics are used, the timing of initial treatment is crucial. Studies have shown that antibiotics taken within the first 48 hours of a strep infection actually *increase* the risk of a recurrent infection by two to eight times.[286] If antibiotics are used, concurrent nutritional support should definitely be used. Whatever the cause of the sore throat, the nutritional supplementation is the same.

Lifestyle/Dietary Recommendations:
1. Licorice root tea or a teaspoon of licorice tinctract in a cup of water has an anesthetizing effect. It helps to soothe the throat and suppress coughs.[287]
2. Jim Duke, Ph.D., U.S. Department of Agriculture's expert on medicinal plants, recommends: "pineapple juice with a pinch or so of ginger, nutmeg, rosemary and spearmint and a bit of licorice as a sweetener." Thyme and cardamom may also be added.[288]
3. Hot liquids such as chicken soup are always of benefit for respiratory illness and sore throats.
4. If sore throat is due to dry indoor air, use a clean humidifier. If due to allergens in home, consider an air purifier.
5. Change toothbrush every 1 to 2 months.
6. Investigate for milk allergy if recurrent tonsillitis is a problem.
7. Eat blackberries. Their astringent tannins may help.

Nutritional Supplement Recommendations:
1. LymphaRub by Mother's Choice™ contains essential oils that work extremely well for sore throats. The product may be rubbed on the throat 3 to 6 times daily.

Family members other than a pregnant mom may decide to put one to three drops in a cup of water and sip slowly one to three times daily. Essential oils should not be taken internally during pregnancy.

2. Zinc lozenges containing at least 23mg of zinc may be taken every 2-4 hours. This amount of zinc should not be taken for more than one week.

3. A warm fenugreek tea or sage tea gargle may help relieve sore throats due, respectively, to their high mucilage and astringent tannins content.[289] [290]

4. Even the FDA calls slippery elm "an excellent demulcent" (soothing agent).[291] It is available in lozenges, teas or liquid combinations.

5. Echinacea may be taken at first sign of a sore throat to aid the immune response. 500 - 1,000mg every 2 to 4 hours.

STRENGTHEN BLADDER FUNCTION

I have included this here to help those moms who may have poor bladder muscle tone. This condition most often occurs at the end of pregnancy when baby's head may make it difficult to completely empty the bladder when urinating or after a pregnancy where the walls of genital area were weakened.

Lifestyle/Dietary Recommendations:
1. Exercise the pubococcygeal (PC) muscle by doing 100 -200 Kegel exercises daily.
2. Do not Kegel while on the toilet. This can lead to urine retention.
3. Relax pelvic floor muscles entirely when urinating and just let it flow.

Nutritional Supplement Recommendations:
1. Nettle and dandelion tea is very helpful in improving bladder and kidney function. 3 - 4 cups daily.

TOOTHACHE

A toothache anytime is anything but pleasant. There are several natural remedies that may be used for a toothache.

A visit to the dentist is appropriate to identify the cause of the toothache. It may be that a build-up of plaque and bacteria have caused inflammation around a particular tooth. A thorough cleaning with a six-month follow-up can help prevent many problems. X-rays should be evaluated for the place they fit into your personal family's healthcare routine. We, Parkers, once eschewed all dental x-rays, then we allowed them when we felt they were necessary for diagnosis. Now, we have settled upon a schedule that suits our own family's dental needs. Each family must weigh the risks versus benefits for themselves. Our own family friend, and dentist, Jeffrey McCarty, DDS, of Weatherford, Texas, says "Dental x-rays confer no more radiation than living atop a mountain in Colorado." I always replied, "Well, we don't choose to live atop a mountain in Colorado, either." After re-evaluating our own dental health combined with other lifestyle choices, we've decided to allow x-rays to be done on a schedule that doesn't make me worry a great deal about the x-ray exposure.

Lifestyle/Dietary Recommendations:

2. Regular brushing (at least twice daily) and flossing (at least once daily) is essential for dental care. Our family does not use fluoride toothpaste because of our concern about the toxicity of fluoride. The book, *Fluoride: The Aging Factor* by John Yiamianis, 6439 Taggert Road, Delaware, OH 43015, is an excellent resource on fluoride as well as *The Fluoride Report: The Truth in H$_2$O Foundation*, PO Box 219, Buckeyestown, MD 21717-0219 or 301-874-2948. We use herbal toothpaste instead. Just as an aside, the natural flouride toothpaste in the health food store is still flouride, so if your family chooses to avoid flouride, be aware of this fact.

3. A diet of whole, natural foods promotes health in all the body's structures. Dried fruits should be limited in the amounts eaten due to their high natural sugar content and stickiness. If we do eat them, we brush our teeth immediately afterwards.

4. A warm cloth over the facial area in pain may be helpful and soothing.

Nutritional Supplement Recommendations:

1. Dip a cotton swab into a mixture of: Essential oil of Clove - 15-20 drops, Olive Oil Extra Virgin - 1 teaspoon, Brandy - 1 teaspoon. Rub the saturated cotton swab on tooth and surrounding gum every 2 hours. Do not overuse. Clove extract has shown the ability to suppress plaque formation, specifically active against streptococcus mutans, a major cause of dental carey (cavity) formation.[292]

2. Echinacea, Myrrh, and Yarrow help stimulate the immune system and fight inflammation. Christopher Hobbs in his book, *Echinacea: The Immune Herb!*, recommends applying drops of tincture right on the tooth every 15 minutes until pain is relieved.

3. Sedative herbs such as valerian, skullcap and chamomile may be used for short periods to relieve toothache pain. 1 teaspoon of herbal tinctract combination, Peace Treaty from Mother's Choice,™ every 2 to 3 hours.

4. For those having dental surgery, bromelain has been shown to reduce swelling by 7.5% one day after surgery at a dosage of 240mg daily. The study was done on patients with impacted or dislocated lower wisdom teeth.[293]

5. Vitamin B6 and zinc supplementation may lead to a reduction in dental caries (cavities), even in those who consume a diet that leads to caries.[294]

TOXOPLASMOSIS

Toxoplasmosis is a protozoal infection caused by the intracellular parasite *Toxoplasma gondii*.[295] Trophozoites in the acute stage pass to the tissue to form cysts which remain viable, and oocysts are passed in cat feces.[296] This disease is transmitted to humans via raw or poorly cooked meat, as well as cat or bird feces. One third of the population has antibodies to toxoplasmosis. Symptoms may manifest as a mononucleosis-type illness: fatigue and malaise; muscle pain; and swollen lymph nodes. However, most cases are sub-clinical or asymptomatic.

This infection crosses the placenta resulting, if contracted by baby, in first trimester miscarriages or malformation of the baby. If contracted later in pregnancy, problems such as prematurity, central nervous system defects, anencephalus, hydrocephalus and destructive changes in the eyes or brain may be seen.

Virology testing is available to check antibody status although it is not performed routinely. Kitty may be tested by the vet. Many adult cats will have previously contracted the disease, thus will no longer be at risk.

Lifestyle/Dietary Recommendations:

1. Avoid cleaning cat litter boxes or working in dirt where cat feces may be present.
2. Cook all meats thoroughly before consuming. Microwaving and stir-frying do not destroy toxoplasmosis.
3. Wash hands thoroughly after touching raw meat or wear gloves when handling raw meat and wash gloves with soap and hot water.
4. Do not buy kitten or bird during pregnancy.

Nutritional Supplement Recommendations:

1. Echinacea - 500 - 1,000mg every 2 hours if infection is suspected.
2. Garlic - 2 to 3 cloves daily or their supplemental equivalent.
3. Bayberry - 1/2 teaspoon of tincture or tinctract twice daily or 500mg of powdered herb twice daily. Exceeding these dosages may result in an upset of the sodium/potassium ratio of the body.

URINARY TRACT INFECTION

The most common urinary tract infection is called cystitis, which is an infection of the bladder. We women are much more likely to have UTIs than men. This may be for a variety of reasons, some of them being:

1) Our urethra is closer to the anus than men;
2) Sexual relations (intercourse) can deposit bacteria near the urethra;
3) Improper wiping after pottying;
4) Using feminine hygiene sprays, douches and bubble baths - these irritate the normal cleansing process of our bodies;
5) Wearing synthetic-material panties when plain (or pretty), breathable cotton is best;
6) Not drinking enough to supply the urinary tract with a constant supply of urine to flush it out.

Lifestyle/Dietary Recommendations:
1. Wipe from front to back after bowel movements.
2. Urinate after sexual relations, and practice good hygiene (washing up) afterwards.
3. Avoid feminine hygiene sprays, douches (not to be used during pregnancy except under direction of caregiver), and bubble baths.
4. Wear loose clothing and cotton underwear.
5. Drink 2 quarts pure water daily. Add lemon for increased urine acidity. Urinate often. Do not "hold" urine while finishing a task — urinate then come back to finish the task.
6. If urinary symptoms persist with a negative urinalysis - suspect yeast (See Vaginal Infection).
7. If dad is having symptoms too, suggest he follow supplement guidelines.

Nutritional Supplement Recommendations:
1. Cranberry juice concentrate capsules - 1 three times daily with 8 ounces of purified water.[297] [298]
2. Buffered vitamin C or Ester-C — 500 - 1,000mg every 4 hours until infection has cleared. Maintenance - 1,000 - 1,500mg daily.
3. Uva ursi, grindelia, pipsissewa, and couchgrass are all herbs that research has shown to be beneficial to the urinary system especially in the treatment of cystitis.[299] Uva ursi should not be used in large amounts during pregnancy due to its uterine stimulant properties.

Vaginal Infections

The most common vaginal infections are: yeast (*Candida albicans*), *Trichomonas vaginalis*, and *Bacteriosis vaginosis* (often caused by *Gardnerella*). As always, prevention is the best course of action. I will list the lifestyle and dietary recommendations first, then I will list each infection separately along with the specific supplement recommendations.

Lifestyle/Dietary Recommendations:
1. Wear cotton underpants.
2. Eliminate or decrease sugar and refined carbohydrate consumption.
3. Use perfume/dye-FREE toilet paper and laundry detergent.
4. Use no feminine hygiene products such as sprays, powders, etc. Daily bathing is sufficient.
5. Clean hands and body before and after intimate relations with husband (this implies relations only with husband - chastity is necessary for the avoidance of some vaginal infections, which are sexually-transmitted).
6. Eat one cup of plain yogurt with live cultures daily.
7. Eat plenty of garlic and make sure the mainstay of the diet is complex carbohydrates and fiber from vegetables, fruits and legumes.

Yeast or *Candida Albicans*:

Symptoms include genital itching, dryness and inflammation, discharge is heavy, thick, white cottage-cheese-like clumps smelling "yeasty." Antibiotic therapy is a common cause.

Nutritional Supplement Recommendations:
1. Microwave underpants.[300]
2. Place pure acidophilus capsules high in the vagina at bedtime. Be careful not to push capsule(s) into the opening of the cervix.
3. An acidophilus powder or cranberry concentrate powder (1 tablespoon to 1 quart of water) as a douche may be helpful. Douching during pregnancy is a definite risk to mom and baby. Douching should only be done during pregnancy under the care and instruction of a professional health care provider.
4. Mom may peel clove of garlic (without damaging clove or it will be very irritating (burning) to vaginal tissue) and insert into vagina for overnight stay. Anytime mom inserts anything into her vagina, she should be careful not to push it (capsule or clove) into cervix.

5. Take 1/2 teaspoon acidophilus powder with 1/2 teaspoon Inner Strength™ (EN). Combine with warm water and drink 4 to 6 times daily during infection to resupply body with "friendly" bacteria.

6. Swab tea tree oil mixture around vagina using gauze soaked in: 1 cup water with 3 drops of tea tree oil or use a tea tree oil suppository once daily for 7 to 10 days.[301] Some women may experience a burning sensation vaginally with intravaginal use of tea tree. Proceed with caution. Do not use un-diluted tea tree oil. This will burn and cause tissue swelling. Experience speaking. Ouch!

7. Echinacea may be taken orally. Initial dose: 1,000mg or 2 mg tincture/tinctract; then 500-1,000mg every 2 to 3 hours for 2 days; then three time daily for 3 days; finally twice daily for 5 more days.

8. Pau D'Arco - 500 - 1,000mg twice daily for 2 to 3 weeks. Caution in pregnancy.

9. Grapefruit seed extract - 130 mg twice daily with plenty of water. This option as well as #8 are short term therapies - 2 - 3 weeks maximum.[302]

10. A product by Nutrition Now called Yeast Defense was very helpful for me during a pregnancy in which I had to take antibiotics for a terrible sinus infection. I used 2 capsules of Yeast Defense plus one tablet of Garlic every 3 hours plus 1 tablet of pure Grapefruit Seed Extract 3-4 times daily. Continued therapy for at least 10-14 days. Yeast infection totally resolved.

Trichomonas vaginalis:

Symptoms include: itching and inflammation of vulva and vagina and a prurient greenish-yellow discharge that is slimy or foamy. Anal sexual contact is a major cause of "Trich" because Trich normally resides in the rectum. Trich may only be passed through sexual contact. Men may harbor the organism in their penis without symptoms. It is imperative that both mom and dad be treated. Since trich cannot live in an acidic environment, the goal is to acidify the vagina.

Nutritional Supplement Recommendations:

1. For dad: 1 to 2 teaspoons Goldenseal/Myrrh tincture or tinctract three times daily for 10 days plus use a Pau D'Arco sitz bath to wash dad's penis: Make a strong infusion of Pau D'Arco (Taheebo or Lapacho). Soak penis 15 minutes twice daily. Instructions for making infusion: Steep 1/2 ounce of Pau D'Arco in 2 cups of water for 20 minutes.

2. Mom can take 2 tablespoons of apple cider vinegar or lemon juice in water twice daily plus 5,000mg vitamin C.

3. A douche of: 2 tablespoons white vinegar and 1 tablespoon activated charcoal powder to 1 quart of water may be used daily for 1 week, then every other day for the following week and then twice weekly for 2 more weeks.

4. Garlic cloves (as described for yeast) may be used every 3 hours for 3 days, then once a day for overnight for 4 more days. The third week, garlic suppositories or capsules may be used every other day then twice in the fourth week.[303]

5. In one study Pau D'Arco (lapacho) extract was applied in the vagina using gauze soaked in the extract. A fresh-soaked gauze was renewed every 24 hours. The treatment was highly effective.[304]

6. A lactobacillus vaccine called Solcotrichovac was used in a study of 444 women which yielded a 92.5% cure rate after one vaccination of the inactivated microorganisms.[305]

7. Bee propolis extract has been shown to have lethal effects on Trich in vitro.[306]

Bacteriosis vaginosis (Gardnerella)

Symptoms may include: itchy, inflamed vagina with a white or yellowish, thin, highly odorous (fish odor) discharge that may be blood streaked; frequent, painful urination, cramps or lower back pain may also be present. Dad needs treatment too.

Nutritional Supplement Recommendations:

1. Echinacea - 1,000mg four times daily or 1/2 teaspoon Echinacea tincture or tinctract.

2. An echinacea infusion (1 ounce to 2 cups boiling water, steep 10 hours) may be used for douching - 3 tablespoons infusion to 1 quart water. Douche daily for 7 days. May also douche with Bayberry bark. Douching during pregnancy is a risk for mom and baby. Douching during pregnancy should only be done under the care and direction of a professional health care provider.

As We Acquire Wisdom... and Gray Hairs

ALZHEIMER'S/MEMORY LOSS

Alzheimer's disease is characterized by progressive mental deterioration, loss of memory and cognitive function, and an inability to carry out daily activities. Although Alzheimer's may occur at any age, it most often appears after the age of 50. Currently, the only way to definitively diagnose Alzheimer's is by post mortem biopsy of the brain. Primary treatment is prevention. Several causative factors have been identified:

- A curious and persistent association between Alzheimer's disease and Down's syndrome;
- High body aluminum and silicon levels;
- Serum vitamin B12 levels are significantly lower in patients with Alzheimer's disease;
- Degeneration of the central nervous system may be secondary to decreased blood and oxygen supply to the brain;
- Increasing cholinergic neurotransmission may offer some benefit to patients already showing some signs of dementia.

Dietary/Lifestyle Recommendations:
1. Have fingerprint pattern analyzed by an expert as Alzheimer's patients tend to have an increased number of ulnar loops (loop pointing toward the ulnar bone, away from the thumb) on all ten fingertips and radial loops (loops pointing toward the thumb) that shift away from the index and middle fingers, where they most commonly occur, to the ring and little fingers. If your fingerprint pattern is characteristic of Alzheimer's disease, initiate an aggressive preventive approach immediately.
2. Avoid exposure to aluminum and silicon.
3. Correct any underlying thyroid abnormality.
4. Maintain adequate blood and oxygen flow to the brain.

Nutritional Supplement Recommendations:
1. Take supplements containing antioxidants such as carotenes, flavonoids, vitamins C and E, zinc and selenium.
2. Add ginkgo biloba extract (containing 24% ginkgo heterosides) at a dosage of 40mg three times daily to supplement regimen. Ginkgo is known to increase blood flow and prevent many aging diseases.

ATHEROSCHLEROSIS

Atheroschlerosis is a degenerative condition of the arteries, primarily characterized with a build-up of lipids (cholesterol bound to proteins and cholesterol eshers) within the artery. The disease is usually silent. Even young children can have arterial plaque accumulation. The condition is diagnosed when insufficient blood flow and blood clot formation bring on a health-threatening condition. A diagnostic sign that commonly occurs in those with atherosclerosis is the presence of a diagonal crease on the earlobe.[307] Prevention is the key with sound, whole foods intake and a lifestyle free of smoking and ingestion of the standard American diet.

Dietary/Lifestyle Recommendations:
1. Reduce serum cholesterol levels by consuming a wide variety of whole foods, concentrating on a vegetable- and fruit-rich diet.
2. Get regular physical exercise.
3. Cease cigarette smoking.
4. Limit coffee consumption to less than 6 cups daily. Tea consumption does not appear to be a problem.
5. Eliminate alcohol consumption as this leads to an increase in serum cholesterol triglycerides and uric acid levels, as well as blood pressure.
6. Increase dietary fiber intake, especially the gel-forming or mucilaginous fibers (flax seed, oat bran, pectin, etc), cold-pressed oils and fish.
7. Ginger, garlic and onions should be used liberally in foods.
8. Limit refined sugar consumption.

Nutritional Supplement Recommendations:
1. Begin supplement program with a high-quality multi-vitamin and mineral daily supplement.
2. Make certain that vitamin C intake equals at least 2,000mg daily.
3. Vitamin E intake should at least be 200 IU daily.
4. A fiber supplement of psyllium seed, guar gum or other water soluble fiber should be taken in quantities of 5,000mg (5 grams) daily.
5. Flaxseed oil, 1-2 tablespoons daily.
6. Omega EPA oils, 5-10g daily.
7. Carnitine has been shown to effective therapeutically in the treatment of atherosclerotic heart disease. Heart function depends on an adequate carnitine supply. Carnitine also increases HDL levels, while decreasing triglyceride and cholesterol levels.[308] 900mg daily.

8. Bromelain, the proteolytic enzyme found in pineapples, has been shown to inhibit platelet aggregation, improve angina pain, reduce blood pressure and break down atherosclertic plaques. Take 300 - 500mg three times daily at least 30 minutes before meals.

9. To improve the structure, function and integrity of the arteries, mesoglycan may be used supplementally, 100mg daily.[309]

10. Ginkgo biloba capsules may be taken twice daily in the morning and again 30 minutes before bedtime to improve blood flow.

ARTHRITIS

Arthritis has three major forms: osteoarthritis, rheumatoid arthritis and gout. We will address the first two types in this section.

Osteoarthritis is degenerative joint disease and the most common form of arthritis. Many elderly people suffer from this malady. The disease occurs when the collagen matrix (support structure) of the cartilage is damaged resulting in the release of enzymes that destroy structural components. As we age, our ability to restore and manufacture normal cartilage decreases, and our activity of repair enzymes is reduced, making the joints prone to damage. Morning joint stiffness is often the first symptom. With disease progression, pain occurs when the affected joint is in motion, worsened by prolonged physical activity and relieved by rest.

Rheumatoid Arthritis (RA) is a chronic inflammatory condition that affects the entire body, but especially the synovial membranes of the joints. RA is an autoimmune disease, meaning the body's immune system is attacking the body's own tissue. Involved joints typically are the hands and feet, wrists, ankles and knees. The onset may be gradual with fatigue, low-grade fever, weakness, joint stiffness and vague joint pain preceding the appearance of painful, swollen joints by many weeks. Involved joints will be quite warm, tender and swollen, and the skin will take on a ruddy purplish hue. Joint deformities may result in the hands and feet.

Both types of arthritis are generally treated allopathically by nonsteroidal antiinflammatory drugs (NSAIDS). Toxicity is quite likely with the high doses necessary to therapeutically treat. Tinnitus (ringing in the ears) and gastric irritation are often the earliest manifestations of NSAID toxicity.

Dietary/Lifestyle Recommendations:
1. Focus on a plant-food diet, while limiting animal foods. Plant foods contain those very important anti-oxidants, which protect against cellular damage, including damage to our joints.
2. Eliminate cigarette smoking.
3. Don't ingest fried foods.
4. Follow the whole foods diet discussed in *The Naturally Healthy Pregnancy*.
5. Eat plenty of flavonoid-rich fruit such as any of the berries.
6. Consume plenty of sulfur-containing vegetables: legumes, garlic, onions, brussel sprouts and cabbage.
7. Eliminate the nightshade family of vegetables: potatoes, tomatoes, eggplants, peppers and tobacco.
8. Eliminate any food allergens.

9. Add juicing of vegetables to the daily whole foods regime.
10. Consume cold-water fish (deep sea fish) such as mackerel, herring, sardines and salmon. Fish oil (EPA supplements) may be an alternative for those who do not eat fish. 1.8 grams of the supplement daily.

Nutritional Supplement Recommendations:
1. Provide the body system with a high-potency multi-vitamin and mineral formula daily.
2. Add antioxidants such as vitamin C and pycnogenols.
3. Glucosamine sulfate, 500mg three times daily.
4. Omega-3 EPA oils, 1.8 grams daily.
5. Bromelain, an excellent antiinflammatory enzyme from pineapples, at a dosage of 400 to 500mg three times daily taken 30 minutes before meals. The most beneficial range of activity of bromelain is from supplements providing between 1,800 to 2,000 m.c.u. activity (milk clotting units).
6. Tumeric (curcuma longa) has an active component, curcumin, that functions as a powerful, safe antiinflammatory. Curcumin has direct antiinflammatory effects as well as enhances the body's own antiinflammatory mechanisms including potentiating cortisone. The standard dosage is 400mg curcumin three times daily. Bromelain and curcumin function very well as a pair.
7. Boswellia serrata contains boswellic acids that demonstrate anti-arthritic effects in various animals. Treatment is long term at 400mg three times daily. No side effects are reported.
8. Feverfew is also used to treat arthritis as well as reducing the number and severity of migraine headaches. 1-2 grams taken three times daily for rheumatoid arthritis of the dried leaves or infusion, 1-2ml of the fluid extract three times daily or 250-500mg three times daily of the powdered solid extract.
9. Licorice root is one of the most extensively investigated botanical medicines. Licorice exerts both a direct and indirect (stimulating body's own mechanisms) effect on the health of the adrenal glands. Three times daily dosages are: powered root - 1-2 grams per day; fluid extract - 4-6ml; solid (dry powered) extract: 250-500mg.
10. Capsaicin, the active component of cayenne pepper, may be applied topically to stimulate and then block small-diameter pain fibers by depleting them of the neurotransmitter substance P. Commercial ointments containing 0.025% or 0.075% capsaicin are available over-the-counter.

Sources: *Natural Alternatives to Over-the-Counter and Prescription Drugs*, Michael T. Murray, N.D. Prima Publishing, Rocklin, CA: 1994 and 1995 Gaia Symposium Proceedings Book, "Clinical Applications of Botanical Medicine."

LUPUS

Lupus, most often referring to systemic lupus erythematosus, a condition that affects many body systems, including the skin, joints and kidney. Lupus is an auto-immune disorder in which the body's immune system attacks connective tissue. Lupus may become life-threatening when the kidneys become involved.

Dietary and Lifestyle Recommendations:
1. Consume a whole foods diet.
2. Avoid animal products with the exception of cold-water (deep sea) fish: salmon, mackerel, herring, halibut, sardines.
3. Identify and eliminate food allergens.
4. Eliminate alcohol, refined sugar and caffeine.
5. Exercise regularly.
6. Drink at least 48 ounces of purified water daily.

Nutritional Supplement Recommendations:
1. High-potency multi-vitamin and mineral supplement.
2. Vitamin C, 500 to 1,000mg three times daily.
3. Vitamin E, 400 to 800 IU daily.
4. Flaxseed oil, 1-2 tablespoons daily or equivalent in capsules. Keep refrigerated to avoid rancidity.
5. Pancreatin (8-10x), 350 - 700mg three times daily between meals.
6. Adrenal cortex extract, start at one-third the dosage on the bottle increasing the amount every two days until a stimulatory effect is noticed.

Source: *Encyclopedia of Nutritional Supplements*, Michael T. Murray, N.D. Prima Publishing, Rocklin, CA, 1996.

MENOPAUSE

Menopause is commonly referred to as "the change" women go through as they pass from their childbearing years to the years of being an "older woman who teaches the younger women." We are finding more and more that it is those habits we employ in our early years of womanhood that cause us to be able to embrace this change in a healthful fashion or have to persevere through a fiery trial. The osteoporosis risk increase after menopause are thought to be caused by a lack of estrogen; however, new evidence is coming to light that shows that it is the amount a girl child's bones are properly calcified prior to the onset of menses that protects her from osteoporosis later in life. Another increased risk factor of difficult menopausal years is not properly taking care of oneself during the childbearing years. Women who choose not to let pregnancy slow them down at all and bounce back into normal activity within days of giving birth appear to be more likely to suffer the ill effects of menopausal symptoms.

There are natural alternatives to hormonal replacement therapy as prescribed by allopathic and osteopathic physicians. In my opinion, trying the natural alternatives is preferable to going straight to pharmaceuticals due to the fact that HRT carries its own risks and side effects. I've seen women begin HRT only to have their blood pressure increase, so they take another med, then their thyroid goes haywire hence another med, and so on and so forth until they are a walking pharmaceutical carrying case.

Dietary and Lifestyle Recommendations:
1. Mothers, begin now to give daughters calcium supplements each day prior to the onset of their menses.
2. Take care of yourself during the childbearing years. Slow down and enjoy the babe in the womb and rejoice in those first few weeks of cuddling your new blessing. All the other activities will still be there later.
3. As the menopausal years begin, exercise regularly, consume the whole foods diet with an emphasis on soy products, fennel, celery, parsley, nuts and seeds which contain natural estrogen precursors as well as protect against breast cancer.

Nutritional Supplement Recommendations:
1. Take a flax oil supplement daily - 1-2 tablespoons or the equivalent in capsules. Keep refrigerated to avoid rancidity.
2. Take a phytoestrogen-rich herb formula such as Femtrol (Enzymatic Therapy), Change-O-Life (Nature's Way), FemChange (Nature's Herbs) or Men-O-Pause (Liquid Light).
3. For hot flashes, the specific herbal helps are: angelica or dong quai (Angelica sinensis), licorice root (Glycyrrhiza glabra), chaste berry (Vitex agnus-castus) and

black cohosh (Cimicifuga racemosa). The above formulas should contain these herbs and may be taken at a dosage of 2 capsules three times daily.

4. If additional help is needed, gamma-oryzanol (ferulic acid), a growth-promoting substance found in grains and isolated from rice bran oil, may be taken at a dosage of 300mg daily. Gamma-oryzanol also helps to lower blood cholesterol and triglyceride levels.

5. Calcium should be supplemented at 1200mg daily with magnesium at 600mg daily.

6. Vitamin C at 2-3 grams daily and Vitamin E at 800 IU daily with meals.

Sources: *Dr. Whitaker's Guide to Natural Healing* by Julian Whitaker, M.D. Prima Publishing: Rocklin, CA, 1995 and *Herbal Prescriptions for Better Health* by Donald J. Brown, N.D., Prima Publishing: Rocklin, CA, 1996.

MULTIPLE SCLEROSIS

Multiple sclerosis is a syndrome of progressive nervous system disturbances occurring early in life. There are still many questions about the progression and cause of MS. The proposed causative factors include viruses, autoimmune factors and diet.

Dietary and Lifestyle Recommendations:
1. Eat the whole foods diet, concentrating primarily on a vegetarian diet with the exception of cold-water (deep sea) fish: salmon, herring, halibut, mackerel, etc.
2. Avoid any food allergens. Test for any suspected.
3. Eliminate processed foods, alcohol, refined sugar and caffeine.
4. Exercise regularly.
5. Drink at least 48 ounces of purified water daily.

Nutritional Supplement Recommendations:
1. Take a high-potency multi-vitamin and mineral supplement daily.
2. Add vitamin C, 500 to 1,000mg daily.
3. Add Vitamin E, 400 to 800 IU daily.
4. Flaxseed oil, providing essential fatty acids, 1 or 2 tablespoons daily or equivalent in capsule form. Keep refrigerated to avoid rancidity.
5. Methylcobalamin (active vitamin B12), 1,000mcg twice daily.
6. Pancreatin (8-10x), 350-700mg three times daily between meals.
7. Ginkgo biloba extract (24% ginkgo flavonglycoside), 40 - 80 mg three times daily.

Source: *Encyclopedia of Nutritional Supplements*, Michael T. Murray, N.D., Prima Publishing, Rocklin, CA, 1996.

Part Six

THE
HEALTH
DEPOT

Resources for Food and Products

Food Cooperatives

This list was compiled by Vickilynn Haycraft, published in the Spring 1997 issue of *An Encouraging Word* magazine published by Nick and Cathy White of Idabel, Oklahoma (see address in magazine section). Vickilynn's article actually contains much more useful information about food cooperatives. We are simply giving the sources here.

AZURE STANDARD
79709 Dufer Valley Rd.
Dufer, OR 97021
541-467-2230

BLOOMING PRAIRIE WAREHOUSE
2340 Heinz Rd
Iowa City, IA 52240
800-323-2131

BLOOMING PRAIRIE NATURAL FOODS
510 Kasota Ave SE
Minneapolis, MN 55414
800-322-8234 (in MN)
800-328-8241 (outside MN)

COUNTRY LIFE NATURAL FOODS
PO Box 489
Pullman, MI 49450
616-236-5011

FEDERATION OF OHIO RIVER COOPERATIVES (FORC)
320 Outervelt St., Suite E
Columbus, OH 43213
614-861-2446

FRONTIER COOPERATIVE HERBS
3021 78th St
PO Box 299
Norway, IA 52318
800-669-3275

HUDSON VALLEY FEDERATION OF FOOD CO-OPS
6 Noxton Rd
Poughkeepsie, NY 12603
914-473-5400

MOUNTAIN PEOPLES WAREHOUSE
12745 Earhart Avenue
Auburn, CA 95602
800-679-6733

MOUNTAIN PEOPLE'S NORTHWEST
4005 Sicth Ave. South
Seattle, WA 98108
800-462-0211 (in WA)
800-336-8872 (outside WA)

NORTH FARM COOPERATIVE
204 Regas Rd
Madison, WI 53714
800-236-5880

NORTHEAST COOPERATIVES
PO Box 8188, Quinn Rd
Brattleboro, VT 05304
802-257-5856

OZARK CO-OPERATIVE WAREHOUSE
Box 1528
Fayettville, AR 72702
501-521-4920 (2667)

SOMETHING BETTER NATURAL FOODS
614 Capitol Ave NE
Battle Creek, MI 49017
616-965-1199

TUCSON COOPERATIVE WAREHOUSE
350 South Toole Ave
Tuscon, AZ 85701
602-884-9951

WHEAT MONTANA FARMS, INC.
10778 Hwy 287
Three Forks, MT 59752-0647
(406) 285-3614

WALTON FEED
135 North 10th (PO Box 307)
Montpelier, ID 83254
800-847-0465 or 208-847-0465

For other cooperatives, you may send a self-addressed stamped envelope to Co-op Directory Services, ATTN: Kris Olsen, 919 21st Ave. S, Minneapolis, MN 55404. No phone calls, please. They have a free packet of information that you will find most useful, sayeth Vickilynn.

ORGANIC PRODUCE SUPPLIERS

Finding organic produce suppliers is a little more difficult than finding whole foods cooperatives warehouses. Some co-operative warehouses offer organic produce as well as bulk foods and supplements. State agricultural agencies are usually good resources for finding organic farmers within one's state. One option may be contacting your local health food store and asking if your co-op could order organic produce through them at a reduced cost for volume sales. While this may not be welcomed, it doesn't hurt to ask.

COMMUNITY ALLIANCE WITH FAMILY FARMERS
PO Box 363
Davis, CA 95617
916-756-8518 or 800-852-3832 for ordering, www.caff.org
Publishes a directory, *The National Organic Directory*, selling for $44.95 + shipping & handling. This directory lists farms, wholesalers, farm suppliers, resource groups, organic standards per state, support businesses and a commodities sold and bought index per state. 386 pp.

NATIONAL INSTITUTE FOR SCIENCE, LAW AND PUBLIC POLICY
Publishes Healthy *Harvest III, A Directory of Sustainable Agriculture Organizations* that lists organic growing associations, food distributors, journals of organic farming, seed sales, training programs and so forth in the U.S. and abroad. May be purchased for $10.95 (plus $1 postage) from
Potomac Valley Press
1424 16th St., NW, #105
Washington, D.C. 20036

MAIL-ORDER HEALTHY
LIVING SUPPLIERS

There are several different mail-order businesses that supply tools, supplements, kitchen equipment, whole grains, etc. The following list is by no means comprehensive. These are just the suppliers that I personally know or have purchased from in the past few years. Just because a business is listed here does not imply a Naturally Healthy™ endorsement. Educated consumers must decide for themselves whom they can support with their dollars.

The Healthy Baby Supply Company
Department D
323 W Morton Dr
St Paul, MN 55107
612-225-8535
Company supplies cloth diapers, herbs for mom and baby, organic baby food, healthcare books and products.

Herbs from God's Garden
103 New Braintree Rd W
Brookfield, MA 01581
508-867-6214
Organically grown and wild-crafted herbs.

Joyful Living Distributors
1601 Kelly Rd
Aledo, TX 76086
817-441-7074 or e-mail 102554.3643@compuserve.com
Kristy Bell and husband, Bill, have a large selection of kitchen equipment, long-storage grains, books, and food and nutritional supplement supplies.

Mother's Choice™
11358 Tyler Ft Rd
Nevada City, CA 95959
800-HERB-KID or 888-HERB-MOM
Mary Bennett and husband, Lyle, produce liquid herbal TincTractTMs that are sold direct to moms at wholesale cost when they order in sufficient bulk quantities ($25 minimum order) to encourage mothers to stock their herbal medicine cabinet.

Self-Care Catalog
104 Challenger Dr
Portland, TN 37148-1716
800-345-3371 or e-mail SlfCare@aol.com
A catalog with a large number of home health tools.

Spirit-Led Childbirth
PO Box 1225
Oakhurst, CA 93644
209-683-2678 or 888-683-2678
Leslie Parrish provides a good selection of birth and parenting supplies as well as natural health care books and supplements.

Urban Homemaker
PO Box 440967
Aurora, CO 80044
1-800-55-BREAD or 303-750-7230 for inquiries
Marilyn Moll and husband, Duane, have a full catalog of products, including the Liquid Light™ herbal TincTracts,™ that assist families in healthy living. Marilyn also publishes a magazine called *The Homemaker's Forum.*

Nutritional Supplement Companies

The companies listed sell primarily to health food stores or professional providers. Some sell directly to consumers. These are noted with an asterisk (*).

American Health
15 Dexter Plaza
Pearl River, NY 10965
(800) 445-7137

Maker of Super Papaya digestive enzymes as well as other products.

bio/chem Research
865 Parallel Dr.
Lakeport, CA 95453
(800) 225-4345

Producers of Citricidal, a grapefruit seed extract antimicrobial.

Biotec Foods
2639 S. King St. #206
Honolulu, HI 96826
(800) 331-5888

High-potency, enteric-coated antioxidant enzyme formulas to include superoxide dismutase and glutathione peroxidase.

Blessed Herbs
109 Barre Plains Rd.
Oakham, MA 01068
(800) 489-HERB

Company providing herb tinctures, bulk herbs, oils, salves, tea bags, soaps, shampoos and books.

Cardiovascular Research/
Ecological Formulas
106 "B" Shary Circle
Concord, CA 94518
(800) 888-4585
510-827-2636 (in CA)

Advanced nutritional medicine line specializing in immune support, yeast problems and allergies.

Eclectic Institute, Inc.
11231 S.E. Market St.
Portland, OR 97216
(800) 332-HERB

Maker of Opti-Natal prenatal vitamins as well as other multiple vitamin and mineral formulas specifically designed for certain health conditions. Only source I know of that carries the freeze-dried herbal products such as nettles that has received so much research attention in the past few years.

*The Pure Body Institute
423 East Ojai Ave. #107
Ojai, CA 92303
(800) 952-PURE

Makers of the best internal cleansing program I've tried. It is gentle yet very effective. "Nature's Pure Body Program" is my personal choice for pre-pregnancy detoxification.

Enzymatic Therapy
825 Challenger Dr.
Green Bay, WI 54311
(800) 648-8211

Top-quality line of nutritional products. Michael Murray, N.D. is on their Scientific Advisory Board, which tells me this company is committed to excellence. ET has been the first to provide U.S. consumers with nutritional supplements common on the European market because of their research-proven benefits.

*Frontier Cooperative Herbs
Box 299
Norway, IA 52318

Full-line of bulk herbs. Now expanding their encapsulated product line.

Kal Healthway Vitamins
P.O. Box 4023
Woodland Hills, CA 91365
(818) 340-3035

Nutritional product company that has been around for a long time. Many times available through food co-ops.

McZand Herbal, Inc.
P.O. Box 5312
Santa Monica, CA 90405
(310) 822-0500

A limited line of herb supplements primarily designed for immune and respiratory support.

Metagenics, Inc./Ethical Nutrients
971 Calle Negocio
San Clemente, CA 92672
(800) 692-9400

Quality and excellence are found in this company's products that are sold under the brand of Metagenics for practitioners, Ethical Nutrients for health food stores. I especially like their line of Intestinal Care products. They have the only milk thistle extract tablets standardized to contain 80% silymarin that I have been able to find.

Miracle Exclusives, Inc.
P.O. Box 349
Locust Valley, NY 11560
(800) 645-6360

Floradix liquid vitamin and herb supplements are made by this company including Floradix Liquid Iron mentioned in the section on anemia.

*Mother's Choice™
11358 Tyler Foote Rd
Nevada City, CA 95959
1-888-HERB-MOM, toll-free

Excellent liquid line of herbal TincTracts™ sold directly to mother's at wholesale cost. Sister line of the Liquid Light™ herbs. Carries my midwife formulas.

Natren
3105 Willow Lane
Westlake Village, CA 91361
(800) 992-3323
(800) 992-9292 (CA)

Maker of probiotics such as "Life Start" containing *Bifidobacterium infantis* and "Bio Nate," an improved strain of *acidophilus.*

Nature's Apothecary
997 Dixon Road
Boulder, CO 80302
(303) 581-0288

Source of herbal products.

Nature's Sunshine Products, Inc.
P. O. Box 1000
Spanish Fork, UT 84660

A line of products sold through distributors in a multi-level organization.

Nature's Herbs
P.O. Box 335
Orem, UT 84059
(800) HERBALS

Owned by Twinlab, a company producing excellent herbal products certified both for potency and organic.

Nature's Way
10 Mountain Spring Pkwy.
Springville, UT 84663
(800) 9-NATURE

Superior quality nutritional and herbal products easily found in the health food store and in many food co-ops.

NF Formulas, Inc.
805 S.E. Sherman
Portland, OR 97214
(800) 547-4891

A full line of naturopathic products including my favorite prenatal supplement, Prenatal Forte. Their Echinacea products are some of the best. Professional only.

Phyto-Pharmica
  (see Enzymatic Therapy)

Progressive Labs/ *Kordial Products
1701 W. Walnut Hill Lane
Irving, TX
(800) 527-9512

Extensive line of dietary supplements certain to please both health practitioners and consumers due to their commitment to excellence in product and customer service.

Rainbow Light Nutritional Systems
207 McPherson St.
Santa Cruz, CA 95060
(800) 635-1233

Maker of a quality line of supplements to include one of my favorite menstrual cycle regulators, Fem-a-Gen.

Schiff Products
180 Moonachie Ave.
Moonachie, NJ 07074
(800) 526-6251

Full line of products available in many health food stores.

Standard Process Laboratories
12209 Locksley Lane, Ste. 15
Auburn, CA 95603
(800) 662-9134
(916) 888-1974 (in CA)

Extensive line of naturopathic formulas sold only to chiropractors and naturopaths. Some midwives may be able to distribute them.

Traditional Medicinals
4515 Ross Road
Sebastopol, CA 95472

A quality line of herbal teas sold for specific health conditions such as "Pregnancy Tea" and "Mother's Milk."

Tri-Light, brand name Liquid Light™
11358 Tyler Foote Road
Nevada City, CA 95959
(800) HERB-KID

My personal favorite for liquid herbs. This company uses a unique multi-staged process that captures the optimum benefits from the herbs while preserving enzymes and preventing oxidation. Children love the flavor (glycerine is naturally sweet) and adults like the potency. No alcohol, no sugar, in squeeze bottles - standard glycerites, these are not. Yes, they do process my Midwife Formulas, and no, I do not receive any financial gain from their sales. Lyle and Mary are kind, generous Believers concerned with family health.

Twin Labs
2120 Smithtown Ave.
Ronkonkoma, NY 11779
(800) 645-5626

A complete line of nutritional supplements commonly found in health food stores and food co-ops.

UAS Laboratories
9201 Penn Ave. S., #10
Minneapolis, MN 55431
(800) 422-DDS-1

Maker of the DDS Acidophilus, a high-potency strain.

Magazines and Journals:

Herbalgram
American Botanical Council
P.O. Box 201660
Austin, TX 78720
(512) 331-8868

Published quarterly by the American Botanical Council and the Herb P.O. Box 201660 Research Foundation. Subscriptions: $25/yr. This is THE best source for up-to-date research news, legal and regulatory information regarding nutritional supplements and the ABC mail-order bookstore offerings include basic herbals as well as more scientific works for the professional herbalists (or consumers desiring to truly educate themselves for family herbal care). No home considering botanical medicine should be without this journal.

Herb Research Foundation
10007 Pearl St., Ste. 200
Boulder, CO 80302

*Membership to HRF is $35/yr and includes a subscription to *Herbalgram*. Both ABC and HRF are non-profit educational organizations and need our support to continue their very valuable work. HRF members also receive the *Herb Research News* quarterly edited by Rob McCaleb, HRF President.
**For a small increased member donation, the Herb Research Foundation will also include a subscription to *Herbs For Health*, my very favorite herb magazine!

Protocol Journal of Botanical Medicine
Herbal Research Publications
12B Lancaster County Road
Harvard, MA 01451

A peer-reviewed publication offering current and thoroughly referenced material for use in both clinical and educational settings. Each issue offers therapeutic protocols with descriptions of contra-indications, underlying chemistry and pharmacology and complete citations from research from around the world. Subscriptions: $96/yr. Quarterly.

Quarterly Newsletter of The American Herb Association
P.O. Box 1673
Nevada City, CA 95959

This 20-page newsletter is always packed with an array of information from case studies and research news to book reviews my personal favorite section. AHA is an association of medical herbalists; however because of AHA's commitment to promoting the use, understanding and acceptance of herbs, anyone interested in herbs will benefit from regular reading of the *Newsletter*. Subscriptions: $20/yr. Quarterly.

Digest of Alternative Medicine
P.O. Box 2049
Sequim, WA 98382
(360) 385-0699 (FAX)

An offshoot of the *Townsend Letter for Doctors* that is designed for use by patients. Write for subscription information.

Townsend Letter for Doctors
Townsend Letter Group
911 Tyler Street
Port Townsend, WA 98368
(360) 385-6021

This 150+ page journal is written for and by health care providers. Published 10 times per year at $49 subscription price, it is an incredible value to those interested in the technical, scientific side of nutritional healing. Many naturopathic researchers publish their findings in this journal.

Books:

Botanical Medicine

The ABC Herbal by Steven Horne. Wendell Whitman Co., 302 E. Winona Avenue, Warsaw, IN 46580. 1992. 82 pp. $7.95.

A quick afternoon read that will give parents the very basics of herbal care with an obvious leaning to Thomsonian practice. The aspect I like best about this book is the guidelines for using the Tri-Light Liquid Light TincTracts (the formulas mentioned in the book are those that Tri-Light processes).

The Alternative Health & Medicine Encyclopedia by James E. Marti.

The Encyclopedia is basically a guide to alternative therapies. The botanical and nutritional medicine information is good; however, there are therapies I personally have a caution about using.

Botanical Influences on Illness: A Sourcebook of Clinical Research by Melvin R. Werbach, M.D. and Michael T. Murray, N.D.

This book is not a guide as to what to use or how to use it; rather, it is more an annotated bibliography that most herbalists will find most helpful when called upon to cite scientific safety and efficacy documentation for clients.

The Clinician's Handbook of Natural Healing by Gary Null, Ph.D.

An enormous resource book for research studies regarding nutritional supplements and their effects upon health. This books make for an excellent tool for those wishing to fully research the medicinal aspects of foods and medicines.

The Complete Botanical Prescriber by John A. Sherman, N.D.

A wonderful book for those who counsel others in use of herbs or for those consumers who wish to be highly informed. The price is a little steep at $59.95, but well worth it for professionals.

The Complete German Commission E Monographs: Therapeutic Guide to Herbal Medicines, edited by Blumenthal, Busse, Goldberg, Gruenwal, Hall, Klein, Riggins & Rister.

No other book will be as important to the budding herbalist's bookshelf as this one. Although the cost (around $200) may seem prohibitive, complete safety guidelines for herbal medicine that are recognized around the world make this one well worth the money.

Encyclopedia of Natural Medicine by Michael Murray, N.D. and Joseph Pizzorno, N.D.

Dr. Murray and Dr. Pizzorno, authors of The Textbook of Naturopathic Medicine which is the definitive text for naturopathic physicians, have written this book as a comprehensive guide for consumers detailing how to use herbs, vitamins, minerals as well as diet and other nutritional supplements. The book employs an easy-to-use style which lists health conditions followed by natural treatments for said conditions.

Foundations of Health: The Liver & Digestive Herbal by Christopher Hobbs. Botanica Press, P.O. Box 742, Capitola CA. 1992. 321 pp. $12.95

Most of us might skip this book thinking we do not have a problem with our livers. How much we would miss if we did. The longer I practice herbal health care with an emphasis on pregnancy and childbirth, I find the liver to be an organ not to be ignored if one seeks a healthy pregnancy. Mr. Hobbs does an excellent job of explaining liver and digestive function, and his recommendations for keeping our liver happy and healthy are superb.

The Green Pharmacy by James Duke, Ph.D.

This book is a treasure chest full of wisdom in using herbs medicinally. Dr. Duke is one of the leading experts in using plants for medicine. This book combines his down-home style with specific guidelines as to which herbs are best used to treat specific illnesses. I've enjoyed this book greatly!

Gynecology and Naturopathic Medicine, A Treatment Manual by Tori Hudson, N.D.

An excellent "treatment manual" is what I would call this spiral-bound book. All practitioners who combine botanical medicine with women's health care will want this one in their library. Consumers who want to participate more in their preventive health plan than simply doing what someone else recommends without knowing why will also benefit from the reading of this book.

The Healing Herbs by Michael Castleman.

This book is a wonderful introduction to the "scientific" side of herbal medicine. Castleman lists the historical usage of herbs, herbal healing information based on scientific research, safety concerns for specific herbs where appropriate as well as herb-growing guidelines. The only thing I do not agree with in this book is the advice to not give herbal medicines to children under 2 years of age or older people over 65 or pregnant women. My own family has chosen to inform ourselves of the risks versus benefit of both herbal medicine and modern pharmaceuticals and choose herbal medicine (wise and prudent use) the majority of the time.

The Healing Power of Echinacea & Goldenseal by Paul Bergner.
For those wishing to keep echinacea and goldenseal as mainstays in their herbal medicine cabinet, this book is a worthy one to give some very explicit education and direction regarding usage and safety concerns.

The Healing Power of Herbs by Michael T. Murray, N.D.
The subtitle of this book is "The Enlightened Person's Guide To The Wonders Of Medicinal Plants." Dr. Murray does not mean mystically enlightened; rather, this title appropriately refers to the scientific enlightenment that occurs when we begin to dip into the great body of research regarding botanical medicines. After reading this book, which is so well documented, one will know botanical medicine yields results that not only compete with modern pharmaceuticals, but actually outperform them in many instances.

Herbs for Health and Healing by Kathi Keville, Director of the American Herb Association.
Easy to read. Plenty of make your own formulas. Kathi is an authority in the professional herbalist field, and it shows in her book.

Herbal Prescriptions for Better Health by Donald J. Brown, N.D.
Currently one of my favorite herbals. Excellent scientific documentation along with well-researched toxicity information. A very readable writing style makes this book one of the most essential for families who are practicing herbal medicine at home.

Herbal Remedies for Women by Amanda McQuade Crawford, M.N.I.NM.H.
I really like the complete coverage of women's health issues in this book. If there is a woman of childbearing age, experiencing gynecological difficulties in the household, get this book.

Herbal Tonic Therapies by Daniel B. Mowrey, Ph.D.
Another great book due to the abundance of scientific citations for each herb discussed. The format follows herbal support for the body systems which does include a section on gynecological health which I have found particularly helpful.

Herbs of Choice by Varro Tyler, Ph.D., Sc.D.
Although Dr. Tyler and I would not agree on every point of what defines herbalism, I feel this book will serve as a bridge between the informed natural health community and the all-too-often misinformed medical community. This is not a "starter" book into

herbal healing unless one has a command of pharmaceutical terms and a good knowledge of biochemistry. Dr. Tyler does present meticulous documentation that makes further study a breeze.

Herbs That Heal by Michael A. Weiner, Ph.D. and Janet Weiner.

This book is extremely user-friendly. A number of herbs are presented complete with their history, recent scientific findings, preparation instructions and some caution information. Since the material is not foot- or end-noted, further study proves difficult for those of us who want to see the source.

Natural Alternatives to Over-the-Counter and Prescription Drugs by Michael T. Murray, N.D.

This book is my favorite book to recommend to those who are new to botanical medicine. Dr. Murray provides excellent information about drugs commonly used for the health complaints he addresses in the book, and then he follows this with excellent lifestyle/dietary and nutritional supplement recommendations. Must have this book when practicing herbal medicine.

Natural Prescriptions by Robert M. Giller, M.D. and Kathy Matthews.

I found this book to be more about vitamins, minerals and other nutritional supplements than about botanical medicine; however, I have included it in this section because I liked the background information given on each health condition. Health problems are listed alphabetically with treatment options in a shaded box at the end of each section.

The Natural Pharmacy by Skye Lininger, D.C., Editor-in-Chief, Jonathan Wright, M.D., Steve Austin, N.D., Donald Brown, N.D., Alan Gaby, M.D.

An excellent sourcebook for specific illness recommendations, detailed information, including toxicity risk, of nutritional supplements.

No More Amoxicillin by Dr. Mary Ann Block.

How many physicians do you know who would endeavor to teach parents about how to avoid antibiotics by giving them clear and simple directions for natural healing methods? Dr. Block does. This book should be in the home of every parent with children, even if your children have not had to use antibiotics. We should understand how they function and how to avoid them.

No More Ritalin by Dr. Mary Ann Block.

The drug used to control America's children finally meets its match, Dr. Block, who gives parents a treatment approach to ADHD without drugs. This book is always my first recommendation to parents who call our Institute for Family Herbal Care looking for information on ADHD.

Nutrition:

Fertility, Cycles and Nutrition by Marilyn M. Shannon. The Couple-to-Couple League Int'l. Cincinnati, OH. 1992. 167 pp. $10.95.

Marilyn Shannon offers in this book the basics of nutrition coupled with specific nutritional recommendations to positively affect fertility. I especially like the tone of this book — favorable to large families, breastfeeding and natural family planning.

Food - Your Miracle Medicine by Jean Carper. HarperCollins Publishers, Inc., 10 E. 53rd St., New York, NY. 1993. 528 pp. $25.00.

This is my favorite and most-often reached for book on nutritional healing. The format listing disorders by body system and then alphabetically within that system is so easy to use. Even critics of "alternative medicine" cannot argue with research proving Grandma's chicken soup really is good for respiratory bugs.

Encyclopedia of Nutritional Supplements by Michael T. Murray, N.D.

Murray completely covers all nutritional supplements with information on how to obtain through diet and supplementation, correct dosages and toxicity information.

The Healing Power of Foods by Michael T. Murray, N.D. Prima Publishing, P.O. Box 1260BK, Rocklin, CA. 1993. 438 pp. $16.95.

Yes, I do have every one of this man's books, and the reason is I have found every single one of them to be a source of solid education on nutrition and herbs. This particular book educates one on the nutrient content of different foods as well as provides an ample section on health conditions that may be treated with food recommendations given.

What Every Pregnant Woman Should Know by Gail Sforza Brewer with Tom Brewer, M.D. Penguin Books, 375 Hudson St., New York, NY. 1985. 260 pp. $9.95.

This information contained in this book arms women with the nutritional guidelines that help to prevent the pregnancy complication, metabolic toxemia of late pregnancy. While I do believe protein is important to prevent MTLP, I believe that it is beneficial to obtain said protein from a variety of sources that excludes liver.

What the Bible Says About Healthy Living by Rex Russell, M.D.

I am so thankful for this book. Finally, a book on the biblical aspects of healthy living that gives guidelines for ideal eating without placing legalistic burdens upon us in our eating practices. Consequences of poor body stewardship are discussed according to medical findings to support biblical principles without placing our body's salvation upon our eating practices. A must have for the home library!

Pregnancy and Childbirth

A Good Birth, A Safe Birth by Diana Korte & Roberta Scaer.

This is a must read for a thorough understanding of the risks and benefits regarding the technology of birth especially for those planning a hospital birth. Those planning a home birth will also benefit from this information. Do not assume having a midwife will mean no intervention; be informed.

Birth After Cesarean. Bruce Flamm, M.D.

Extensive documentation of the safety of vaginal birth following a cesarean section. De-bunks the myth of "Once a cesarean, always a cesarean."

The Birth Book. William Sears, M.D. and Martha Sears, R.N.

This is a comforting and reassuring book about the natural-ness of childbirth. The Sears clearly and simply share with us the benefits of "low-tech, high-touch" birth. Options are discussed openly and honestly. Illustrations are some of the best I've seen of birth positions. My favorite quote from the book, "While you can't totally orchestrate the perfect birth—birth is full of surprises—you can create the conditions that increase your chances of having the birth you want."

Childbirth Without Fear. Grantly Dick-Read.

Helen Wessel Nickel has revised this edition of Mr. Dick-Read's classic on natural childbirth. An excellent book for the parent-to-be.

Emergency Childbirth. Gregory White.

A small, basic manual for those who are concerned about not making it to the hospital or their midwife not making it to the home for delivery. Step-by-step instructions are clear and easy to understand.

Heart and Hands. Elizabeth Davis.

A guide written for midwives, but useful for mothers planning home-birth, on caring for pregnant women.

The Joy of Natural Childbirth, A Revised Edition of Natural Childbirth and the Christian Family. Helen Wessel-Nickel.

Helen walks one through the beginning of pregnancy to the completion of a joy-filled birth in this book. An essential book to understand God's design for birth. Keep in mind that while His design is perfect, our fallen world may yield a not-quite-perfect birth. I suppose what I am trying to say is that although pain in childbirth may not be a curse from God, most women do experience some (or a great deal) pain during their childbirth experience. The perception of pain in daily life has an impact on the perception of pain during birth.

The Naturally Healthy Pregnancy by Shonda Parker, Professional Family Herbalist

How can I toot my own horn? I wrote the pregnancy book to meet the needs of mothers wishing to have a book entirely devoted to those herbs and foods that are wholesome and considered safe for pregnancy. The nice thing is that with over 70 illnesses discussed that any family member may encounter, the book can be used by all the family.

Under the Apple Tree. Helen Wessel Nickel.

Once again, Helen imparts to us her expansive knowledge of Christian parenting and birth. Her personal style of writing makes the book a very easy read.

Understanding Diagnostic Tests in the Childbearing Year. Anne Frye.

This new revised edition is Frye's best yet. While I do not practice midwifery, therefore I am not the book's target group, I do prefer to have my own information available at home to go over my lab results and aid in self-diagnosis where possible. I found this book to be the one most referred to during my childbearing years (my midwife kept calling me for the answers—she didn't own the book until I sold her one of her own).

Breastfeeding

Bestfeeding. Renfrew, Fisher and Arms.

A basic guide to breastfeeding. Accurate information and helpful pictures.

Breastfeeding and Natural Child Spacing. Sheila Kippley.

Discusses and details the "ecological" method of natural child spacing. The information is accurate and scientific on the natural amenorrhea imparted through breastfeeding which I believe is God's perfect design for a woman's healing and rest for baby's first year.

Keys to Breastfeeding. William and Martha Sears.

Practical advice for new and expectant moms on nutrition, dietary needs and advantages of breastfeeding.

The Womanly Art of Breastfeeding. La Leche League International.

Don't throw out the baby with the bath water. While I may disagree with much of the childrearing information promoted through La Leche League, this organization should be recognized for being highly instrumental in a resurgence in breastfeeding in this country. Their breastfeeding support is invaluable for many women. I was told to call La Leche League when I had my first child prematurely. I did not. I now wish I had as he was bottle-fed, developed allergies and chronic ear infections until I finally got him off formula and cow's milk.

Marriage and Family

Titles by Patrick L. Hurd: *Separation of Church and Family; Sexual Purity; Covenant Succession: Transferring Godly Convictions to our Children; The High Calling of Covenantal Fatherhood; Training Godly Rulers: Apprenticing in Statecraft; Solidarity vs. Separatism: In Search of Effectual Alliances; Our Heritage of Citizenship; The Effectual Kingdom Family.*

Reforming Marriage by Douglas Wilson.

This is a wonderful book on marriage. I've never seen a clearer presentation of the Christ-Bride/Husband-Wife relationship.

The Fruit of Her Hands by Nancy Wilson.
     This is an excellent book for women on "our part" in the marriage relationship.

Other family titles by Douglas Wilson: *Her Hand in Marriage, Standing on the Promises.*

Family Planning
All the Way Home by Mary Pride

The Art of Natural Family Planning. John and Sheila Kippley.

The Bible and Birth Control. Charles D. Provan.

A Full Quiver: Family Planning and the Lordship of Christ. Rick and Jan Hess.

Letting God Plan Your Family. Samuel A. Owen, Jr.

Children: Blessing or Burden (Exploding Myth of the Small Family). Max Heine.

Grand Illusions: The Legacy of Planned Parenthood. George Grant.

The Way Home by Mary Pride

Child Training
     I recommend the books below knowing that they offer practical suggestions to loving our children by training our children; however, I want to add that whatever training we do, we need to realize that the sin nature of our children cannot be trained out. Our children can learn to obey, but they will disobey (sin) because of their flesh's cry for willfulness. Do not be discouraged! God is at work in all of us. Let us be diligent in our daily training and be not angry when they fail.

The Heart of Anger by Lou Priolo.
     This bok is an excellent resource to teach parents how to not provoke their children to wrath.

The Mother at Home by John S.C. Abbott.
     While this book is on child training, the book really centers more on mothers disciplining themselves to be a good example unto their children. I loved this book. Buy it!

Seminars by Jonathan Lindvall.
     My church family has benefited from the shared wisdom of this man's experience with child training and suggestions for protecting our children.

Shepherding a Child's Heart by Ted Tripp.

This book gets to the heart of the disobedience matter. A good book to provide some insight for our children into the "why" of their behavior.

Hints on Child Training. H.C. Trumbull.

A classic written over a hundred years earlier, this book still hits right on target. The truth of: discipline-only promoting wrath, love-only promoting self-adoration is clear as Trumbull promotes a loving discipline method of child training.

To Train Up a Child. Michael and Debi Pearl.

The Pearl's have written a concise book on building family ties and gentle use of the rod for training. I do not particularly promote the early toilet training exampled in this book (I think it's parent-training; if parents want to be trained this way, fine). This book offers very practical "remedies" to rebellious behavior.

Part Seven

STRUCTURAL INTEGRITY

BREAD, THE STAFF OF LIFE

B read. We all have eaten bread or have at least eaten a poor nutritional substitute that calls itself bread. White flour bread was the last item to go as my family moved to more nutritious meals. This was due in large part to me because I was unwilling to eat bitter 100% whole wheat bread found in grocery stores everywhere. I did not realize how very wonderful "good" bread could taste until I tasted a homemade loaf made by someone who grinds her own grains right before baking.

At last, I was a convert, but the question remained, "How could I inexpensively eat this delicious bread every day?" My friend answered with "You need to buy a mill to grind your grains and a bread machine to properly mix and knead the dough." Another question from me "That sounds great, but how am I, woman of few cooking or baking skills going to be able to make these light and fluffy loaves of bread, those mouth-watering cinnamon rolls, that yummy pizza dough, those dinner rolls, breadsticks, burger buns, AAAAHHHH?"

I still am a woman of few cooking and baking skills, but I have learned the keys to baking good bread. Before we enter into the technique area, I think it would be prudent to answer the question of "Why should I bake my own bread?" The answer is so simple. It is the healthiest choice.

Whole grains are touted today as a preventive for a number of diseases (See Figure 1) as well as an excellent source of vitamins, minerals, and protein. Grains have a protective outer coating called bran that prevents the grain from spoiling or "going rancid." I will address the grain, wheat, since it is the most popular grain used for bread. The wheat kernel is a gold mine of nutrients. Once the wheat kernel is cracked or ground, the bran no longer is able to protect the grain from spoilage. The flour will begin to lose nutrients immediately after milling. In only seventy-two hours, flour that has been milled from whole grains will be rancid, and most of the nutrients will be gone. Rancid flour contains free radicals that have been shown to cause numerous health problems including cancer. The bran is extracted during the white flour refining process thus causing a loss of the following percentages of nutrients originally in whole wheat flour: 86% of the niacin, 73% of the pyridoxine, 50% of the pantothenic acid, 42% of the riboflavin, 33% of the thiamine, and 19% of the protein. We all have read about the health benefits of fiber, which the bran supplies.

Constipation	Gallstones and Kidney Stones
Colon Cancer	High cholesterol levels
Irritable Bowel Syndrome	Diverticulitis
Hemorrhoids and Varicose Veins	Obesity
Diabetes	Ulcers

Figure 1: Diseases Related to Low Fiber Intake.

Another part of the wheat kernel is the endosperm, the inner part of the kernel. The endosperm is primarily made up of starch and is the source for white flour. The endosperm contains the following percentages of nutrients: 43% of the pantothenic acid, 32% of the riboflavin, 12% of the niacin, 6% of the pyridoxine, 3% of the thiamine, and 70 - 75% of the protein. While the endosperm still contains a large amount of protein, alone (as in the case of white flour), it is very deficient in the B vitamins as well as severely lacking in fiber.

The other portion of the wheat kernel is the germ or embryo. This is what causes the wheat to sprout and grow into a plant. Wheat germ contains essential oils, which cause whole-wheat flour to go rancid if not used within a few days. The germ is extracted from white flour because of the difficulty in preserving the flour's quality. The bitter taste in 100% whole-wheat flour and bread purchased in food stores results from the wheat germ spoiling or turning rancid. The nutrients lost when milling out the wheat germ are: 64% of the thiamine, 26% of the riboflavin, 21% of the pyridoxine, 7% of the pantothenic acid, 2% of the niacin, and 8% of the protein.

Obviously, bread made from white flour is an inferior product (I would not even call it food) that can cause health problems from lack of fiber and lack of those incredible B vitamins. We also need to recognize that bread made from flour that was milled seventy-two hours or more ago lacks healthful qualities. This 100% whole wheat bread *had* all the healthy nutrients, but the flour sat too long before being made into bread, which allowed the nutrients to oxidize and the oils to turn rancid. One would think bread that is frozen in health food stores would be an acceptable alternative; however, the vitamin E is lost when flour or bread is refrigerated or frozen. The other reason this is not a good alternative is because of the difficulty in ascertaining when the flour used to bake the bread was milled.

How do we make certain we are eating quality bread? Grind our own grain and bake immediately. If the Lord has not provided the means at present to purchase a mill and bread machine, the other healthy alternatives are to: buy bread from someone who mills the grains fresh before baking (typical cost $2.50 or more per loaf; this is a more expensive alternative in the long run); at least purchase a home grinding mill and bake bread by hand (if baking by hand proves difficult, baking quick breads with the fresh flour or making pancakes and such is an option); or purchase freshly ground flour from someone and bake or cook with it at home.

What is the approximate cost of baking loaves of bread at home using one's own mill and bread machine? The initial cost of a quality mill and bread machine is substantial (around $200 and $400 respectively); however, savings are realized in a variety of ways. There will no longer be a need to purchase expensive cereals, fiber supplements, and a reduced likelihood of having to visit the doctor for hemorrhoids or high cholesterol among other things. The cost per loaf of bread when baking at home is in the range of $ 0.25 - 0.65 (depending on wheat prices and bulk-buying capabilities). When families consume one or more loaves per day (as we should), the initial investment of the equipment soon yields healthy returns.

Once we have purchased our home baking equipment, how do we bake bread the family will appreciate? The key to successful bread baking is quality wheat for grinding into flour. I have struggled in years past with poor bread results. Finally, I was able to get some of this year's crop of Prairie Gold Hard Spring Wheat. The difference in my dough and the resulting bread was amazing. I followed the same process I always have, yet my dough turned out shiny, smooth, stretchy and easy to work with. The bread fluffed up beautifully instead of being dense and crumbly. The reason the Montana Prairie Gold Spring Wheat results in good bread is that it is very high in protein (17 - 19%). Canadian Red Wheat is also high in protein with the Hard Red Winter Wheat being the lowest of the three in protein content. Growing seasons affect the wheat as well. The 1993 wheat crop did not produce light, fluffy loaves of bread because of all the flooding in the wheat-growing regions. Ask suppliers which years' crops they have available. If wheat has a few weevils in it, do not worry. They are not bad for the health. I am not recommending eating weevils - you can freeze the wheat and kill the few weevils. A weevil infestation is not good, though, because many weevils in wheat will bore holes in the grain and cause it to grow rancid.

So, we have our equipment and our high-quality wheat, now we bake. The following recipe is for the Bosch Universal Bread Mixer. Those with the Magic Mill Classic should decrease the amount of water to only 5 cups and decrease the amounts of the other ingredients by a small amount.

6 cups of warm water (110 F)
- 2/3 cup of oil - applesauce may be substituted for half or all this amount for low-fat bread
- 2/3 cup honey - pear juice may be used for diabetics or 1/3 honey, 1/3 cup black-strapmolasses for added iron content of bread
- 2 T sea salt

Pour the above ingredients into the mixer bowl. Then add:
- 5 cups freshly, ground flour
- 2 tablespoons of yeast (SAF yeast is the best; after opening vacuum-sealed package, store in sealed container in the refrigerator)
- 2 tablespoons of dough enhancer
- For added nutrition, extra lecithin may be added or blended sesame seeds for extra calcium.

Begin adding more flour slowly. Recipes usually call for 1/3 more flour than needed for machines so that the dough can be worked by hand. Do not measure flour. Wait until it begins to pull away from the sides (it does not have to stay away) and let it knead for 6 minutes. If more flour is added after kneading is begun, the gluten bonds that have already formed will be broken resulting in crumbly bread.

After dough is kneaded, pour and spread a palm-full of oil onto kitchen counter, then dump dough onto oiled surface. Cross dough over itself a couple of times to strengthen the fiber by crossing grains.

Bread pans may be sprayed with cooking sprays, or oiled with a mixture of 1/2 liquid lecithin/1/2 oil, as a healthier alternative. Smaller loaf pans produce the lightest loaves.

Pinch off a section of dough (1.5 lbs for medium-sized loaf pans; .14 oz. for small pans). Leave top nicely rounded and place in pan. Do not try to reshape the loaf in the pan. This will cause the loaf to lose its smooth, rounded top. Let the dough rise in the pan until it has doubled in size.

Place dough in a cold oven. Turn oven on to 350 F. This gives dough an extra lift. After bread is nice and golden brown, take out of oven. Butter may be rubbed on top to make the loaf look professional. Sesame seeds, rolled oats, cracked grains or poppy seeds can be sprinkled on the loaf after rubbing the butter on to give it a "fancy" look.

For cinnamon rolls: Pinch off amount of dough for one loaf, roll out on counter as for pie crust. Rub butter on dough then sprinkle cinnamon. Be careful to get cinnamon on all edges of dough. Sprinkle Sucanat™ or spoon applesauce or honey for sweetening. Roll dough away from body until it is in a roll. Place a length of dental floss under dough roll and cross over at top to cut the cinnamon rolls. Place in pan, let rise and bake at 325 F.

For a yummy topping, place 1 egg white in Bosch mixer. Whip into meringue. Add a little honey and a little butter (oil in bowl will not work). Dollop on top of cinnamon rolls.

For pizza: Roll out dough (approximately 1/2 loaf worth of dough) until thin. Cook 8 minutes at 425 F on pizza stone. For thick crust, let it rise a little before pre-baking. Add ingredients such as pasta sauce or mix 1 can tomato paste, 1 can water with 1 tablespoon of pizza sauce mix with Italian seasoning for pizza sauce. Cover sauce with toppings of choice and cheese. Bake at 425 F until cheese melts.

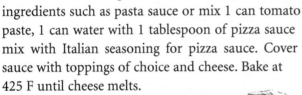

Troubleshooting dough/bread problems:

Problem	Possible Cause
Dough doesn't rise well	Overkneading, adding flour too slowly; Adding too much flour; Putting in 200 F oven to rise - kills yeast; Using hot water for ingredients - kills yeast
Bread sinks in middle	Too long rising time - if dough more than doubles, punch down, reshape and let rise again
Sticky, sticky dough	Adding too little flour
Dry, crumbly bread	Adding too much flour; Using poor-quality wheat
Bread hard as a rock or hockey puck	Using an auto-bakery - if yeast works well, bread rises to the top then falls

LIVING WATER

Water is the primary constituent of our body; over 60% of our body weight is water. Water makes up our body fluids, which fill and bathe our cells; and it washes waste products from our body. Water nourishes all of our body processes. Without it, we would perish.

Such a vital source of nutrition should be a pure source. The sad fact is, today, water that nourishes and promotes health is harder to find than one would think. An increasing number of reports from government agencies and private organizations point to our water supply as a major factor in disease: gastrointestinal illnesses, lead poisoning, even certain types of cancer. Most of us rely on government agencies such as the Environmental Protection Agency (EPA) to protect us from any contaminants or dangerous chemicals in our water. Our personal responsibility is to provide healthful food and drink to our families. What are the current dangers in our nation's waters, and can we really count on municipal water systems for safe water?

What Can Water Do To Us?

Today, a tall glass of tap water from most cities' water supply is equivalent to drinking a chemically loaded cocktail. A U.S. News and World Report article in 1991 (July 29) began with these startling facts: 1 out of 6 people drink water with excessive amounts of lead; in the early summer, 1/2 the rivers and streams in America's Corn Belt are laced with unhealthy levels of pesticides; microbes in tap water may be responsible for 1 in 3 cases of gastrointestinal illness; and most alarming, chlorine used widely to disinfect water supplies combines with other substances in water to form known carcinogens.310 While our water supply does not pose the same overt threat of disease as in developing and war-torn countries in other parts of our world, our nation's drinking water has been labeled by the EPA as one of the top four environmental threats to health. The threat to our health is subtle. Many times we are not aware that it is our water causing our health problems.

Chlorine

Chlorine was first added to our drinking water in the 1900s to control the spread of typhoid, cholera and other water-borne diseases. It was not until almost 20 years ago that chlorine was identified as a potential health hazard. Chlorine, the same active ingredient in household bleach bottles, reacts with organic material (decaying plant matter) to form trihalomethanes (THMs). Chloroform is an example of a THM. Trihalomethanes are carcinogenic compounds as shown in laboratory tests. Two other by-products of water, DCA and TCA, are even more potent carcinogens. There are more chlorine by-products formed that have not been studied at all.

Chlorine's carcinogenic factor has finally begun to gain much-needed attention in the scientific community. A study at the National Cancer Institute involving 3000 people revealed that drinking chlorinated water may double a person's risk of bladder cancer.[311] Drinking chlorinated water is definitely a health risk. Bathing or showering in chlorinated water increases one's risk of disease as well. In fact, during a bath or shower, our skin absorbs many contaminants. This is even worse in a hot shower during which the contaminants are heated. These harmful vapors released into the enclosed shower space thus are inhaled into the body posing a threat to all body systems, particularly the delicate mucous membrane of our respiratory system. Some authorities believe skin absorption and respiratory inhalation may prove more harmful than drinking the same water.

Other forms of city water disinfection that are currently being "tried out" scare some chemists. Frank Scully, chemist at Virginia's Old Dominion University, says these alternative forms of disinfection are "frightening." Scientists know less about these forms than they know about chlorine. What will be tomorrow's headline?

Nitrates

Just when those of us with our own private water wells were breathing a collective sigh of relief that *we* were not having to drink that terrible city water...Well water can be just as dangerous to our health. Nitrates are commonly used to "cure" bacon, hot dogs, luncheon and deli meats, sausage, etc. Cooking these products causing the nitrates to transform into nitrosamines which are potent cancer-causing chemicals. Our well water may contain nitrates as well, and it doesn't have to be cooked for the nitrates to transform into nitrosamines. Our mouth, stomach and bladder perform this transformation too efficiently.

Tests by the EPA in 1992 found that 1,130 community water-system wells and 254,000 rural domestic wells had nitrate levels that exceeded the agency's proposed health advisory levels.[312] The maximum levels allowed by the EPA typically are higher than that most of us would be comfortable with if we knew the health risks of contaminants. Nitrates get into groundwater or aquifers from animal manure on farms and feedlots, sewage systems as well as from nitrates in agricultural and lawn fertilizers. Nitrate contamination in water has been associated with "blue baby syndrome" which causes babies to suffocate when nitrate is converted into a substance that keeps red blood cells from absorbing oxygen. The prudent homeowner drinking well water would be well-served by having the water tested for nitrate contamination at a reliable laboratory.

Radon

"Radon is a colorless, odorless, tasteless gas that occurs naturally in the ground, particularly in the Northeast and the Southwest; under some circumstances it can enter the drinking water. Radon must be removed during treatment. If not, when the water is heated in cooking or agitated in a shower or washing machine, the gas vaporizes and becomes breathable. Inhaling radon increases the risk of lung cancer," says Jeanne Briskin, special assistant to the director of the Environmental Protection Agency Office of Drinking Water in Washington, D.C.[313] A risk of lung cancer is not the only cancer associated with radon-filled water. Studies in Maryland and Virginia suggest drinking radon-loaded water may double the risk of several soft-tissue cancers.

The EPA estimates that as many as 17 million people may have excessive levels of radon in their water.[314] It has become fairly commonplace in "at-risk" regions for officials to recommend testing for radon gas that can seep through cracks in basements or home foundations, but warnings of the more-likely danger of water contamination are missing. The EPA waited until June 1991 to propose radon limits in drinking water, and water suppliers had until 1996 to comply with the new limits. Regulations on lead in the water supply have been delayed even more.

Lead

Lead is a toxic metal associated with neurological and developmental problems in children. Lead ingestion during pregnancy is also associated with premature birth, slow mental and nervous system development and shorter stature.[315] Even in minute quantities, lead can cause lowered intellectual abilities. With all this information disseminated widely, we still have 1 in 6 children under the age of 6 with elevated levels of lead in their bloodstream.

Water treatment facilities are generally lead-free. Lead contamination comes from: service lines piping the water into homes that are often made of lead; solder used in home plumbing often contains lead and brass fixtures containing lead in kitchens and bathrooms leach the lead into running water. "Soft" (low mineral content) water corrodes pipes thus allowing lead into the home's water supply. Contamination with lead is a problem. We also face a threat to our health through the mass addition of flouride to our municipal water supplies.

Flouride

Flouride is added to our water supplies because of well-meaning folks who believe that the addition of flouride to our diet and application to our teeth strengthens our teeth and prevents decay. This is far from the complete truth. Flouridation of of water supplies began in the 1960s even after research by Dentist Donald J. Galagan, published in the *Journal of the American Dental Association* in 1943, showed that dental fluorosis (mottling of the teeth) increased and became more severe as the fluoride concentration in the water increased. This study showed no decrease in the number of decayed, missing or filled teeth per child.

Flouride is toxic in large doses, a large dose being a tube of toothpaste. Ever wonder why the dentist tells us not to eat our toothpaste or swallow the gel during fluoride treatments? Severe reactions, even death, has occurred in some children using fluoride in some form who had an unknown allergy to fluoride. Other health risks associated with fluoridation include loss of collagen causing premature aging, chromosome damage, disruption in enzyme production, arthritis and allergies. A book that offers more detail about the health risks of fluoride is *Fluoride: The Aging Factor* by John Yiamiannis. Even if we manage to avoid all of the chemical contaminants in our water, we have to contend with the little beastly microbes.

Microbial Contamination

Microorganisms from human and animal waste still pose a health threat to us, even with chlorinated treatment systems. Many microbes *can* be killed by chlorine treatment; however, there are some microorganisms that defy the toxic chlorine bath to live on and infect the public. Giardia, a single-celled animal (protozoan), can survive some chlorine treatment and infect humans causing symptoms such as diarrrhea, nausea, vomiting and cramps that may last for months. Other protozoans that may contaminate our water supply making us ill are *Entamoeba histolytica, Shigella,* and *Blastocystis hominis.* One doctor speculates that nearrly seven million people in the United States alone are infected. He estimates that in the New York area 25 percent of the population is infected. The amazing thing is that he estimates that 15 percent of these infected people have no symptoms, 25 percent have symptoms that can be ignored and 55 percent have a compromised quality of life and 5 percent are disabled.[316]

Many times the public is not made aware of the danger of microbial contamination because of the anxiety and public outcry this might cause. I recall an instance several years ago in Louisiana where we in the city of Shreveport were told that tests confirmed that a high number of microbes were in the water but "The public does not need to be concerned about their health. This level should not cause any problems." Perhaps every member of the city did not need to be concerned, but it certainly concerned those of us who were making very frequent bathroom visits.

Toxic Leaks

Perhaps the most frightening aspect of contamination is the possibility of hazardous wastes seeping or leaking into our water supply. A 1987 review of the 1,000 top priority "Superfund" sites (the nation's worst hazardous-waste dumps) showed 4 out of 5 sites were leaking their poisonous mixture into the ground water.[317] Our own lawn maintenance may be poisoning us as well. Residents of suburbs use up to two and one-half times more pesticide per acre than farmers do to keep their fields weed-free. Toxic water does increase one's risk of miscarriage, stillbirth, birth defects, cancer and other body system malfunctions. Now that we know what water can do to us, now we must find out...

What Does Water Do For Us?

Water is life unto our body as Jesus is life unto our spirit. Perhaps this is why He referred to himself as "the Living Water" in the Gospel of John, chapter 4. Our major body organs are like waste treatment facilities. The liver, kidneys, skin, respiratory system and bowels all work to filter out "toxins" from our body system. Water is the substance these organs are dependent on to filter or flush out unneeded or harmful materials which find their way into our body. Some of the most common health problems in our country may be partially or completely treated with this simple, yet precious liquid: constipation, bladder infections, kidney stones, arthritis, respiratory infections and obesity are just a few.

The minimum amount of water we should be consuming in one day is 8 - 10, 8 ounce glasses or 2 quarts. Most of us do not drink until we feel thirsty. This practice is not in the best interest of our health. As we become dehydrated (not the severe dehydration which may need to be medically treated), our hypothalamus sends out a message of thirst so we will drink to rehydrate our body. Unless we heed this message, our body will not function appropriately. Mothers of preborn children need a plentiful water intake to keep up with the increased blood volume of pregnancy. A decline in water intake equals a decline in blood volume which equals a decline in nourishment for mom's growing baby. A good rule of thumb would be to drink more water than we feel we need. Drink past the thirst stage.

Our daily water loss is equal to the minimum of two quarts we must ingest (for an average person weighing 130-155 lbs.). We eliminate 50 percent of our body's water through urine, 25 percent through our skin, 19 percent through our lungs (as water vapor in air) and 6 percent in feces.[318] One should not count the water in fruits and vegetables as part of the two quart minimum of drinking water daily. The extra water we naturally get in our "eating" foods constitute another quart that we need in our daily diet.

Pure Water

Pure water will not flow from our taps whether we are drinking water from a city municipal system, well water or mountain spring water. The responsibility for pure water does not belong with government legislators; we each are responsible to purify our own water supply. There are many treatment systems available. It is hard to decide which to use without first knowing what each form of treatment does to the water. I will provide a brief description of the common types of filtration.

Carbon filtration is an effective method of removing chlorine from water when the filter is new. This is the least expensive method of filtration; however, carbon filters are the least effective filtration method. Carbon filters trap debris, chlorine, bacteria, some parasites, most viruses and heavy minerals such as lead or mercury. This removes the unsightly appearance, odor and taste from the water. Carbon filters can collect bacteria and sediment, allow the bacteria to breed and allow it to be dumped back into the water. Hot water run through a carbon filter increases the risk of contaminant release. Carbon is not effective in removing inorganic minerals including flouride. Some carbon filters are "silver-impregnated." These filters using silver are very controversial due to their ineffectiveness and possible silver toxicity caused by their use. The major disadvantage of carbon filtration alone is its limited use and safety concerns. Even the widely used carbon-block filtration does not remove all lead (some carbon-block filters can do this), does not remove viruses from the water, only suceeds with arsenic reduction, not elimination and leaves in after filtration: salts, aluminum, flouride, nitrates, sulfates, phosphates, detergents, dead dirt and minerals. Minerals, while certainly essential for our health, are best absorbed in the body from plant form, not the inorganic minerals found in our water. The inorganic minerals found in water are the type most associated with excess build-up in body tissue causing disease conditions.

Distillation is a process of vaporizing water (heating the water until it becomes steam) in one chamber, then condensing it again in another chamber. Distilled water should be free of chlorine, fluoride, bacteria, parasites, chemicals, minerals and heavy metals. Many experts on water purification are concerned about the possibility of certain organic chemicals recondensing after vaporization into the second chamber's "pure" water. To prevent this from occurring, a pre-filter of solid carbon should be employed. Others have expressed concern over the possible biochemical effect of water that has been heated to 212 degrees Fahrenheit. One of the main disadvantages of distillation is the initial cost coupled with an ongoing cost for the electricity needed to operate the unit.

Reverse Osmosis is the filtration method most authorities recommend as the best method of purifying water. The reverse osmosis process uses water pressure from the tap. Water flows through special membranes with microporous holes the size of the water molecule. These very small holes allow the water molecule to pass through while rejecting the larger inorganic and organic materials. Reverse osmosis alone removes fluoride, bacteria, viruses, parasites, chemicals, minerals and heavy metals. Since it does not remove chlorine, most

RO (reverse osmosis) units also use carbon filtration to remove the chlorine. The best RO units use a pre-sediment filter, which allows particulate matter to settle and a post-filter made of carbon which removes the chlorine. This filtration system is virtually 100 percent pure. The main disadvantage to a reverse osmosis system is water waste. For every ten gallons of water passed through the unit, only one gallon of pure water is made.

Although bottled water is not a filtration method, I mention it because so many rely on bottled water as their "pure" water source. Buying bottled water can lead to a false sense of security. Some bottling companies may not process or purify their water beyond minimum standards. Other companies may use spring water, which can be good if the water is from a pure spring source high in the mountains where no humans or animals have ever lived or bad if the spring has been contaminated somehow. If bottled water is to be used, it should state the type of purification process employed and should preferably be a three-stage RO process.

Water purification is a must for us at this point in our society. The only negative is that the process of purification if successful removes even the minerals beneficial to us from our water. To prevent a lack or deficiency of minerals, we should consume mineral-rich foods and perhaps even supplement with a natural mineral supplement.

Deciding on the purifier that is right for our particular family is difficult. There are many to choose from. I have found that it is always best to begin with a water test to check for the types of contaminants in the water supply. After we know what we need to get rid of, the next step is to find the type of purifier that will best meet our needs. There is one company I recommend to those seeking water purification. The company will send water samples to an independent water testing laboratory to determine the client's individual purification needs. The name of this company is:

Fred's Essential Water and Air
1092 Shady Trail Ste. 102
Dallas TX 75220
(800) 964-4303

Fred Van Liew is an internationally recognized expert on water treatment systems. The advantages to purchasing through this company is Fred's commitment to providing top-quality water systems in a variety wide enough to meet the needs of families, businesses, even ranches and farms. Fred has 120 different filters and systems including shower and bath filters. Fred's Essential Water and Air also has air purification systems available. As stated before, this company will has water tested at an *independent* laboratory.

For independent water analysis, there are three laboratories that specialize in testing drinking water:

National Testing Laboratories
6151 Wilson Mills Rd
Cleveland, OH 44143
(800) 458-3330 (in Ohio, 216-449-2525)

WaterTest
33 South Commercial Street
Manchester, NH 03101
(800) 426-8378

Suburban Water Testing
4600 Kutztown Road
Temple, PA 19560
(800) 433-6595 (in Pennsylvania, 800-525-6464)

A LAND FLOWING WITH MILK...

Milk is a food that God promised to the children of Israel in the Promised Land.[319] Contrary to the philosophy that milk is only meant for infants, milk from cows, sheep or goats is definitely designed by our Creator as a food for children and adults (the only milk an infant needs is mother's breastmilk). Milk has a great number of positive qualities: naturally-occurring enzymes to aid its digestion, antibodies, and nutrients (vitamins and minerals). Milk also has received negative attention recently. We have read and heard a great deal of information about the health risks associated with milk consumption: heart disease, diabetes, ear infections, intestinal difficulties, even some types of cancer and allergies. This information is true. It is also true that milk is good for you. How do we sift through the propaganda to arrive at the truth?

First we go to the Truth, the Written Word of God. Milk directly from creatures God designed for human consumption (those listed in the Bible as food) is a healthful food. Milk as man has tried to improve it (homogenized, pasteurized, chemically-altered) has been linked to multiple health problems. For the sake of understanding the big difference between these types of milk, some helpful definitions follow:

- Raw milk is a term used to describe milk that has not been homogenized or pasteurized.
- Certified raw milk is milk from dairies that are regularly inspected and found to be clean and the cows free from disease.
- Homogenized milk is milk that has gone through the process of homogenization: The fat particles of the cream are broken up by straining the fat through tiny pores under immense pressure. The fat particles are changed from large to very tiny (one-millionth of a meter) so they stay suspended (distributed evenly) throughout the milk.
- Pasteurized milk has been heated (parboiled) to at least 145 F to supposedly kill bacterial contaminants and make it "safe" for us to drink.
- Genetically-engineered milk is a term scientists use to describe milk from cows injected with bST or rBGH (recombinant bovine growth hormone). This hormone is a genetically-engineered version of the naturally-occurring bovine growth hormone in cows. After the cows have been injected with rBGH, their milk production increases...so does the amount of mastitis infections the dairy herd experiences...so does the amount of antibiotic use necessary to treat the mastitis infections.
- IGF-1, insulin-like growth factor I, is a substance that mediates the effects of growth hormones. It is naturally present in bovine and human milk as well as human saliva. IGF-I is present in increased amounts in milk from cows treated with rBGH.

Most of us have been drinking milk from the supermarket or corner grocery, not fresh and raw from the local dairy, for most of our lives. I grew up on a farm. As a child, we had fresh milk from our milk cow (yes, her name was Bossy!). I can remember my fascination and longing to have "store-bought" milk. The lack of rich taste in this "store-bought" milk did not matter; I just wanted the kind from the store. My thinking was like most of the people who made that switch from fresh, raw milk to processed milk, "If the processed kind is being sold publicly and promoted as 'safe,' it must be the better choice." How wrong was this attitude! And how long this attitude is enduring!

Dairymen, grocers, legislators, neighbors and friends are not deliberately trying to deceive us when they tell us raw milk is dangerous. They do believe what they are saying, but is what they are saying really true?

Homogenization

Homogenization is a process employed primarily for aesthetic purposes. If milk were not homogenized, we would see the layer of milk fat, cream, at the top of our milk jugs. Many people used to the smooth appearance of milk might find the cream layer repugnant. The problem with homogenization is the studies by Doctors Oster, Zikakis, Ross as well as other investigators. These doctors' research implicates homogenization as a factor in coronary heart disease.

Oster, Zikakis and others found that plasmalogen (a substance or tissue essential to the integrity of outer cell membranes in the artery lining, as well as parts of the heart muscle) was depleted in the areas of the heart where a blockage had formed. In the areas where the arteries had hardened, XO (xanthine oxidase, an enzyme) had replaced the naturally occurring plasmologen. Dr. Kurt A. Oster postulates that angina (heart pains) may be caused by the interaction of xanthine oxidase and plasmalogen. This interaction occurs as xanthine oxidase enters the bloodstream and interacts with plasmalogen. Superoxide (toxic to cell membranes in the inner artery wall) is produced which allows xanthine oxidase to eat the arterial lining and attack the walls of the heart muscle.[320]

Since the body's natural response is to protect the plasmalogen tissue from damage is to produce scar tissue and calcifications, arteriosclerosis (hardening of the arteries) results. High blood pressure is also likely since a narrowed blood vessel makes the heart work harder to supply blood to the body systems. As the researchers began to search for dietary sources of XO, they discovered that the *only* dietary source of XO are dairy products. How could dairy products be the culprit since they have been consumed almost from the beginning of time and heart disease is a modern disease (becoming common in the 20th century)?

The major changes that took place in the dairy industry were pasteurization and homogenization. As Oster investigated the homogenization process further, he found that XO is attached to the fat globules of milk. Normal (raw milk) fat globules are too big to go through the gut wall and into the bloodstream. Homogenization alters the fat by changing it into tiny molecules that pass easily through the intestinal wall and into the bloodstream. As these tiny fat molecules now populate our bloodstream, so does XO.

Some have argued that XO cannot survive the digestive process. It might not, except that XO is protected by liposomes, which function as a taxi to carry XO into the bloodstream. Pasteurization kills some of the XO (up to 60%), but the milk producers add vitamin D3 to our milk, which activates that remaining XO into doing its number on our arterial walls. The male sex hormone, testosterone, also activates XO.

Dr. Oster did find that folic acid protects against the destructive effects of XO. This does not mean we should continue drinking homogenized milk. We have other factors to consider. Scientists have long been suspect of cow's milk as a causative factor in diabetes. Diabetes, like heart disease, is a modern disease. Diabetes is believed to be an autoimmune disease in which the body makes antibodies that attack its insulin-producing cells.

Since diabetes is common in countries where milk is popular, Canadian and Finnish researchers did studies to try to ascertain what initiates the rogue antibodies in diabetics. The research results point a finger to an immune reaction to proteins in cow's milk.[321] I think this could be entirely possible when dealing with homogenized, pasteurized milk since the molecular structure of raw milk is altered during processing resulting in missing proteins, micromolecules of fat being absorbed when they should not be. Until further research is done, it certainly behooves those of us at risk for diabetes (most all of us consuming a processed-food diet) to avoid processed milk.

Pasteurization

Pasteurization has been lauded as the best thing to happen to our food supply. We are told that pasteurization has little effect on the nutritional status of milk and rids milk of contaminants. Professor Fosgate of the Dairy Science Department of the University of Georgia refutes this, "If milk gets contaminated today, the chances are that it will be after pasteurization. Pasteurized milk and raw milk are equally susceptible to contamination by pathogenic bacteria…"[322] Actually, raw milk may be less susceptible to pathogenic bacteria than pasteurized milk because of its enzymes and antibodies. Pasteurization was begun due to literal filth in the milk industry. Sanitation was not the strong suit of the industry. Many diseases were spread by milk. The fact that the milk was raw was not the issue. At issue was the filthy way the cows were milked (no cleaning of the cow, especially of the hind legs, udder and teats) as well as the people who handled and coughed into the milk on its way to the consumer.

While there is not doubt that disease was spread by raw milk contaminated with handler's disease, pasteurization of milk can unfortunately be a way of allowing some of the same unclean practices of yesterday to continue. Pasteurized milk is not tested more than twice per month by the Department of Health. When it is tested, a certain number of aerobic (needing air to survive) bacteria are "okay" to still have in the pasteurized milk. Anaerobic bacteria such as the *Clostridium* species as well as the aerobic *Streptococcus* in pasteurized milk are not tested for in any state.[323] Bacteria grow very rapidly in pasteurized milk because the friendly acid-forming bacteria natural to raw milk has been destroyed by the pasteurizing process. This "friendly" bacteria in raw milk helps to slow the growth of bacteria that may be present in the milk. The fact I found most interesting as I read Dr. William Campbell Douglass' *The Milk Book* was that pasteurized milk may not have a coliform bacteria count exceeding 10 per ml. This is the same maximum allowable amount of coliform in certified raw milk, and milk planned for pasteurization may have a leukocyte count up to 1,500,000 per ml, as compared to a maximum of 500,000 per ml in certified raw milk.[324]

The pasteurized variety of milk so common to our supermarkets does not sour. This heat-altered product instead goes rancid within a few days then decomposes. Raw milk keeps at good quality for at least two weeks under constant refrigeration and then begins to sour. This allows mom to use it to make butter, cottage cheese, sour cream, etc. Raw milk is a product usable fresh and sour.

The nutrient content of pasteurized milk is significantly lowered as compared with the 100% of all natural enzymes, vitamins, minerals, protein and fat available in raw milk. While many argue that pasteurized milk may be a less nutritious but safer product than raw milk, the Centers for Disease Control has had more disease outbreaks from pasteurized milk than raw milk since pasteurization was begun. Outbreaks of *salmonella* poisoning and *listeriosis* blamed on raw milk were actually caused by pasteurized milk.

Milk sensitivity or allergy seems to be an issue for many today. Parents such as myself find that illnesses such as ear infections many times cease after eliminating pasteurized, homogenized milk products from the diet. The surprising fact was that as I introduced raw milk products into my family's diet, the milk allergy did not rear its ugly head. After reading about processed milk versus raw milk, it is my opinion that a true milk intolerance (characterized by a lack of the enzyme lactase which digests the milk sugar lactose) in a person will not allow the drinking of cow or goat milk. A person with milk allergy or sensitivity may be able to consume raw milk products. I believe this is due to homogenization's changing milk's normal molecular structure into very tiny molecules that are absorbed into the bloodstream possibly causing an allergic reaction. Pasteurization may be a causative factor as well since the high temperature used to pasteurize destroys milk's natural enzymes that aid a person's digestion of the milk. It is worth a try if a family enjoys milk and cheese.

rBGH or Genetically-Engineered Milk

Much of the furor over milk in the past few years has come from the approval by the FDA for milk producers (actually dairy farmers; the cows produce) to inject their herd with rBGH (bST) to increase milk production by 10-20%. The use of rBGH causes an increase of mastitis infections which then are treated with antibiotics. The public consuming the milk then could possibly end up with milk containing rBGH residue, antibiotic residue or a higher amount of IGF-1. FDA Commissioner, David Kessler, M.D. states that "no current techniques" can distinguish between genetic milk and regular pasteurized, homogenized milk.[325]

Other researchers and physicians disagree. David Kronfield, Ph.D., a professor of veterinary medicine at Virginia Polytechnic Institute and veteran rBGH researcher, in a reinterpretation of data from a Monsanto (maker of rBGH) report showed that administration of bST into cows does increase rBGH residue in milk. He also contends that the genetically engineered bovine somatotropin (bST or rBGH) is not identical to its naturally occurring cousin. Kronfield feels this may cause "possible immunogenic and allergenic responses" in humans.[326] Dr. Jay Gordon, a Los Angeles pediatrician who specializes in pediatric nutrition is also concerned about the immune implications of using rBGH in cattle, "Children exposed to the milk of these highly medicated cows could develop allergies to antibiotics and this could create large problems in treating serious infections later in life..[L]ong term exposure to multiple chemicals only serves to strengthen the argument against their use," he explains.[327]

An increase in drug residue in cattle is not something we should ignore. A 1992 report release by the General Accounting Office (GAO), an independent investigating arm of Congress, pointed out that the Milk Monitoring Program tests for only 12 of the 64 drugs that are commonly administered to dairy cows, 35 of which are not approved for bovine use. The GAO also found that only 500 samples are analyzed per year. This amounts to only a little over one analysis per state per month. Dairies are notified ahead of time which could enable them to change results by withdrawing any unapproved drug from the herd prior to inspection.[328]

The increase in IGF-1 in cows treated with rBGH is another cause of concern. Critics of genetically-engineered milk argue that IGF-1 might cause premature growth in children and abnormal proliferation of intestinal cells.[329] Studies cited by William Daughaday, M.D. and David Barbano, Ph.D., who published an article on rBGH in the Journal of the American Medical Association (Aug. 22, 1990), claim that the increased presence of IGF-1 in rBGH milk is "modest...well within the levels [already present] in bovine and human milk" and has "no impact" on human health.[330] However, Monsanto's own corporation-sponsored study published in Science(1990),which they interpreted had no effect on the "rat participants" [quotes are Shonda's],was reviewed by Michael

Hansen, Ph.D., research associate at the Consumer Policy Institute, a division of Consumers Union in Yonkers, N.Y. who stated that the male rats consuming IGF-1 showed significant increases in body weight gain and tibia (leg bone) length. The rats did get bigger.[331] The question has been raised by some and deserves some thought, "If IGF-1 causes abnormal growth of cells, what increase in our cancer risk in long-term use can we expect?"

Conclusion

The preceding information certainly raises some legitimate health questions in regard to processed milk products. One would do well to examine the role milk is playing in the family's health. Our own choice has been to consume raw milk products such as raw milk cheese and raw milk from cows that we know (a friend's dairy, someone we know's cow, certified raw milk dairies, etc). Please note: In light of the recent rise in *listeria* infections which almost always cause miscarriage or stillbirth in babies whose mothers have contracted the infection prenatally, I have decided to become even more vigilant in assuring the safety of the dairy products our family ingests, particularly me while pregnant.

As in all things, prayer and supplication before our Lord to determine how He may lead us in the health care of our families is the best choice. The information provided here is simply a starting point, we hope, for you to begin your research and praying for an answer to the milk question. Since milk is spoken of so often and so positively in scripture, I find it difficult to rule milk out of the family dietary enjoyment, yet with the information I found above, I feel it prudent to avoid processing of a food so naturally provided by God.

AND HONEY...

Who of us does not have a sweet-tooth craving now and then? The difficulty lies in trying to decide what sweetener is the best choice. Refined cane sugar (white, table sugar) is called "the natural choice" in the industry's ads and even natural foods magazines are telling us refined cane sugar is not all that bad for us. The truth is that no matter what the industry's ads say, refined cane sugar does decrease immune response by lowering white blood cells for four hours after ingesting sugar. Even natural sugar from honey, maple syrup, date sugar, dried cane juice (Sucanat®) fructose or fruit juices will have this same immune system effect.

The benefit of using natural sources of sweeteners rather than refined cane sugar is natural sweeteners do not have the up/down effect on the blood sugar like refined cane sugar does. Refined cane sugar is addictive and stimulating to the adrenal glands which over time can cause depletion of adrenal sufficiency. In addition, refined cane sugar is the harbinger of dental caries. In third world countries today, dental caries are not found in the inhabitants until refined cane sugar consumption becomes prevalent.

Artificial sweeteners such as aspartame (Nutrasweet), saccharin, sorbitol all carry some health risk to sensitive individuals. The best thing I can say about these artificial sweeteners is that they are not a whole food; therefore, we do not eat them.

Most of us who have made the move to natural medicine turn our noses up to refined sugar (well, most of the time, perhaps), yet we indulge our desire for sweets abundantly with more "natural" forms of sugar. Is this healthier? Are there any problems associated with these "natural" sugars?

One certainty is that refined sugar, the most refined being made primarily from sugar beets and bleached after processing, has no health-building qualities. In fact, many writers have pointed out health problems believed to be created, in part, by regular ingestion of refined sugar: intestinal disease, heart disease, glandular problems, chronic infections, structural deficiencies, to name a few.

Another definite health problem that comes directly from sugar ingestion is lowered immune response (up to 30%). This lowered immune response continues for four hours after the consumption of sugar.

Could We Have Any of the Above Problems With Natural Sugars Also?

Certainly, if we have to choose between refined sugar and a sugar that is naturally provided by God in nature, we will choose the natural sugar. The big question comes down to what defines refined and a natural sugar.

I believe the answer is quite simple, yet the answer will bother most of us who yearn for sweets at certain times of our lives.

Define: Refined Sugar - Any sugar created by a process of extracting out or "cooking down" certain parts of a natural food (fruit, cane, vegetable, sap, etc.). For example, maple syrup and sugar cane syrup are created in much the same way: the juice from the tree (or plant) is put into a pan over heat until slowly the juice thickens creating syrup. If this process is taken just a bit further, maple sugar and cane sugar will be created just by allowing the syrup to cook more until sugar crystals are formed. White table sugar is taken a step further by bleaching which I find most offensive of all.

Dried fruit is also considered a refined sugar in that it has been dried which concentrates the sugars. Our very wise dentist, Jeff McCarty of Weatherford, TX, tells us that we should always brush after eating dried fruit because of tooth decay problems associated with this fruit sugar sticking to the teeth.

We should note that during an infection, we should avoid all refined sugars, even those considered natural. This includes fruit juice since we have extracted out and concentrated the sugars by eliminating the fiber. All of the above sugars can cause the 30% immune depletion up to four hours which is not a good idea during an illness.

Define: Natural Sugar - Any sugar found naturally in a God-made food. For example, pears, apples, watermelon, dates, figs, plums, grapes are all quite naturally sweet. Eaten as a whole food (eating the whole fruit), we can satisfy our sweet craving and still benefit from the fiber in the fruit that buffers the effects of the sugar. Honey is also an example of a God-given sugar, so busily produced by bees. Honey has many health benefits. The key to honey or even fruit consumption is moderation. The Word tells us that too much honey is not good for us (make us vomit, Ewww!). Too much fruit will also cause a bodily reaction (most often while on the toilet). I believe fruit to be a good choice during an illness and not detrimental to immune function. Honey has its place in limited quantities during illness.

Am I Saying We Should Only Eat Natural Sugar?

No. I am saying that it is the most healthful and should be the one we eat most often. I would add that we should weigh the processing factor in as we choose between refined sugars.

Because of the bleaching factor of white sugar, we Parkers do try to avoid it (except for a few times a year when our children lose teeth - then it's off to Braum's we go! Gee, could there be a correlation? Actually, these "lost" teeth are baby teeth). We should at least be aware of the consequences of our eating habits so that we may either alter them as our health needs require or antidote them as our every-so-often indulgences require.

Sugar Equivalents:

1c Sugar =   1/2c Raw Honey   2/3c Maple Syrup
               2/3c NutriCane Sugar   1/2c - 1c Fructose
               1c Date Sugar   1c Sucanat
               1/2c Frozen fruit juice concentrate
               1c Fruit juice

Food Combining

Food combining is a system of eating that involves an intricate combining of certain acceptable foods and non-combining of so-called non-compatible (digestively-speaking) foods. Harvey and Marilyn Diamond, authors of *Fit for Life*, popularized this method of eating in the 80s. Many other authors and health-food enthusiasts maintain that proper food combining is the key to digestive health.

The primary rules in food combining are: fruits and fruits alone, melons separate from any other fruit, acidic fruit not allowed with alkaline fruit; vegetables may be combined with a starch or with a protein but not both a starch and protein.

As you can see with the above rules, meal times could become quite a chore in terms of figuring out what to serve, although some people have found it to be freeing in that they only have to serve one or two items at meal time. Personally I find this to be too restrictive for the average family and not based on a biblical foundation.

Food combining can be beneficial for those with digestive difficulties or illnesses that require a light load on the digestive system. I do not want to intimate that those who choose to use food combining methods are engaging in sin; what I do want to stress is that those who do not use food combining are equally without sin in this area.

What do the Scriptures say about food combining?

Interestingly, there are no indications in scripture that tell us to refrain from combining certain foods. In Levitical law, we are told what foods God considered clean, but He did not demand a certain way of presenting or eating them. In fact, when God, Himself, visited Abraham by the terebinth trees of Mamre, Abraham had Sarah make bread (starch), a young man prepared a tender, young calf (protein), and Abraham took butter and milk (more protein) and gave these to God to eat, which He did eat (Genesis 18:6-8). When Jesus miraculously fed the five thousand, He fed them bread (a starch) and fish (protein) (Matthew 14:13-21).

My point is: if God considered this good eating, why do we choose to exalt our own knowledge about the human body and create burdensome food rituals on our people, His people. This legalism (extra-biblical rules made by man) is just what Jesus was righteously angry about as He spoke to His disciples about the scribes and the Pharisees in Matthew 23.

RAW FOODS DIET AND VEGETARIANISM

The raw foods diet has been around for a long time, but in recent years has become more popular among Christians due in large part to the ministry of Hallelujah Acres headed by Reverend George H. Malkmus, author of *Why Christians Get Sick*. Rev. Malkmus was cured of cancer and other assorted health problems and believes that all illness comes from violation of "God's Natural Laws." Hallelujah Acres advocates a raw foods vegetarian diet as the only diet man was truly intended to eat for wellness and long life (pp. 108-109, *Why Christians Get Sick*). There are many other ministries and health advocates who promote raw foods, vegetarianism. HA is just the one I am most familiar with, so I am using them as my example.

Before we go further, I would like to say that I agree with many of HA's dietary information. Our bodies do benefit from eating raw fruits and vegetables. My concern is that people who are desperately seeking an alternative to the standard American diet filled with processed foods that do not lead to health, will embrace this diet for the so-called biblical reasons rather than health reasons. We are not in the Garden. We will not be re-creating the Garden just because we eat what was eaten there. Things changed drastically for us after our being expelled from the Garden. I feel we would be better served by following God's dietary directives for what was acceptable outside the garden rather than trying to return to what we lost by our sin.

We would do well to avoid meats that are injected with antibiotics and growth hormones as well as dairy that has been processed so that the dairy becomes a poison to many rather than a food blessing as God intended.

Some questions we need to answer before throwing out our steaks and chicken:

- Are God's Laws and Natural Law one and the same? Is God still in control of Natural Law?
- Was the addition of meat-eating the only reason man's lifespan was shortened after the Flood?
- Is meat-eating prohibited in Scripture?
- Does God make mistakes?

Question #1: God's laws are contained fully and completely in His Law-Word, the Bible. Certainly, He has establisheded order to His creation and some may call this natural law; however, the question we must ask is: Does Natural Law supercede God's Sovereignty? The natural law as applies to man and sickness, according to Rev. Malkmus is "God created man to be well and to have perfect health" (*Why Christians Get Sick* by Rev. George Malkmus, Hallelujah Acres Publishing: Eidson, TN, 1989, p. 94).

The Bible does not support that all illness comes from violating natural dietary law. In fact, the Bible supports that all illness originates in original sin which brought as a resulting curse, death (of which illness is a part). (See Genesis, first several chapters.) If we can prevent illness through following diligently all of natural law, why do we still live only short lives and die? This belief builds up our bodies and natural law as supreme over God, not allowing that sometimes God does indeed use illness as part of our Christian sanctification process. Is this saying that God is to blame? Yes, you might choose to phrase it this way, although saying "blame" is rather inflammatory. God is totally and completely in control of His creation, moving all of creation according to His perfect plan. In Isaiah 44, verses 24-25, God says, "Thus says the Lord, your Redeemer, And He who formed you from the womb: I am the Lord, who makes all things, Who stretches out the heavens all alone, Who spreads abroad the earth by Myself; Who frustrates the signs of the babblers, And drives diviners mad; Who turns wise men backward, And makes their knowledge foolishness." In Isaiah 45, 6-7, God says, "I am the Lord, and there is no other; I form the light and create darkness, I make peace and create calamity; I, the Lord, do all these things." God says Himself, that He alone is in charge of all matters of creation.

Violating natural law is not what we need to be concerned about; rather, we should concern ourselves with not violating God's Law Word, which has provided very clear directions for all areas of our lives. Natural law does not save us from the effects of original sin: death with attending sickness in many instances. God's grace alone is sufficient for our salvation, yet bodily death (and yes, sickness) is still a part of His plan.

Question #2: Actually this question about shortened life spans after the Flood would best be answered by a creation scientist. From what I've learned and gleaned from reading books on creation science, there are several reasons why man's life span was shortened including the absence of the canopy of water in our atmosphere that God used to rain upon the earth for 40 days and 40 nights. The lack of vegetation certainly may have contributed to the shortened life span; however, who gave the direction for Noah to eat meat after the flood? God did.

Question #3: Meat eating is not prohibited in scripture. God and God alone instructed Noah that meat-eating was a gift from God in His covenant with Noah (Genesis 9:1-4). God ate meat with Abraham (Genesis 18:6-8). God gave Moses the Levitical law concerning which foods He considered clean and acceptable for food. Leviticus 11 God's instruction came through Peter and Paul in the New Testament concerning the acceptability of eating all things with thanksgiving (with the exception of blood) (Acts 15:19-20, Acts

10:28-29, Acts 21:25, Romans 14:1-23, 1 Timothy 4:4-5). Jesus ate meat with the multitudes for whom He miraculously provided food (John 21:1-14, Mark 6:30-44). In fact, in 1 Timothy 4: 1-5, there is a reference to the end times when there will be a turning away from the faith and people commanding to abstain from meats. Now, I'm not saying that those who choose a vegetarian diet have turned away from the faith; rather, I am saying that those who command all to abstain from meats as a biblical directive are misguided in their interpretation of what God has designed, because…

Question # 4: God does not make mistakes. Not to belabor the point, but God gave the directive to eat meat, God ate meat and God considered this meat-eating to be okay. Would our Creator who loves us enough to die for our sin choose to tell us to eat a food (and eat it himself) that He never designed us to eat? Where was God's foreknowledge in the beginning if this is true? God is the Creator. If He didn't want us to eat meat, He would have said so. He did not remain quiet when it was important to Him for there to be specific dietary instructions (Leviticus 11).

To sum up, there is nothing generally wrong with choosing to eat plenty of raw foods in our diets or even choosing a vegetarian diet for the treatment of certain illnesses. The danger lies in writing into scripture directives that God left out (1 Corinthians 10:25). Our wisdom is still considered foolishness to God. Why can we not just accept His word as the final authority and be satisfied with the fruit and blessing of following His Authoritative Word?

About the Author

Shonda Parker is the mother of five delightful children and the wife of the wonderful Keith. Shonda is also a Professional Family Herbalist and Certified Childbirth Educator. She and her family are currently enjoying life in the Blue Ridge Mountains of North Carolina, learning about the herbs native to the mountains and planting their own gardens. Shonda is a firm believer in a parent's God-given right and responsibility to direct family health care. She encourages all parents not merely to read and accept what another might say, but to research on their own and discover their own family way of health.

INDEX

ENDNOTES

1. Castleman, Michael. *The Healing Herbs*. Emmaus, PA: Rodale Press. 1991. p. 135.

2. Ames, Bruce, et al. *Science* 236:271, 1987.

3. Castleman, p. 113.

4. Castleman, p. 112-14.

5. Akron, Ohio Regional Poison Control Center's national database.

6. Weiner, Ph.D., Michael A. & Janet A. *Herbs That Heal*. Mill Valley, CA: Quantum Books, 1994. p. 286-87.

7. Ibid. p. 289-90.

8. Murray,N.D., Michael T. *Natural Alternatives to Over-the-Counter and Prescription Drugs*. New York, NY: William Morrow & Co., Inc., 1994. pp. 114-15, 237-239,224,228.

9. Weiner, p. 95.

10. Castleman, p. 199.

11. Roufs, J.B. Review of L-tryptophan and eosinophilia-myalgia syndrome. *J Am Diet Assn*,92:844-850, 1992.

12. Murray, p. 227, 228.

13. Caston, J.C., Roufs, J.B., Forgarty, C.M., et al. Treatment of refractory eosinophilia-myalgia syndrome associated with the ingestion of L-tyrptophan-containing products. *Adv Ther* 7:206-228, 1990.

14. Schilcher, Heinz Prof. Dr. *Phytotherapy in Paediatrics Stuttgart*, Germany: medpharm GmbH Scientific Publishers, 1997. P. 25.

15. Nelson, Waldo, E., M.D. Behrman, Sliegman, Arvin. *Nelson Tetbook of Pediatrics*, 16th Ed. Philadelphia, PA: W.B. Saunders Company, 1996. P. 872.

16. Ibid, p. 877-878.

17. Ibid, p. 776

18. Nelson, *Textbook of Pediatrics*, p. 777

19. Nelson, *Textbook of Pediatrics*, p. 776.

20. Ibid, pp. 779-780.

21. Centers for Disease Control and Prevention. Pertussis in the Netherlands: an Outbreak Despite High Levels of Immunization with Whole-Cell Vaccine, April-June 1997. *Emerging Infectious Diseases* 1997; 3:175-178.

22. Nelson, *Textbook of Pediatrics*, pp. 780-781.

23. Centers for Disease Control and Prevention, 1997, Information regarding disease clinical features, current morbidity and morality, epidemiology, culturing recommendations and sensitivity, treatment and prevention guidelines downloaded from website, www.cdc.gov October, 1997.

24. Information obtained during class on Infectious Disease Prevention taught by Carolyn Boozer, B.S.N., Infectious Disease Specialist, November, 1997.

25. Schilcher, *Phytotherapy in Paediatrics*, p. 38-39.

26. Nelson, *Textbook of Pediatrics*, pp. 815-817.

27. Miller, Neil Z. *Immunizations: The People Speak!* Sante Fe, NM: New Atlantean Press, 1996. P. 22.

28. Nelson, *Textbook of Pediatrics*, p. 877-878.

29. Ibid, p. 882.

30. Ibid, p. 763.

31. Barbour, Marina L., D. Phil., M.R.C.P. "Conjugate Vaccines and the Carriage of Haemophilus influenzae Type B," *Emerging Infectious Diseases* 2(3), July-September 1996. www.cdc.gov/ncidod/eid/vol2no3/barbour

32. Ibid.

33. Ibid.

34. Bisgard, Kristine, M., et al. "*Haemophilus influenzae Invasive Disease in the United States*, 1994-1995: Near Disappearance of a Vaccine-Preventable Childhood Disease," EID, 4(2), April-June 1998. www.cdc.gov/ncidod/eid/vol4no2/bisgard

35. Nelsons, *Textbook of Pediatrics*, p. 763.

36. Barbour, Marina, L., *EID*.

37. Nelson, *Textbook of Pediatrics*,p. 764

38. Bisgard,et al. *EID*.

39. Null, Gary, Ph.D. *The Clinician's Handbook of Natural Healing* NY, NY: Kensington Publishing Corp. 1997. P.693.

40. Bassett I.B., Pannowitz D. L. and Barnetson RSC, "A comparative study of tea tree oil versus benzoyl peroxide in the treatment of acne," *Med J Australia* 153: 455 - 458, '90.

41. Lininger, Skye, Wright, Jonathan, Austin, Steve, Brown, Donald, Gaby, Alan. *The Natural Pharmacy*. Rocklin, CA: Prima Publishing, 1998. p. 6.

42. L.H. Leung, "Panthothenic Acid Deficiency as the Pathogenesis of Acne Vulgaris," *Med Hypoth*, 44(6) June 1995, p. 490-492.

43. M.G. Longhi, et. Al., "Activity of Crataegus Oxyacantha Derivatives in Functional Dermocosmesis," *Fitoterapia*, L(2), 1984, P. 87-99.

44. Shirakawa, T. and Morimoto, K.: "Lifestyle effect on total IgE," *Allergy*, 46:561-569, 1991.

45. Freedman, B.J. A diet free from additives in the management of allergic disease. *Clin Allergy*, 7:417-421, 1977.

46. Lindahl, O. Lindwall, L., Spangberg, A., et al. Vegan diet regimen with reduced medication in the treatment of bronchial asthma. *J Asthma*, 22:45-55, 1985.

47. Johnston, C.S., Retrum, K.R., and Srilakshmi, J.C. Antihistamine effects and complications of supplemental vitamin C. *J Am Diet Assoc*, 92:988-989, 1992.

48. Foreman, J.C. Mast cells and the actions of flavonoids. *J Allergy Clin Immunol*, 127:546-50, 1984.

49. Taussig, S. The mechanism of the physiological action of bromelain. *Med Hypoth*, 6:99-104, 1980.

50. Simon, S.W. Vitamin B-12 therapy in allergy and chronic dermatoses. *J Allergy*, 2:183-185, 1951.

51. Garrison, R. and E. Somer. *The Nutrition Desk Reference*, Chapter 5 - Vitamin Research: Selected Topics. New Canaan, CT: Keats Publishing, 1985. pp93-94.

52. Collip, P. J., Goldzier, S.III, Weiss, N., et al. Pyridoxine treatment of childhood asthma. *Ann Allergy*, 35:93-97, 1975.

53. Kasahara, Y., Hikino, H., Tsurufuji, S., et al. Anti-inflammatory actions of ephedrines in acute inflammations. *Planta Medica*, 54:325-331, 1985.

54. Weil, M.D. Andrew. *Natural Health, Natural Medicine*. Boston, Mass: Houghton Mifflin Co., 1990. p.254.

55. Weiner, PhD, Michael and Janet A. Weiner. *Herbs that Heal*. Mill Valley, CA: Quantum Books, 1994. p166. Actual studies listed p. 358.

56. Fu, J.S. Measurement of MEFV in 66 cases of asthma in the convalescent stage and after treatment with Chinese herbs. *Chinese Journal of Modern Developments in Traditional Medicine*, 9(11): 658-659, 644, 1989.

57. Li, Y.P. & Wang, Y.M. Evaluation of tussilagone: a cardiovascular repiratory stimulant isolated from Chinese herbal medicine. *General Pharmacology*, 19(2): 261-263, 1988.

58. Frye, p. 132-133.

59. el-Chobaki, F.A., Saleh, Z.A., & Saleh, N. The effect of some beverage extracts on intestinal iron absorption. *Journal of Nutritional Sciences*, 29(4): 264-269, 1990.

60. Null, Gary, Ph.D. *A Clinician's Handbook for Natural Healing*, p. 831.

61. Weiner, Michael, A. Ph.D. & Janet A. *Herbs That Heal*. Mill Valley, CA: Quantum Books, 1994.

62. Null, Gary Ph.D. *The Clinician's Handbook of Natural Healing*. p. 450.

63. Murray, Michael, T. N.D. *The Healing Power of Foods*. Rocklin, CA: Prima Publishing, 1993. p. 273-74.

64. Ellis, J.M., Folkers, K. Shizukuishi, S., et at., Response of Vit B6 Deficiency & the Carpal Tunnel Syndrome to Pyridoxine. *Proceedings of National Academy of Science*, USA. 79:749-98, 1982.

65. Ellis, J., Folkers, K., Watebe, I., et.al. Clinical Results of a Cross-over Treatment with Pyridoxine and Placebo of the Carpal Tunnel Syndrome. *American Journal of Clinical Nutrition*, 32: 2040-46, 1979.

66. Ellis, J.M., Azuma, J. Watanebe, T. et.al. Survey and New Data on Treatment with Pyridoxine of Patients Having a Clinical Syndrome Including the Carpal Tunnel and Other Defects. *Research Committee on Clinical Pathology & Pharmacology*, 17: 165-67, 1977.

67. Hamfelt, A. Carpal Tunnel Sundrome & Vit B6 Deficiency. *Clinical Chemistry*. 28:721, 1982.

68. Phalen, G.S. The Birth of a Syndrome, or Carpal Tunnel Syndrome Revisited. *Journal of Hand Surgery*. 6:109-10, 1981.

69. Fraser, G.E., Sabate, J. Beeson, W.L., and Strahan, T.M. A possible protective effect of nut consumption on risk of coronary heart disease. *Arch Int Med* 152: 1416-24, 1992.

70. Satyavati, G.V. Gum guggal (Commiphora mukul) - The success story of an ancient insight leading to a modern discover. *Ind J Med Res* 87: 327-35, 1988.

71. Nityanard, S., Srivastava, J.S., & Asthana, O.P. Clinical trials with gugulipid, a new hypolipidaemic agent. *J Assoc Phys India* 37: 321-28. 1989.

72. Lau, B.H., Adetumbi, M.A. & Sanchez, A. Allium sativum (garlic) & atherosclerosis: a review. Nutr Res 3:119-28, 1983.

73. Carper, Jean. *The Food Pharmacy*. NY,NY: Bantam Books, 1989.

74. Murray, Michael T., N.D. *The Healing Power of Foods*.Rocklin, CA: Prima Publishing, 1993. p. 115-17.

75. Arsenio, L. Bodria, P., Magnati, G., et al. Effectiveness of long-term treatment with pantethine in patients with dyslipidemias. *Clin Ther* 8: 537-45, 1986.

76. Gaddi, A., Descovich, G., Noseda, G. et. al. Controlled evaluation of pantethine, a natural hypolipidemic compound, in patinets with different forms of hyperlipoproteinemia. *Atheroscl* 50:73-83, 1984.

77. Murray, Michael T., N.D. *Natural Alternatives to Over-the-Counter and Prescription Drugs*. NY,NY: Wilaim Morrow & Co., Inc., 1994. p. 140.

78. Giller, Robert M. & Matthews, Kathy. *Natural Prescriptions*. NY,NY: Carol Southern Books, 1994. p. 84.

79. Eby, G.A., Davis, D.R., & Halcomb, W.W. Reduction in duration of common colds by zinc gluconate lozenges in a double-blind study. *Antimicrob Agents Chemother* 25: 20-24, 1984.

80. Murray, Michael T., N.D. *Natural Alternatives to Over-the-Counter and Prescription Drugs*. NY,NY: William Morrow & Co, Inc., 1994.

81. Murray, Michael T., N.D. *The Healing Power of Herbs*. Rocklin, CA: Prima Publishing, 1994.

82. Weiner, Michael A., & Janet A. *Herbs That Heal*. Mill Valley, CA: Quantum Books, 1994. p. 213 & p. 73-74.

83. Murray, Michael T., N.D. *The Healing Power of Foods*. Rocklin, CA: Prima Publishing, 1993. p. 60-63.

84. Murray, Michael T., M..D. *Natural Alternatives to Over-the-Counter & Prescription Drugs*. NY,NY: William Morrow & Co., 1994, p. 174.

85. Ibid, p. 174.

86. Anderson, J.W. & Ward, K. High carbohydrate, High Fiber Diets for Insulin-treated Men with Diabetes Mellitus. *American Journal of Clinical Nutrition* 32: 2312-21, 1979.

87. Anderson, J. *Diabetes: A Practical Approach to Daily Living*. NY,NY: Arco Press, 1981.

88. Vahouny, G. & Kritchersky, D. *Dietary Fiber in Health and Disease*. NY, NY: Plenam Press, 1982.

89. Hughes, T., Gwynne, J. Switzer, B., et.al. Effects of Caloric Restriction and Weight Loss on Glycemic Control, Insulin Release and Resistance and Atherosclerotic Risk in Obese Patients with Type II Diabetes Mellitus. *American Journal of Medicine* 77: 7-17, 1984.

90. Murray, N.D., Michael T. *Natural Alternatives to Over-the-Counter and Prescription Drugs*. NY,NY: William Morrow & Co., 1994.

91. Carper, Jean. *Food - Your Miracle Medicine*. NY,NY: HarperCollins Publishers, Inc., 1993. p. 120.

92. Carper, p. 124-125.

93. Ibid, p. 125.

94. Ibid, p. 124.

95. Ibid, p. 123.

96. Pedersen, Mark. *Nutritional Herbology*. Bountiful, UT: Pedersen Publishing, 1991. p. 154.

97. Castleman, Michael. *The Healing Herbs*. Emmaus, PA: Rodale Press, 1991. p. 60.

98. Casteman, Michael. *The Healing Herbs*. Emmaus, PA: Rodale Press, 1991, p. 187.

99. Ibid, p. 191.

100. Castleman, Michael. *The Healing Herbs*. Emmaus, PA: Rodale Press, 1991. p. 152.

101. T. Ovesen, et at., "Local application of N-acetylcysteine in Secretory Otitis Media in Rabbits," *Clinical Otolaryngol*, 17(4), August 1992, p., 327-331.

102. Murray, Michael T., N.D. *The Healing Power of Foods*. Rocklin, CA: Prima Publishing, 1993. p. 290.

103. F.A. Bahmer & J. Schafer, "Treatment of Atopic Dermatitis with Borage Seed Oil (Glandol) - A Time Series Analytic Study," *Kinderarztl Prax*, 60(7), October 1992, p. 199-202.

104. Evans, F.Q. The Rational Use of Glycyrrhetinic Acid in Dermatology. *British Journal of Clinical Practice* 12:269-74, 1958.

105. Mann, C., and Staba, E.J. The Chemistry, Pharmacology and Commercial Formulation of Chamomile. *Herbs, Spices, and Medicinal Plants: Recent Advances in Botany, Horticulture and Pharmacology* 1: 235-80, 1986.

106. Weiner, Michael A., Ph.D. & Janet A. *Herbs That Heal*. Mill Valley, CA: Quantum Books, 1994. p. 131.

107. Castleman, Michael. *The Healing Herbs*. Emmaus, 1991. p. 134.

108. Giller, Robert.M., M.D. & Matthews, Kathy. *Natural Prescriptions* NY,NY: Carol Southern Books, 1994. p. 133.

109. Murray, Michael T., N.D. *Natural Alternatives to Over-the-Counter & Prescription Drugs*. NY,NY: William Morrow & Co., 1994.

110. Frye, Anne. *Understanding Lab Work in the Childbearing Year*. New Haven, CT: Labrys Press, 1990. p322.

111. Hanshaw, James B., Dudgeon, John A. & Marshall, William C. *Viral Diseases of the Fetus & Newborn*. Philadelphia, PA: W.B. Saunders Co., 1985. p. 209.

112. Carper, Jean. *Food - Your Miracle Medicine*. NY,NY: HarperCollins Publishers, 1993. p. 362-65.

113. Haas, Elson M., MD. *Staying Healthy with Nutrition*. Berkeley, CA: Celestial Arts Publishing, 1992. p. 272.

114. Weiner, Michael A., Ph.D. & Janet A. *Herbs That Heal*. Mill Valley, CA: Quantum Publishers, 1994. p. 213.

115. Haas, *Staying Healthy with Nutrition*, p. 288.

116. Mowrey, Daniel B., Ph.D. *Herbal Tonic Therapies*. New Canaan, CT: Keats Publishing, Inc., 1993. p. 78.

117. Campos, R., Garrido, A., Guerra, R. & Valenzuela, A. Silybin dihemisuccinate protects against glutathione depletion & lipid peroxidation induced by acetaminophen on rat liver. *Planta Medica* 55: 417-19, 1989.

118. Weiner, Michael A., Ph.D. & Janet A. *Herbs That Heal*. Mill Valley, CA: Quantum Books, 1994. p. 333.

119. Castleman, Michael. *The Healing Herbs*. Emmaus, PA: Rodale Press, 1991. p. 252, 371.

120. Murray, Michael T., N.D. *The Healing Power of Foods*. Rocklin, CA: Prima Publishing, 1993. p. 201.

121. Heinerman, John. *Science of Herbal Medicine*. Orem, UT: Bio-World Publishers, 1984. p. 125.

122. Castleman, Michael. *The Healing Herbs*. Emmaus, PA: Rodale Press, 1991. p. 86.

123. Mowrey, Daniel B., PhD. *Herbal Tonic Therapies*. New Canaan, CT: Keats Publishing, Inc., 1993. p. 56.

124. Castlleman, *The Healing Herbs*, p. 152.

125. V. Esanu, et al., "The Effect of an Aqueous Propolis Extract, of Rutin and of a Rutin-quercetin Mixture on Experimental Influenza Virus Infection in Mice," *Virologie*, 32(3), July-September 1981, p. 213-215.

126. Conversation regarding gallbladder attacks with Chris Marquart, M.D., June 30, 1992.

127. Carper, Jean. *Food - Your Miracle Medicine*. NY,NY: HarperCollins Publishers, Inc., 1993. p. 187.

128. Ibid.

129. Carper, *Food - Your Miracle Medicine*, p. 188.

130. Ibid.

131. Carper, *Food - Your Miracle Medicine*, p. 189.

132. Hobbs, Christopher. *Foundations of Health*. Capitola, CA: Botanica Press, 1992. p. 226.

133. Murray, Michael T., N.D. *The Healing Power of Herbs*. Rocklin, CA: Prima Publishing, 1992. p. 74-75.

134. M.S. Hussain & N. Chandrasekhara, "Effect on Curcumin on Cholesterol Gall-stone Induction in mice," *Indian Journal Medical Research*, 96, October 1992, p. 288-291.

135. Niu & B.F. Smith, "Addition of N-acetylcysteine to Aqueous Model Bile Systems Accelerates Dissolution of Cholesterol Gallstones," *Gastroenterology*, 98(2), February 1990, p. 454-463.

136. Carper, Jean. *Food - Your Miracle Medicine*. NY,NY: HarperCollins Publishers, In.c, 1993. p. 139-141.

137. Carper, p. 142.

138. Carper, p. 141.

139. Hobbs, Christopher. *Foundations of Health*. Capitola, CA: Botanica Press, 1992. p. 197.

140. H. Hertel, et al., [Low Dosage Retinol and L-cystine Combination Improve Alopecia of the Diffuse Type Following Long-term Oral Administration], *Hautarzt*, 40(8), August 1989, p. 490-495.

141. Murray, Michael T., N.D. *Natural Alternatives to Over-the-Counter & Prescription Drugs*. NY,NY: William Morrow & Co., 1994.

142. Ibid.

143. Ibid.

144. Ibid.

145. Weiner, Michael A. Ph.D. & Janet A. *Herbs That Heal*. Mill Valley, CA: Quantum Books, 1994. p. 154-55.

146. Carper, Jean. *Food - Your Miracle Medicine*. NY,NY: HarperCollins Publishers, Inc., 1993. p. 311

147. Carper, p. 314.

148. Carper, p. 321.

149. Castleman, Michael. *The Healing Herbs*. Emmaus, PA: Rodale Pres, 1991. p. 188.

150. Carper, *Food - Your Miracle Medicine*, p. 322.

151. Carper, Jean. *Food - Your Miracle Medicine*. NY,NY: HarperCollins Publishers, Inc., 1993. p. 149-153.

152. Weiner, Michael A., Ph.D. & Janet A. *Herbs That Heal*. Mill Valley, CA: Quantum Books, 1994. p. 227.

153. Mowrey, Daniel B., Ph.D. *Herbal Tonic Therapies*. New Canaan, CT: Keats Publishing, Inc., 1993. p. 188.

154. Murray, Michael T., N.D. *The Healing Power of Foods*. Rocklin, CA: Prima Publishing, 1993. p. 156.

155. Frye, Anne. *Understanding Lab Work in the Childbearing Year*. New Haven, CT: Labrys Pres, 1991. p. 215.

156. Weiner, Michael A., Ph.D. & Janet A. *Herbs That Heal*. Mill Valley, CA: Quantum Books, 1994. p. 196, 241, 247, 340-41.

157. Frye, p. 215.

158. Weiner, p. 102.

159. Weiner, p. 84.

160. Hanshaw, James B., Dudgeon, John A., & Marshall, William C. *Viral Diseases of the Fetus & the Newborn*. Philadelphia, PA: W.B. Saunders Co., 1985. p. 184.

161. Ibid.

162. Frye, Anne. *Understanding Lab Work in the Childbearing Year*. New Haven, CT: Labrys Press, 1991. p. 332.

163. Hanshaw, p. 185.

164. Hanshaw, p. 186.

165. Hanshaw, p. 188 - 191.

166. Frye, p. 335.

167. Hanshaw, p. 190 - 191.

168. Hanshaw, p. 195-96.

169. Hanshaw, p. 196.

170. Frye, Anne. *Understanding Diagnostic Tests in the Childbearing Year*. New Haven, CT: Labrys Press, 1993. p. 387.

171. Willson, J.Robert & Carrington, Elsie Reid. *Obstetrics and Gynecology*. 8th Ed. St. Louis, MO: The C.V. Mosby Co., 1987. p. 330.

172. Weiner, Michael A., Ph.D. & Janet A. *Herbs That Heal*. Mill Valley, CA: Quantum Books, 1994. p. 139, 234.

173. Mowrey, Daniel B., Ph.D. *Herbal Tonic Therapies*. New Canaan, CT: Keats Publishing, Inc., 1993.

174. Ibid.

175. Mowrey, p. 40-45.

176. Castleman, Michael. *The Healing Herbs*. Emmaus, PA: Rodale Press, 1991. p. 152-53.

177. Weiner, Michael. A. Ph.D., & Janet A. *Herbs That Heal*. Mill Valley, CA: Quantum Books, 1994. p. 142-42.

178. Mowrey, p. 55-59.

179. Weiner, p. 73-75.

180. V.I. Komar, [The Use of Pantothenic Acid Preparations in Treating Patients with Viral Hepatitis A], *Ter Arkh*, 63(11), 1991, p. 58-60.

181. S. Iwarson & J. Lindberg, "Coenzyme-B12 Therapy in Acute Viral Hepatitis," *Scandinavian Journal of Infectious Disease*, 9(2), 1977, p. 157-158.

182. I.V. Komar, [Use of Vitamin B12 in the Combined Therapy of Viral Hepatitis], *Vopr Pitan*, (1), February 1982, p. 26-29.

183. W. Li, et atl, [Preliminary Study on Early Fibrosis of Chronic Hepatitis B Treated with Ginkgo Biloba Composita], *Chung Kuo Chung His I Chieh Ho Tsa Chih*, 15(10), October 1995, p. 593-595.

184. Shonda Parker as noted while working as a medical assistant for Dr. James R. Bergeron in Shreveport, LA - 1984.

185. Frye, Anne. *Understanding Lab Work in the Childbearing Year*. New Haven, CT: Labrys Press, 1990. p. 338.

186. Willson, J. Robert and Carrington, Elsie Reid. *Obstetrics and Gynecology*. St. Louis, MO: The C.V. Mosby Co., 1987. p. 609-10.

187. Varney, Helen. *Nurse-Midwifery*. St. Louis, MO: Blackwell Scientific Publications, Inc., 1987. p. 169.

188. Frye, Anne. *Understanding Lab Work in the Childbearing Year*. New Haven, CT: Labrys Press, 1990. pp. 339-40.

189. Carper, Jean. *Food - Your Miracle Medicine*. NY,NY: HarperCollins, Inc., 1993. p. 362.

190. Murray, Michael T., N.D.*The Healing Power of Foods*. Rocklin, CA: Prima Publishing, 1993. p. 307.

191. Murray, *The Healing Power of Foods*, p. 307.

192. Giller, Robert M., M.D. & Matthews, Kathy. *Natural Prescriptions*. NY,NY: Carol Southern Books, 1994. p. 184.

193. Weiner, Michael A. & Janet A. *Herbs That Heal*. Mill Valley, CA: Quantum Books, 1994. p. 79.

194. Weiner, p. 84.

195. Weiner, p. 97.

196. Weiner, p. 141-42.

197. Weiner, p. 276-77.

198. Weiner, p. 296.

199. Mowrey, Daniel B., Ph.D. *Herbal Tonic Therapies*. New Canaan, CT: Keats Publishing, Inc., 1993. p. 67, 323.

200. Weiner, p. 126, 319.

201. D.B. Mowrey, *The Scientific Validation of Herbal Medicine*, New Canaan, CT, Keats Publishing, 1986, p. 73.

202. M. Amoros, et al., "Comparison of the Anti-herpes Simplex Virus Activities of Propolis and 3-methyl-but-2-enyl Caffeate," *Journal of Nat Prod*, 57(5), May 1994, p. 644-647.

203. IuF Maichuk, et al., [The Use of Ocular Drug Films of Propolis in the Sequelae of Ophthalmic Herpes], *Voen Med Zh*, (12), December 1995, p. 36-39.

204. Frye, Anne. *Understanding Lab Work in the Childbearing Year*. New Haven, CT: Labrys Press, 1990. p. 258.

205. Willson, J. Robert & Carrrington, Elsie Reid. 8th Ed. *Obstetrics and Gynecology*. St. Louis, MO: The C.V. Mosby Co., 1987. p. 308.

206. Mowrey, Daniel B., Ph.D. *Herbal Tonic Therapies*. New Canaan, CT: Keats Publishing, Inc., 1993. pp. 55-58.

207. Castleman, Michael. *The Healing Herbs*. Emmaus, PA: Rodale Press, 1991. pp. 58, 353.

208. Weiss, Rudolf F., M.D. *Herbal Medicine*. Beaconsfield, England: Beaconsfield Publishers, Inc., 1991. p. 279.

209. Murray, Michael T., N.D. *The Healing Power of Foods*. Rocklin, CA: Prima Publishing, 1993. p. 313.

210. Giller, Robert M., M.D. & Matthews, Kathy. *Natural Prescriptions*. NY,NY: Carol Southern Books, 1994. p. 203.

211. Frye, Anne. *Understanding Lab Work in the Childbearing Year*. New Haven, CT: Labrys Press, 1990. p. 250.

212. Giller, Robert M., M.D. & Matthews, Kathy. *Natural Prescriptions*. NY,NY: Carol Southern Books, 1994. p. 205.

213. Willson, J. Robert, & Carrrington, Elsie Reid. *Obstetrics & Gynecology*. 8th Ed. St. Louis, MO: The C.V. Mosby Do., 1987. p. 308.

214. Frye, Anne. *Understanding Lab Work in the Childbearing Year*. New Haven, CT: Labrys Press, 1990. p. 262.

215. Frye, p. 261.

216. Murray, Michael T., N.D. *The Healing Power of Foods*. Rocklin, CA: Prima Publishing. p. 70.

217. Frye, p. 261.

218. Mowrey, Daniel B., Ph.D. *Herbal Tonic Therapies*. New Canaan, CT: Keats Publishing, Inc., 1993. pp. 194-99.

219. Jones, V.; McLaughlin, P.; Shorthouse, M.; et al. Food Intolerance: A Major Factor in the Pathogenesis of Irritable Bowel Syndrome. *Lancet 2*: 1115-18, 1982.

220. Petitpierre, M.; Sumowski, P.; and Dirard, J. Irritable Bowel Sundrome and Hypersensitivity to Food. *Annals of Allergy* 54: 538-40, 1985.

221. Carper, Jean. *Food - Your Miracle Medicine*. NY,NY: HarperCollins Publishers Inc., 1993. p. 163.

222. Ibid.

223. Carper, p. 167.

224. Murray, Michael, T., N.D. *The Healing Power of Foods*. Rocklin, CA: Prima Publishing, 1993. p. 320.

225. Ibid.

226. Murray, *Natural Alternatives to Over-the-Counter & Prescription Drugs*, p. 201.

227. Brochure *Nutritional Research News* Issue 2 provided by the Foundation for the Advancement of Nutritional Education, PO Box 4621, San Clemente, CA 92672.

228. Murray, Michael T., N.D. *Natural Alternative to Over-the-Counter and Prescription Drugs*. NY,NY: William Morrow & Co., 1994.

229. Giller, Robert M., M.D. & Matthews, Kathy. *Natural Prescriptions*. NY,NY: Carol Southern Books, 1994. p. 213.

230. Ibid.

231. Carper, Jean. *Food - Your Miracle Medicine*. NY,NY: HarperCollins Publishers, Inc., 1993. p. 134.

232. Murray, Michael T., N.D. *The Healing Power of Foods*. Rocklin, CA: Prima Publishing, 1993. pp. 147, 149.

233. Murray, *The Healing Power of Foods*, p. 114.

234. Murray, Michael T., N.D. *Natural Alternatives to Over-the-Counter & Prescription Drugs*. NY,NY: William Morrow & Co., 1994. p. 226.

235. Giller, Robert, M., M.D. & Matthew, Kathy. *Natural Prescriptions*. NY,NY: Carol Southern Books, 1994. pp. 218-19.

236. Trowell, H.; Burkitt, D.; and Heaton, K. *Dietary Fibre, Fibre-Depleted Foods and Disease*. NY,NY: Academic Press, 1985.

237. Murray, Michael T., N.D. *The Healing Power of Food*. Rocklin, CA: Prima Publishing, 1993. p. 321.

238. Trowell, H. & Burkitt, D. *Western Diseases: Their Emergence and Prevention*. Cambridge, Mass.: Harvard University Press, 1981.

239. Carper, Jean. *Food - Your Miracle Medicine*. NY,NY: HarperCollins Publishers, Inc., 1993. p. 192.

240. Murray, pp. 322-23.

241. Rose, G., and Westbury, E. The Influence of Calcium Content of Water, Intake of Vegetables and Fruit and of Other Food Factors Upon the Incidence of Renal Calculi. *Urological Research* 3: 61-66, 1975.

242. Shaw, P., Williams, G. and Green, N. Idiopathic Hypercalciuria: Its Control with Unprocessed Bran. *British Journal of Urology* 52: 426-29, 1980.

243. Seeling, M.S. Vitamin D - Risk vs Benefit. *Journal of American College of Nutrition* 4: 109-10, 1983.

244. Murray, p. 323.

245. Prien, E. and Gershoff, S. Magnesium Oxide-Pyridoxine Therapy for Recurrent Calcium Oxalate Calculi. *Journal of Urology* 112: 509-12, 1974.

246. Gershoff, S. andPrien, E. Effect of Daily MgO and Vitamin B6 Administration to Patients with Recurring Calcium Oxalate Stones. *American Journal of Clinical Nutrition* 20: 393-99, 1967.

247. Giller, Robert M., M.D. & Matthews, Kathy. *Natural Prescriptions*. NY,NY: Carol Southern Books, 1994. p. 228.

248. Weiner, Michael A., Ph.D. & Janet A. *Herbs that Heal*. Mill Valley, CA: Quantum Books, 1994. p. 132.

249. Weiner, p. 136.

250. Weiner, p. 156.

251. Weiner, p. 197.

252. Mowrey, Daniel B., Ph.D. *Herbal Tonic Therapies*. New Canaan, CT: Keats Publishing Inc., 1993. p. 270.

253. Weiss, Rudolf F., M.D. *Herbal Medicine*. Beaconsfield, England: Beaconsfield Publishers Ltd., 1991. p. 185.

254. Frye, Anne. *Understanding Lab Work in the Childbearing Year*. New Haven, CT: Labrys Press, 1991. p. 192.

255. Weiner, Michael A., Ph.D., & Janet A. *Herbs That Heal*. Mill Valley, CA: Quantum Books, 1994.

256. Murray, Michael T., N.D., p. 56.

257. Mowrey, Daniel B., Ph.D. *Herbal Tonic Therapies*. New Canaan, CT: Keats Publishing, Inc., 1993. p. 8.

258. Weiner, Michael A., Ph.D. , p. 169.

259. Murray, Michael T., N.D. *The Healing Power of Herbs*. Rocklin, CA: Prima Publishing, 1992. p. 4 - 6.

260. Castleman, Michael. *The Healing Herbs*. Emmaus, PA: Rodale Publishing, 1991. p. 191.

261. Giller, Robert M., M.D. & Matthews, Kathy. *Natural Prescriptions*. NY,NY: Carol Southern Books, 1994. p. 65-67.

  2. Pizzorno, Joseph & Murray, Michael. *An Encyclopedia of Natural Medicine*. Rocklin, CA: Prima Publishing, 1991. p.467.

262. P. J. Leggott, et al., "Effects of Ascorbic Acid Depletion and Supplementation on Periodontal Health and Subgingival Microflora in Humans," *Jrnl of Dental Res*, 70(12), December 1991, p. 1531-1536.

263. R. I. Vogel et al., " The Effect of Folic Acid on Gingival Health," *Jrnl of Periodont*, 47(11), November 1976, p. 667-668.

264. Murray, Michael T. *Natural Alternatives to Over-the-Counter & Prescription Drugs*. NY,NY: William Morrow & Co., 1994. p. 228.

265. Murray, Michael T., N.D. *The Healing Power of Foods*. Rocklin, CA: Prima Publishing, 1993. p. 191.

266. Carper, Jean. *Food - Your Miracle Medicine*. NY,NY: HarperCollins, 1993. p. 444.

267. C. Miyares, et al., [Clinical Trial with a Preparation Based on Propolis "propolisina" in Human Giardiasis], *Acta Gastroenterol Latinoam*, 18(3), 1988, p. 195-201.

268. Weiner, Michael A., Ph.D., & Janet A. *Herbs That Heal*. Mill Valley, CA: Quantum Books, 1994. p. 259.

269. Mowrey, Daniel B., Ph.D. *Herbal Tonic Therapies*. New Canaan, CT: Keats Publishing, Inc., 1993. p. 78-79.

270. Castleman, Michael. *The Healing Herbs*. Emmaus, PA: Rodale Press, 1991. p. 156.

271. Berkow, Robert, M.D. *The Merck Manual*. Rahway, NJ: Merck Research Laboratories, 1992. p. 2428.

272. Weiss, Rudolf Fritz. *Herbal Medicine*. Beaconsfield, England: Beaconsfield Publishers, LTD, 1991. p. 337.

273. Sherman, John A., N.D. *The Complete Botanical Prescriber*. 1993. p. 411.

274. Weiss, p. 337.

275. J. DeBersaques, "Vitamin A Acid in the Topic Treatment of Warts," *Acta Derm Venereol Suppl*, 55(74), 1975, p. 169-170.

276. C Trenkwalder, et al., "L-dopa Therapy of Uremic and Idiopathic Restless Legs Syndrome: A Double-Blind, Crossover Trial," *Sleep*, 18(8), October 1995, p. 681-688.

277. Schmidt, Michael A., Smith, Lendon H. & Sehnert, Keith W. *Beyond Antibiotics*. Berkeley, CA: North Atlantic Books, 1993. p. 30

278. Hoffman, R.L. *Seven Weeks to a Settled Stomach*. NY,NY: Pocket Books, 1990. p. 6.

279. Frye, Anne. *Understanding Lab Work in the Childbearing Year*. New Haven, CT: Labrys Press, 1990. p. 362.

280. Giller, Robert M., M.D. & Matthews, Kathy. *Natural Prescriptions*. NY,NY: Carol Southern Books, 1994. p. 305-307.

281. Carper, Jean. *Food - Your Miracle Medicine*. NY,NY: HarperCollins, Inc., 1993. p. 338-39.

282. Murray, Michael T., N.D. *The Healing Power of Herbs*. Rocklin, CA: Prima Publishing, 1992. p. 183-84.

283. Weiner, Michael A., Ph.D. & Janet A. *Herbs That Heal*. Mill Valley, CA: Quantum Books, 1994. p. 141-42.

284. Castleman, Michael. *The Healing Herbs*. Emmaus, PA: Rodale Press, 1991. p. 152-53.

285. Schmidt, Michael A., Smith, Lendon H. & Sehnert, Keith A. *Beyond Antibiotics*. Berkeley, CA: North Atlantic Books, 1992.

286. Schmidt, Smith, & Sehnert, p. 246.

287. Carper, Jean. *Food - Your Miracle Medicine*. NY,NY: HarperCollins, Inc., 1993. p. 342.

288. Carper, p. 343.

289. Castleman, Michael. *The Healing Herbs*. Emmaus, PA: Rodale Press, 1991. p. 171.

290. Weiss, Rudolf F., M.D. *Herbal Medicine*. Beaconsfield, England: Beaconsfield Publishers Ltd., 1991. p. 228.

291. Castleman, p. 343.

292. Weiner, Michael, Ph.D. & Janet A. *Herbs That Heal*. Mill Valley, CA: Quantum Books, 1994. p. 126.

293. G. Hotz, et al., [Antiphlogistic Effect of Bromelain Following Third Molar Removal], *Dtsch Zahnarztl Z*, 44(11), November 1989, p. 830-832.

294. E. Rapisarda & A. Longo, [Effects of Zinc and Vitamin B6 in Experimental Caries in Rats], *Minerva Stomatol*, 30(4), July-August 1981, p. 317-320.

295. Varney, Helen. *Nurse-Midwifery*. 2nd. Ed./ Boston, Mass.: Blackwell Scientific Publications, 1987. p. 168.

296. Beischer, Norman A. & Mackay, Eric V. *Obstetrics & the Newborn*. 2nd Ed. Artamon, NSW: CBS Publishing Australia Pty Ltd., 1986. p. 250.

297. Giller, Robert, M., M.D. & Matthews, Kathy. *Natural Prescriptions*. NY,NY: Carol Southern Books, 1994. p. 101-103.

298. Weiner, Michael A., Ph.D. & Janet A. *Herbs That Heal*. Mill Valley, CA: Quantum Books, 1994. p. 136.

299. Weiner, p. 79, 188, 264-265, 331-332.

300. Frye, Anne. *Understanding Lab Work in the Childbearing Year*. New Haven, CT: Labrys Press, 1991. p. 381.

301. Belaiche P, Treatment of vaginal yeast infections of Candida albicans with the essential oil of Melaleuca alternifolia. *Phytotherapie* 15:15-16, 1985.

302. Brown, Donald J. *Herbal Prescriptions for Better Health*. Rocklin, CA: Prima Publishing, 1996. p. 240.

303. Frye, p. 384.

304. Mowrey, Daniel B. *Herbal Tonic Therapies*. New Canaan, CT: Keats Publishing, Inc. 1993. p. 80.

305. M.S. Litschgi, et al., [Effectiveness of a Lacctobacillus Vaccine on Trichomonas Infection in Women. Preliminary Results], *Fortschr Med*, 98(41), November 6, 1980, p. 1624-1627.

306. J. Starzyk, et al., " Biological Properties and Clinical Application of Propolis. II. Stidus on the Antiprotozoan Activity of Ethanol Extract of Propolis," *Arzneimittelforschung*, 27(6), 1977, p. 1198-1199.

307. Murray, Michael T. N.D. and Joseph Pizzorno, N.D. *Encyclopedia of Natural Medicine*, Prima Publishing, Rocklin, CA: 1991. p. 157.

308. Murray and Pizzorno, pp. 166-167.

309. Murray and Pizzorno, p. 167 and 170.

310. Carpenter, Betsy with Hedges, Stephen J., Crabb, Charlene, Reilly, Mark and Bounds, Mary C. "Is Your Water Safe?" *U.S. News and World Report* July 29, 1991, p. 48-55.

311. Ibid.

312. Opheim, Teresa "Water Purity" *Country Living* April 1993, p. 80.

313. Castleman, Michael "Is Your Water Safe" *Redbook* July 1988, p. 91.

314. Carpenter, Betsey *U.S. News and World Report*, p. 51.

315. Castleman, Michael *Redbook*, p. 91.

316. Giller, Robert M., M.D. & Matthews, Kathy. *Natural Prescriptions*. NY, NY: Carol Southern Books, 1994, p. 287.

317. Carpenter, et al. *U.S. News and World Report*, p. 53.

318. Haas, Elson, M., M.D. *Staying Healthy with Nutrition*. Berkeley, CA: Celestial Arts, 1992, p. 29.

319. Holy Bible. Exodus 3:8.

320. Frye, Anne. *Understanding Diagnostic Tests in the Childbearing Year*. Portland, OR: Labrys Press, 1993.

321. Weiss, Rick "What's the Matter With Milk?" *Health* January/February 1993, p. 18.

322. Douglass, William Campbell, M.D. *The Milk Book*. Dunwoody, GA: Second Opinion Publishing, 1993.

323. Ibid, p. 67-68.

324. Douglass, M.D. *The Milk Book*, p. 66-75.

325. Arnot, Bob,M.D. "The Great American Milk War" *Good Housekeeping* June, 1994, p. 50.

326. Harris, Mark "The Dairy Debate" *Vegetarian Times*, April 1994, p. 78.

327. Peterson, Natasha "Natural Nutrition, Organic Dairy Products: Are They Something to Moo About?" *Let's Live* March 1994, p. 55.

328. Harris, Mark *Vegetarian Times*, p. 78.

329. Weiss, Rick "What's the Matter With Milk?" *Health* January/February 1993, p.10.

330. Harris, p. 78.

331. Harris, p. 80.